PRAISE FOR
BACK ON THE CAREER TRACK

"Practical help . . . a soup-to-nuts guidebook. Don't miss the tales of high-profile relaunchers such as Supreme Court Justice Sandra Day O'Connor."
—*Boston Globe*

"Comprehensive . . . step-by-step . . . Real-life examples of success stories combined with a multitude of practical advice make this book a unique resource."
—Constance E. Helfat, professor, Tuck School of Business
at Dartmouth College

"Provide[s] guidance in updating skills, networking, and even getting the family on board with the idea of Mom going back to work."
—*Fort Worth Star-Telegram*

"A wonderful and practical road map to 'on ramping' back into the workforce."
—Anne Erni, chief diversity officer, Lehman Brothers

"Candid, constructive, compelling . . . realistic yet optimistic advice with examples on how to relaunch a career successfully."
—W. Stanton Smith, national director, Next Generation Initiatives/Human
Resources, Deloitte & Touche USA LLP

more . . .

"Practical tools *and* an emotional road map for navigating the challenges of relaunching. Cohen and Rabin not only address the how-tos of networking and résumés, but also the subtler personal issues, such as lack of confidence, guilt, and negotiating in marriage. Refreshingly matter-of-fact, Cohen and Rabin are supportive and trustworthy guides."

—Daphne de Marnette, PhD, psychologist, and author of
Maternal Desire: On Children, Love, and the Inner Life

"Offers concrete tools and tips for people wanting to reactivate careers after time off . . . Easy-to-read, no-nonsense."

—Corrie Martin, Tuck Executive Education

"This book takes the voice of the wise mother and practical mentor our generation so badly needs as we navigate uncharted career and parenting waters . . . a very strong, yet warm, guiding hand."

—Jules Pieri, president and COO, Ziggs, Inc.

"Will I be able to find rewarding work? Do I still have what it takes? Will anybody hire me? 'Yes!' say authors Cohen and Rabin who offer stay-at-home moms practical guidance."

—DeAnne Aguirre, senior vice president, Booz Allen Hamilton

"Filled with practical advice and stories from women who have been through the process, BACK ON THE CAREER TRACK is indispensable for moms relaunching their careers."

—Shira Goodman, executive vice president, Staples

BACK
on the
CAREER
TRACK

A Guide for Stay-at-Home Moms
Who Want to Return to Work

Carol Fishman Cohen
and Vivian Steir Rabin

**BUSINESS
PLUS**

NEW YORK   BOSTON

*Good luck on
your relaunch!
Carol Cohen
1-14-09*

Throughout the book, all full names used are those of actual people, usually experts we're quoting. When only first names are used, they represent pseudonyms for women we interviewed, and any other identifying information is also disguised. The exceptions are Carol and Vivian, which refer, not surprisingly, to each of us.

Business Plus
Hachette Book Group USA
237 Park Avenue
New York, NY 10017
Visit our Web site at www.HachetteBookGroupUSA.com.

Originally published in hardcover by Hachette Book Group USA.

Book design by Fearn Cutler de Vicq
Printed in the United States of America

First Trade Edition: August 2008
10 9 8 7 6 5 4 3 2 1

Business Plus is an imprint of Grand Central Publishing.
The Business Plus name and logo are trademarks of Hachette Book Group USA, Inc.

The Library of Congress has cataloged the hardcover edition as follows:

Cohen, Carol Fishman.
  Back on the career track : a guide for stay-at-home moms who want to return to work / Carol Fishman Cohen and Vivian Steir Rabin.—1st ed.
    p. cm.
  Includes index.
  ISBN 978-0-446-57820-2
  1. Vocational guidance for women—United States. 2. Stay-at-home mothers—United States. 3. Women—Employment re-entry—United States. 4. Work and family—United States. 5. Choice (Psychology) I. Rabin, Vivian Steir. II. Title.
  HF5382.65.C64 2007
  650.14085'20973—dc22   2006020986

ISBN 978-0-446-69580-0 (pbk.)

Photo of Carol Fishman Cohen by Lynn Wayne Photography
Photo of Vivian Steir Rabin by Sandra Nissen Photography

To Doug—husband, parent, and friend extraordinaire
—VSR

In memory of my father,
I. William Fishman, who would have been so proud
to see this book, and in honor of my husband, Stephen, who
has been my biggest fan through every stage of my career.
—CFC

Contents

Our Journey from Playdough to Real Dough

Vivian: On May 30, 2001, I boarded a flight from Newark to Boston, ostensibly to attend my fifteenth reunion at the Harvard Business School. In fact, however, it was a pre-reunion program for female alums that had motivated me to make the trip. For a stay-at-home mother of five, clearing out of town for two nights and three days was quite a challenge. To get out of the house that morning, I made arrangements with my husband months in advance, reshuffled several car pools, coordinated numerous after-school playdates, and booked backup care in case one of the kids got sick.

But I was determined to attend. Billed as a forum for exploring back-to-work options for women grads currently out of the full-time labor force, the program seemed tailor-made for me. Just eight months prior, I had begun working part-time from home as an executive recruiter after having spent seven years focused full-time on my children. The recruiting work had sort of fallen into my lap; I was itching to "do something," so I accepted a neighbor's offer to assist him in his executive search business. But I wasn't being paid very much, and I hadn't done any strategic thinking about whether or not this was the right field for me, let alone the right job.

Although I loved mothering and was busy with volunteer work and other activities, I missed the excitement and intellectual stimulation I had enjoyed during my career. Also, as our household's expenses grew,

I began to miss the money. Finally, I felt that the longer I put off trying to reenter, the tougher it was going to get. When I thought about
the specifics of returning to work, however, I was overwhelmed. What
could I do that would be compelling, but also allow me the flexibility
to spend time with my children? Were my skills and experience still
valuable, or was I so rusty that nobody would want to hire me? How
should I present myself to potential employers or clients? What did I
really want to do, anyway, and did I have the ability to do it? And if I
uncovered my dream job, how could I make the transition from full-
time mom to full- or part-time work as problem-free as possible—for
my husband and my children, as well as for myself?

The chance to meet with women in a similar situation and learn
from the experts at Harvard Business School was irresistible.

As it turned out, my logistical wrangling was well worth it. At the
Harvard seminar, I didn't find all the answers. I actually found something more important—a community; fifty women facing the same
questions I was. The group included former investment bankers, marketing managers, technology gurus, and others who felt just as intimidated and frustrated about the prospect of returning to work as I did.
But more importantly, I had a chance to connect with a roomful of
female professionals determined not to be written off just because they
had stepped off the corporate ladder.

Buoyed by this newfound sense of community, and with a few new
self-assessment tools and networking techniques in my back pocket, I
vowed to get my career back on track. I quickly realized, however, that
this job search differed distinctly from any other I'd undertaken. I had
pounded the pavement before, but never had I felt so lacking in confidence as I did this time.

I assumed there would be lots of books and online resources to
help me, but in that summer of 2001, when I Googled "women going
back to work" in every conceivable configuration, I kept coming up
empty. Nor did I fare much better with printed job search literature.
In the books I perused, I never found more than a token reference to

the topic. If I hadn't attended that Harvard Business School seminar, I would have thought I was the only formerly professional, currently stay-at-home, mom in the country looking to get back into the game.

I eventually did manage to relaunch my career. But I was so fascinated by the process itself, and so struck by the lack of information on the issue, that at one point in my odyssey I decided I wanted to write a book on the subject. It was during this period that a mutual friend introduced me to **Carol,** also a Harvard Business School alum.

Up in Boston, Carol had pulled off what I considered the impossible—after eleven years at home with her four children, she had nabbed a coveted full-time job at a premier investment firm. Carol was the first woman I found who had successfully relaunched her career, and I was dying to know how she did it and how she was faring. Carol's story didn't disappoint. It was loaded with emotional ups and downs and tips from which the fifty women at the Harvard Business School seminar could have easily benefited. (In fact, Harvard later made her the subject of a classroom case study so that new MBAs could learn from her relaunch experience.) But I needed to find more stories—more women who had done what Carol had done and what I was trying to do—if I wanted to write a book that would both inspire and counsel women who were thinking about resuming their careers.

Torn between the desire to relaunch my career and the compulsion to write about it, I decided to focus on relaunching, rather than writing, at least initially. But when Carol e-mailed me in the fall of 2003 that she had left her job and was thinking about writing a book on career reentry, we couldn't resist the opportunity to pool our insights and resources and write the book together.

———

Although both of us have MBAs, we decided early on that we didn't want to write this book solely for former businesswomen. Therefore, in researching this book, we made sure to speak to women from a wide variety of backgrounds—including business, of course—in the hope that you will be able to identify with at least one of them. Accordingly, we spoke with more than a hundred women from across the country from the fields of law, medicine, teaching, nursing, banking, advertising, real estate, customer service management, scientific research, psychology, and others who have successfully relaunched their careers. They had been out of the workforce for anywhere from eighteen months to twenty years, and they ranged in age from their early thirties to early fifties when they first tried to reenter. Their approaches to relaunching also differed. Some women returned to the same field, and even the same company, where they had spent most of their initial career. Others relaunched themselves in an entirely new direction. Their work arrangements also ran the gamut—from full-time to part-time, from consulting to entrepreneurship, and everything in between. Through in-depth interviews, we discovered how each woman prepared for her relaunch, both emotionally and logistically; how she found or created her new opportunity; and how her relaunch has affected her life, including her marriage and her children. In this book, we examine their successes *and failures,* extracting lessons from both. And we get personal. Promised anonymity, these women bared their souls about embarrassing interviews, threatened spouses, and initial on-the-job blunders. They also waxed eloquent about the joys of being back at work again.

Despite their differences, we found most of these women grappled with the same questions we had—and that you're probably grappling with, too:

1. Should I go back to work?
2. Why am I intimidated at the prospect?
3. How can I regain my confidence?
4. How can I find or fashion opportunities that will accommodate my family obligations?

5. What are the actual, concrete steps I can take to return successfully?

6. How can I make the adjustment as easy as possible for myself and my family?

Part I of this book addresses these questions. To supplement what we learned from the women we interviewed and our own experience, we consulted career counselors, recruiters, work–life balance experts, relaunchers' husbands, and employers on the topic of career reentry. Vivian's eight years in recruiting and executive search also came in handy. Based on all these sources, we developed a 7-step plan to guide you through the relaunch process. These steps, which we explain in detail in chapters 1 through 7, are outlined briefly below:

Step 1: **RE**launch or not? You decide
Step 2: **L**earn confidence
Step 3: **A**ssess your career options
Step 4: **U**pdate your professional and job search skills
Step 5: **N**etwork and market yourself
Step 6: **C**hannel family support
Step 7: **H**andle the job (or find another one)

But before we go any further, you're probably curious: Why do we use the term *relaunch*? Because what we've found, both in our own experience and among the women we interviewed, is that going back to work after being home full-time with kids is rarely a matter of returning to the job you had. In most cases, women don't end up going back to their old employers, let alone the same jobs. And in many instances, women forge entirely new careers. So just as you had to launch a career after college or graduate school, now you'll have to relaunch one at this stage of your life. Far from being discouraging, however, the chance to relaunch should fill you with the same feeling of anticipation and excitement that you had umpteen years ago when you first entered the world of work. This is your opportunity either to return to your old profession with mature insights and perspectives, to pursue the career dreams you wouldashouldacoulda but for some reason didn't, or simply to work at something you now find fulfilling in some fashion.

Step 1 may strike you as superfluous. After all, if you've bought this book, you're probably sure you want to reenter the workforce, right? Not necessarily. For many women, making the decision to relaunch is not easy. If you've been focused solely on raising your family, you may feel very torn about *when* and even *whether* to return to paid work. For many women, contemplating a relaunch involves a confrontation between dueling aspects of the self—between the mother who wants to be there for her kids and the career woman she suppressed for years, but never quite forgot. You may experience intense internal conflict as you reflect on your current role at home in light of your former and potential role as a breadwinner, independent thinker, leader, and achiever in the conventional sense. You may mull over these conflicts endlessly, repeatedly reworking them with hypothetical career scenarios, discussing them constantly at book groups and PTO meetings, with your husband and even your children.

In considering a relaunch, your level of financial need obviously influences your thinking. If you face a sudden financial crisis, you'll feel pressure to generate income quickly and may believe you have to take whatever job you can get. If your financial requirements are longer-term, however—funding your retirement or your kids' college education, for example—you'll probably be a little more choosy in your search. Finally, if you face no financial pressure, you're likely to be extremely picky about the kind of work you're willing to take on. *Whatever your financial status, however, we believe you'll benefit from a strategic approach in attempting your relaunch.* Even if you believe you need a job tomorrow, you'll improve your chances of success if you approach the market thoughtfully rather than answering the first classified ad for which you feel qualified. And for those on the other end of the financial spectrum, if you've despaired of finding something worth doing that fits into your life, our 7-step approach will enable you to generate options you may find surprisingly compelling.

Deciding to go back to work, however, is only the first hurdle. You'll still face a whole host of internal and external challenges. Internally, you may grapple with a lack of confidence and uncertainty about what you want to do. Externally, you'll face skeptical human resource managers and rigid workplaces. From both perspectives, you may suffer from a lack of role models. Although you probably weren't the first woman in your workplace when you started your career, you may be the first woman you know to return to work after a long absence. Living in neighborhoods filled with either working-mother lifers or confirmed domestic divas, many women wonder whether they are the only ones in the world trying to negotiate the transition. Being a pioneer is tough, but it's also liberating. And most importantly, it enables you to set the agenda—to write the rules. But let us assure you of one thing up front: It *is* possible to relaunch your career and still remain an involved mother (and wife). Just as the women you're about to meet in this book managed to make the transition, you'll discover that you can, too.

Part II of this book is devoted to what we call the Relaunch Movement and Beyond—the whole phenomenon of women returning to work after taking time out to raise children. We begin in chapter 8 by profiling six inspirational relaunchers, women whose second careers have far outshone their first ones, including pioneers such as retired Supreme Court Justice Sandra Day O'Connor. Here you'll also find a list of women from actors to politicians who you probably never knew have gaps on their résumés. And yet they managed to relaunch. Big time.

We also ask the questions: Why are there so many women in this situation today (how many are there exactly?), and what, besides relaunching *ourselves,* can all of us do about it? We make the case for why corporations and other employers should consider hiring relaunchers, and we highlight those that are doing so. The Big Four accounting firm Deloitte & Touche, for example, has an extended leave program complete with mentoring and guaranteed job placement at the end of the leave. *Even if you can't benefit directly from these initiatives, they'll give you ammunition to approach other potential employers about creative solutions to the relaunch issue.* We also take a look at what universities and others are doing to facilitate women's return to the workplace.

Finally, in our epilogue, we glimpse the future. Will relaunching get any easier over the next ten years? What should women who are just *launching* their careers do now to make a potential future *relaunch* smoother? And, what impact will the Relaunch Movement have on the workplace of the next generation?

But we're getting ahead of ourselves. Before you can foment a movement, you've got to take the first step yourself.

PART I

THE
SEVEN STEPS
TO
RELAUNCH
SUCCESS

Relaunch or Not? You Decide

I always assumed I would return to my job at Drexel Burnham Lambert after maternity leave. Three years into a promising investment banking career, I couldn't imagine a better way to spend each day. There was fast-paced excitement, big stakes, challenging work, and a close-knit working team—everything I hoped for in a career when I started business school.

But before I could go back, Drexel collapsed and I was out of work, with a new baby and a serious case of mixed feelings. I loved my firstborn son and was applying my customary intensity to becoming a good mother. At the same time, I wasn't sure I was ready to relinquish my self-image as a career woman. Back in 1990, no one in my female peer group had even been pregnant, let alone left work to stay home with a child. While the same friends and business colleagues who had marveled at my pregnancy now stared curiously at our newborn baby, a part of me longed to be back with them in their high-paying, high-status positions.

As the first year of motherhood passed, I slowly adjusted to my new role. I gradually stopped defining myself in terms of career—or the lack of one. By the time my second child was born seventeen months later, I had thrown myself into motherhood with enthusiasm, and no apologies to myself or anyone else. As any mother knows, there are highs and lows. But I loved it and derived profound satisfaction from providing a caring and enriching environment for my children, including our third and fourth, who arrived within the next four years.

No longer feeling the tug of the workforce, I began to volunteer at our children's school. For the next five years, I poured my energy into making their school the best it could be, serving first as treasurer, then co-president of the school PTO, enlisting scores of talented new volunteers, securing a major technology grant, and leading our school's fight in a contentious citywide redistricting campaign. But as interesting and rewarding as I found these pursuits, there also seemed to be a never-ending pile of laundry, dishes, doctor's appointments, and the like at home. Gradually, troubling questions started to gnaw at me: Why, despite my education and experience, was I in the same place as women of a generation before me—the traditional volunteer/housewife?   —Carol

The Floundering Period

Like Carol, some of you may go through a floundering period during which you feel vaguely dissatisfied with your life, but aren't quite sure what to do about it. You're still deeply enmeshed in your children's routines—getting them up and out in the morning, transporting them to after-school activities later in the day—and in community volunteer projects, especially school-related ones, but you aren't getting the same satisfaction out of them as you once did. Floundering can manifest itself in resentment, anger, desperation, or a combination of these emotions. If it's misplaced, it can be directed at your spouse or kids, but in truth it represents discontent with how you perceive *yourself* after a number of years at home. Once your children become more *independent,* you may start to think of yourself as a *dependent.* This may feel especially awkward to those of you who earned substantial incomes in your former careers. Over time, you may begin to look at your husband's income as *your husband's money*. You may begin to feel guilty about buying things that are splurges just for you (even if you can afford such a purchase). Melissa, a highly accomplished former management consultant, confided: "I would never spend my husband's hard-earned money on anything purely for my own benefit if I didn't perceive it as absolutely crucial."

In addition to unwelcome feelings of dependence, you may experience a sense of worthlessness. Once your children enter grade school, you're no longer critical to their lives on an hourly basis. You still shuttle them to activities, supervise their homework, monitor their free time, and help them solve their childhood or adolescent traumas. Throw in the shopping, the cooking, the housework, and the almost mandatory school-related volunteer work, and you're quite busy. But once the kids are out of the house, motherhood feels less like a full-time job and more like underemployment. And if you had a challenging career before, you may suffer from this syndrome all the more acutely.

Let's start at the beginning. Remember when you first quit work to stay at home with your children? Remember that long, painful adjustment period of feeling like a nobody because your self-image was so tied up in who you were as a career woman? In the introduction to *The Price of Motherhood*, Pulitzer Prize nominee Ann Crittenden poignantly captured this sense of lost identity when she related: "A few years after I had resigned from *The New York Times* in order to have more time for my infant son, I ran into someone who asked, 'Didn't you used to be Ann Crittenden?'"[1]

For Judy, a corporate lawyer, the transition was particularly difficult. "Making the decision to stop working was really traumatic for me. I felt like I was jumping off the edge of the world. I had worked really hard for years, had become a partner with a beautiful corner office, and I'm giving this up? We have all these opportunities, but we also have children."

As emotionally difficult as that transition from work to home might have been, you got over it. You channeled all the energy and talent that had made you successful at work into being the best mother you could be. And most importantly (most of the time), you loved it! Or maybe, like Janice, a former social worker, you didn't: "I feel like all I do is move kids and things from one place to another. That is, when I'm not filling out forms." Shelly, a physician, commented: "When I was working, I was really there for my patients intensely and could be calm 95 percent of the time. But home wasn't the same. I felt more out of control at home. It was tougher to be at home."

Regardless of your reaction to those euphoric/exhausting first few years of at-home motherhood, things shifted when your oldest child started school and you charged into the PTO volunteer arena, finding all sorts of ways to let your professional knowledge seep into the classroom.

Maybe you've only been out for a year or two, or maybe you *thought* you'd only be out for a year or two, but in the wonderful tangle of child rearing, year stretched into year, and suddenly you woke up one morning, like Rip Van Winkle, five or ten years later, only then realizing how much time had passed. In any case, suddenly, for the first time in recent memory, you confront a gaping hole on the fridge calendar— those hours from eight thirty to three when your youngest child spends a full day at school. Even if you still have a toddler at home, you can see it coming—the day when that time will be yours and you are ready to make yourself the priority.

But what does this mean? Should you dust off your old loom sitting in the basement and sign up for a weaving class? Should you join a women's volleyball league to reclaim your college jock status? What about the piano lessons you always wanted to take, but never did? Or should you become a professional volunteer, contributing your time and energy to worthy causes on an unpaid basis? Some of you realize that you would only be satisfied with one thing: a return to the paid workforce. So you begin to contemplate a *relaunch of your career*.

Pros and Cons of a Relaunch

This is no simple decision. Unlike the choice to pursue nonwork passions, the decision to return to work has the distinction of not being completely on your own terms. It involves an obligation to others beyond your family and you. The last thing you want to do is take on a professional commitment and not deliver. Therefore, make sure you decide whether or not to return to work *not* by default, but after exhausting all other ways you may want to spend your time.

On the other hand, returning to work has the potential to satisfy so many of your long-suppressed desires. It allows you to contribute to the family income and be recognized for doing so, interact with adults on intellectual issues, focus on challenging problems for extended periods, and experience the unique sense of accomplishment that comes from finishing a complex project and getting paid for it.

Reasons Behind Your Uncertainty About Returning

Your Husband's Attitude and Work Situation

Before pursuing paid work, you have to consider one of the other major passions in your life, your husband (if you have one). Where is he in his career, and can he be the point person for family-related issues during some predetermined ramp-up period you may require once you start a job? What type of job does he have? If he controls his hours, then taking a job with unpredictability or heavy travel becomes more of a possibility for you. However, if he has a job with a crazy schedule or a huge amount of travel, it will be difficult for you to take a position with similar characteristics.

Another relevant factor is how he handles his own job emotionally. Is he under a lot of job stress? Is he new to his current job or has he held it for a number of years? Is he happy with his situation or will he be looking for a change soon? The more stable his career, the easier it may be for him to help at home.

What kind of money is he earning? If he's making enough to support all of you in style for the foreseeable future, he may legitimately wonder why you see the need to earn money yourself. However, if your income will materially improve your lifestyle, either now or in retirement, he will probably be more gung-ho.

Finally, is he open to the prospect of taking on more domestic responsibilities? Is he threatened by it? Does he think he can't handle it in addition to his workload, or has he become so accustomed to your doing everything at home that he dreads the thought of its being any other way? Even those husbands favorably disposed to the notion of picking up more child- and home-related responsibilities are shocked by the amount of time involved.

We mention husbands here because their employment status and their feelings about your going back to work will have a fundamental impact on your thinking. Nevertheless, if your husband is the only one holding you back, don't necessarily let him stand in your way. You'll have to take his schedule and attitude into consideration, but in most cases, if you're thoughtful, committed, and persistent, you can relaunch in a way that strengthens, rather than threatens, your marriage.

The Impact on Your Children

For most women at home, it's their children who are keeping them there. If you've been a hands-on parent, seeing your children off to school each morning and meeting them at the bus stop or welcoming them home each day, you may be understandably concerned about how your return to work will affect them and in turn, how that will make you feel as a mother. And it's probably not just the logistics of who will get them out of the house in the morning or who will supervise them in the afternoon that worry you. If you've been an at-home parent, you're accustomed to a *parent* kissing them good-bye in the morning and keeping track of their goings-on after school. Peggy, a former advertising executive with two elementary-school-aged daughters, has very strong feelings about the importance of parental influence, *in the moment,* when her kids come home from school. "I know who my kids' friends are and can subtly and gently steer them toward certain friendships and away from others. I could never have this level of awareness if I was working full-time. I think this closeness gives me the ability to set boundaries for my children that I wouldn't be able to set as clearly if I weren't so close to the dynamics of their daily lives."

Although many mothers feel strongly about being home for milk-and-cookie time almost until their children leave for college, some find themselves willing to consider being out of the house a few afternoons a week because they've built up such a cushion of full-time motherhood underneath them. These moms do not think they need that lengthy daily contact in order to feel part of their children's lives. In fact, a few women described having the opposite feeling: *Because* they had been home full-time for so long, they actually *didn't* want to be there full-time anymore.

If you're worried about the emotional and psychological impact of your working on your kids, be aware of the significant research published and dissected since you probably last visited the issue. In *A Mother's Place,* Susan Chira examined several child care studies and concluded that "most studies that have followed children over time . . . have found virtually no differences between children of working or at-home mothers."[2] In fact, "several studies have indicated that children of working mothers, particularly poor children and girls, are more socially adjusted; perform better in school; and have greater self-reliance, higher career aspirations, and more egalitarian views of sex roles."[3] Unless your job hours coincide with those of your children (and we interviewed women who crafted such opportunities), then you're going to have to find some child care and get yourself and your kids comfortable with it. You may have to engage a part-time babysitter or enroll your child in an after-school program, for example, at least a couple of days a week. Our experiences and those of the relaunchers we interviewed suggest that as with any major change, if you still have elementary-school-aged children at home, the transition will be easier for both you and your kids if you return to work *gradually,* rather than going back full-time out of the house from day one.

If a sudden change in financial status requires that you return to full-time work outside the home immediately, so be it. Or if you're offered an incredible full-time opportunity that you don't want to pass up, go for it. But if making the transition smooth is an option, then starting off with a reduced schedule, for example, a full day three days a week, or consulting from home with occasional days out, will help you and your children get used to the idea of your not being home when they get out of school. After an adjustment period, you can then ramp up to five full days without its being such a jolt to your children's routines and expectations. *Presenting yourself consistently as a working parent is the key to making the transition easier.* A steady and gradual relaunch will help you appear more consistent to your kids.

The Difficulty of Relinquishing Control

Although studies suggest that children will survive their mothers' working as long as high-quality care is found for them, you may still be reluctant to relinquish control on the home front. Gloria, a former pharmaceutical sales representative and mother of four, commented: "I'm a control freak. I just can't see myself letting someone else run my household during the day. It would make me crazy."

Although you may think you're indispensable, most school-aged children can fend for themselves when pressed. But as stay-at-home moms, some of you may rarely give your children that opportunity. Monica, a physical therapist, worked while her kids were younger and then took five years off. She was contemplating a return, but was nervous about how the family would cope in her absence. She explained: "I was sick of hearing complaints from my husband and children about breakfasts, lunches, and how things were or were not getting done around the house, but I was nervous about how they would manage without me. Fed up one morning, I decided to take . . . inaction. I stayed in bed and let the children run through the morning routine themselves." Well, the kids (a thirteen-year-old and ten-year-old twins) made their breakfasts and lunches themselves and left on their own. "It was a lesson to me. It was as if someone turned the light on. I realized that a ten-year-old making her own breakfast and going to the bus by herself can be a good thing. She's developing competencies she wouldn't have developed if I were always around. I think about it in terms of competencies developed in the absence or presence of parents." Independence isn't a bad thing to test and encourage. And it may convince you, as it did Monica, that life will go on at home after you go back to work.

The Reluctance to Give Up Your Freedom

In addition to the difficulty of letting go at home, many mothers don't relish giving up their own freedom. Although part of you may long for the paycheck and camaraderie that come with employment, another part of you may be reluctant to give up the flexibility you now have to structure your days and accomplish your obligations as you see fit. Although you may be very busy "doing" for your husband, your kids, your home, and even volunteer assignments, those efforts differ significantly from being obligated to an employer or a client. And while we believe there is greater potential work flexibility now than has existed since the industrial revolution began, flexibility has its limits.

Debbie, a San Francisco mother of three, was a commercial banker who relaunched as a regional sales manager for a women's clothing company that holds trunk shows in women's homes. She gave us her take on the flexibility-versus-commitment issue: "It isn't that these women don't want to work. It's just that they want work to be on their own terms. They want manageable time. They want work to factor into family life rather than the other way around." Debbie took the regional sales job because it allowed her to have this kind of relationship with her work. And she recruits women to be reps who feel the same way. "I recruit women who have entrepreneurial leanings, but who don't want to compromise family for their work." The reps make twenty-five to fifty thousand dollars a year in gross commissions before expenses. For some, this is less than they made in their previous careers, but they willingly pay this price for the flexibility of the job and the ability to have their own business. Some of them do this as a way of keeping their hand in the working world, but in a manageable way.

Low Self-Esteem or Depression

As we mentioned, some women experience dwindling self-esteem the longer they remain home full-time. In extreme cases, this feeling of worthlessness can border on depression.

Kathy, a mother of four who left a public relations career, commented, "There's this whole part of me that doesn't know how I got here. I'm much more tentative in social situations. There are certain topics of conversation I shy away from because I'm afraid I won't have an opinion on them. I don't know what happened to the confident, competent person that I was. All I know is that person is definitely not here anymore. That person has been replaced by a depressed, easily intimidated person who feels socially awkward in groups that include others besides 'mommies' and their kids.

"Complicating this, I also feel as if my life has no meaning. I have no sense of accomplishment in my life, no sense that I'm making a difference for others outside of my immediate family. I use so much energy making everything work for all my kids all day that I am too exhausted at the end of the day to do anything to make myself interesting. I feel completely worthless because I don't have anything to contribute."

We don't mean to imply that depression is an occupational hazard of at-home motherhood, nor that relaunching your career will eliminate your psychological ills. But neither are we the first to notice a correlation between housewives and depression.

Ambivalence and Guilt

Even if you don't become depressed, you may be plagued by doubt: *Do I really want to go back to work? Would my family and I be better off if I simply devoted more time to outside interests, like a hobby or volunteer work? If I don't go back to work, will I harbor anger and resentment toward my family? Is this the right time, in terms of my children's development and my feelings about my life, to return to work? Will my children be okay if I have to hire a babysitter or put them into an afternoon program a couple of days (or more) a week?*

These questions may be prompted by a deep ambivalence about returning to work. Many of you had a hard time deciding whether to leave work in the first place; likewise, you may have just as hard a time deciding when and even whether to return. You shouldn't beat yourself up over this ambivalence. It's only natural. You may have spent a number of years building a life for yourself as a full-time mother and homemaker, investing in your children, in your home, in friendships, in community organizations and routines. The thought of changing all that is frightening.

Some of you experience ambivalence related to your perception of *other people's expectations* of you as a working person. Rebecca, a teacher who was relaunching after five years at home, reflected: "Work takes on an inflated importance when you live in a community like mine. When women here go to work, most of them are doing *important* things like groundbreaking scientific research or AIDS medicine. There is some subtle pressure to have an intense, important job, or not work at all. I had to fight this perception when I chose to take my job as a teacher's aide."

Even if your children are in school all day, if you add up the hours before and after school, during the summer, and on vacation and sick days, you realize that there is a lot of time when your children are at home. And if you're used to being a hands-on parent, you probably can't imagine giving that up. You worry about what impact losing that together time will have on your child, as well as what impact it will have on you and your assessment of yourself as a mother.

A debilitating sense of guilt can permeate your state of mind during this period. Many women feel guilty because they enjoy the luxury of staying home, while others feel guilty at the thought of going back to work: "I actually felt it was the greatest act of selfishness to return to work full-time," Carol once remarked. "This decision was all about me, and only me. Objectively, I thought, it was detrimental to the lives of my husband and children, who relied on me at home. Yet, on the other hand, *I wondered whether an unhappy, impatient, and frustrated wife and mother was really better than one who's around less but in better spirits.*" The media haven't helped, by portraying materialistic house-wives feeding off their husbands on the one hand and career-obsessed working mothers on the other.

What Others Think and Say

Finally, as you flounder over whether or not to try to relaunch your ca-reer, you will be plagued by unsolicited advice, opinions, and just plain interference from well-meaning friends and family. Kim, a former city planner on the verge of becoming an empty-nester, was urged by her mother to "pamper herself." When she decided to relaunch instead, her friends reacted in two different ways. "I was afraid my friends would laugh at me. But most said, 'You can do anything.' One very tough, highly successful friend thought I was overreaching when I applied for certain jobs. It cut me to the quick. And I really wanted to prove her wrong, which I did."

Terry was not prepared for the reaction of some women in her at-home peer group after she relaunched as a full-time software program-mer: "When I first started telling other women that I was returning to work, many were shocked, and *asked if my husband had lost his job. They couldn't believe that I was doing this by choice.* That surprised me."

Bucking the Perfect-Mother Myth and the New Momism

All these concerns about your proper maternal role have crystallized around a peculiar recent malady called the new momism, the über-mom syndrome, or any number of other colorful descriptors. Indeed, according to Judith Warner, author of *Perfect Madness,* the current generation of mothers has "driven themselves crazy in the quest for perfect mommy-dom. . . . I heard of whole towns turning out for a spot in the *right* ballet class; of communities where the competition for the *best* camps, the *best* coaches and the *best* piano teachers rivaled that for admission to the best private schools and colleges."[4]

Although Warner claimed that this affliction strikes both stay-at-home and working mothers, as a stay-at-home mom you may be particularly vulnerable because you've poured all your energies into child rearing. And having invested so much time and trouble into full-time motherhood, you may find it difficult to cut back. The question is: How much of this mania is due to your deeply held beliefs about what constitutes good parenting, and how much is due to keeping up with the Joneses in the motherhood department? In contemplating a relaunch of your career, you need to make sure you meet your own maternal expectations, not someone else's idea of the perfect mother.

Seven Motivators for Relaunching

What are the motivators for making the relaunch decision? If your family has managed to survive this long without your income, why should you return to the rat race, this year, next year, or ever? After all, the choice to return to work is not foreordained. Although most of the women we read about in articles on women leaving the workforce claim that they'll return to work someday, we all know women who are thrilled to be home full-time and may never wish to return.

Although each woman may phrase her reasons for wanting to return to work slightly differently, we've identified seven major motivators, with many women experiencing a combination of these.

1. Money
Not surprisingly, number one on the list for most women is money. According to the Center for Work–Life Policy's March 2005 "Off-

Ramps and On-Ramps" study, 38 percent of on-ramping women cite "household income no longer sufficient for family needs" and 24 percent cite "partner's income no longer sufficient for family needs" as the major factors propelling them to seek jobs.[5] Although your husband may have earned enough to permit you to take time off while your children were young, you may not be able to afford this setup any longer. Or you may be concerned about your financial future. These concerns may not force you to get a job tomorrow, but they may play, more or less subtly, into the calculus of your thinking about returning to work.

Indeed, the very growth of your family may precipitate the need for additional income. For example, you may be busting out of the starter house you bought when you were first pregnant. Feeding, clothing, and entertaining a teenager costs more than doing the same for babies and toddlers. Part of the reason why Judy, the corporate lawyer who gave up her corner office, relaunched her career was that she and her husband wanted to switch their children into private schools. When Bonnie, a former sales manager, ran the numbers on retirement and paying for college, she realized the family would come up short unless she added another income stream into the projections.

Over the last few years in particular, after the bursting of the stock market bubble in 2000, many husbands have encountered career hiccups, for perhaps the first time in their work lives. Even if you managed to stay home during these episodes of reduced or nonexistent spousal income, you may have vowed not to put your family at the mercy of one employer again.

And for better or worse, there are also many of you who are currently single again, whether through widowhood or divorce, who may have enough of a cushion for the next few years but who know, or believe, that the money won't last forever.

We're not arguing that you should take a job on the off chance that you might get divorced, but we do stand by the Girl Scout motto of "Be prepared." Divorce, widowhood, spousal disability, and protracted spousal unemployment can and do happen. Relaunching thus offers a contingency plan in case of a major financial dislocation.

Even though making money may be one of your goals, there may be situations in which it's advantageous to start off by taking a job in which you barely break even financially after accounting for child care, transportation, and other work-related expenses. As we discuss in detail in chapter 3, you should consider such an opportunity if something special about the job content, flexibility, or people will lead to a more lucrative future position. Think of it as an investment, a résumé builder, a way to indicate to future employers you are serious about working and keeping current.

Leah, a primary care physician and mother of two young boys, relaunched by joining the satellite office of a small private practice two mornings a week. After three years, the physicians who owned the practice decided to close the office, and Leah had to reevaluate her options. By then, her older boy was in elementary school and her younger child was in nursery school three mornings a week. She really liked working two mornings a week, but she couldn't find another practice that would allow her to work the same schedule. Finally, she came across an opportunity to work part-time as a clinical instructor at a university medical school residency program located close to her home. Unfortunately, the position was unpaid; typically, paid senior physicians on staff supervised the residents on a rotating volunteer basis.

Leah weighed the pros and cons. She loved the babysitter who had been with her for the last three years, and didn't want to lose her. The university would pick up malpractice insurance coverage that she would otherwise have to maintain herself, and would also give her an associate professorship title. She really liked the people she would be working with. Taking this position was a net loss because of the babysitting and transportation costs, but it was less expensive than covering her own insurance while she continued looking for another job. Her husband questioned the decision. What convinced her (and eventually him) that it was worth doing was that it gave her continuous work experience on her résumé, kept her medical knowledge current, gave her access to a medical community with lots of contacts, and bought her some time to look for the right paid position the following year when her younger child entered kindergarten and she would be available for more hours.

If you can live without a positive income stream in the short term, the intangible future benefits from a job in which you temporarily lose money or only break even may make it worth taking. Make sure you weigh all the benefits, as Leah did, not just the cash compensation, when making a relaunch decision.

2. Validation

When you left work in the first place, you probably couched it as "a good family decision." Unlike the traditional housewives Betty Friedan described in *The Feminine Mystique,* you *chose* to be home *after* proving yourself quite capable of handling a demanding career. Friedan's women never had the opportunity to test their professional potential and experience career success. The big surprise is that despite previous professional accomplishments, today's women who decide to relaunch after taking extended leave from promising careers often experience a kind of delayed and watered-down version of what Friedan's women felt. It is not unusual to experience self-doubt about whether you can still make it professionally, or whether, while at home, you've lost something critical to success. How do you overcome these feelings of self-doubt? You need the validation that will come from resuming your career.

Your contribution to the organization and enrichment of family life only gets you so far. Marla, a lawyer and human resource executive, put it this way: "The idea of being independent and self-determined is paramount to me, and while I love being a mother, it will not solely define my life." According to Peggy, after she quit her job as an advertising executive, "It would kill me not to have an occupation to fill in on forms." For those of you without pressing financial need who are returning to the workforce after raising children, *the job itself* is the validation. The bottom line is that you need to make money again and contribute to the family income, *not for the purchasing power of the income, but simply for the legitimacy and validation that earning it provides.*

3. Leveling the Marriage Playing Field

Pulling in your own income and contributing in a material way to family finances can do wonders for making you feel self-sufficient, confident, and independent within your marriage. Resuming your work status means spending *decisions* replace spending *negotiations.* You put less pressure on yourself to be thrifty when you carry some of the financial burden. You more easily give yourself permission to splurge occasionally.

Yolanda distinctly remembered feeling much freer to go into a store and buy something she liked (maybe even something for herself!) shortly after returning to work. Prior to her relaunch, she rarely shopped except for essentials: "Before I went back to work, I somehow didn't feel justified in making purchases for myself or for the house because I was not contributing directly to our family's income. This feeling was completely self-generated, as my husband never pressured me to limit my purchases when I was home full-time."

Melanie, a relauncher who started her own Web site design business, related, "I was the fourth kid in my family growing up, and my family had to scrape for me to go to college. So I always had discomfort with not being in control financially." Molly, a textile artist and weaver who relaunched as an art teacher for the disabled, explained her delight at receiving her first paycheck: "I told my husband and kids I was taking everyone out to dinner when my first paycheck came in. And I did! It was a terrific feeling to be earning my own money again."

4. Intellectual Stimulation

Most women do enjoy their maternal roles, but being at home full-time makes them stir-crazy. For some of you, a lack of intellectual excitement in your lives drives you to think about reentering.

Vivian craved the company of other bright, high-energy adults. "I missed the sense of accomplishment that comes from completing a difficult project, and I needed to wrap my mind around something other than domestic challenges. Having had an exciting job, with great colleagues and tough assignments, before I decided to stay home with my children whetted my appetite for more. It gave me a kind of high I couldn't get any other way, and once I'd experienced that work-driven adrenaline rush, the desire for it never completely faded."

Charlene, a brand-manager-turned-consultant, cited, among other reasons, the "pride and sense of accomplishment I get from work." Susan, who had been at a large management consulting firm and relaunched by working for the board of education of a major city, mentioned a common theme: "I like working, feeling connected to people, using skills, having an impact, being challenged. I don't like drifting."

5. Avoiding Empty-Nest Syndrome

Although some of you might wonder if it would be better to wait until the kids are in high school or college before going back to work, believing that it's too difficult to juggle a job, along with the car pools, the shopping, and the medical appointments (let alone the housework) that raising teenagers requires, many of you may be haunted by the specter of the unfulfilled lives of your mothers' generation. According to Maxine, a former real estate executive, "I see a lot of at-home mothers whose kids have gone to college, and they are lost. They are leading lives of quiet desperation."

Patty, a psychologist, appreciated the problem from both a personal and professional perspective: "I feel if I don't develop something of my own I'll develop emptiness syndrome"—a condition she had studied in her master's program.

"My mother had gotten kind of depressed in her sixties when she felt like she didn't have much to do, and I didn't want that to happen to me," Kim, the former city planner, confided. For many baby boomers, fear of "becoming our mothers" fueled earlier career ambitions. And that fear returns with a vengeance when you hit forty and see yourself in almost the same position they were in at that age.

Although your sixties may still be decades away, be aware that if you wait until your decks are completely cleared of all child-rearing responsibilities (which your mother will tell you will never happen anyway), you'll find it even harder to pursue professional dreams. So while it may feel a little early in terms of your obligations at home, some of you plunge back into careers, not wanting to put your professional life on hold any longer.

Lindsay, a former chemical engineer, described the life events that propelled her back into the job market: "When my youngest was still in high school (the other two were in college and grad school already), my older brother died suddenly. I also went into menopause. I was faced with my own mortality. I realized you only get one shot. I thought, *Is this it?* I realized I have to take care of doing everything *I* want to do. Even though I still had one child at home and I was busy with the parents' association, I could see that soon I was going to have a lot more spare time. My husband works seven to seven, five days a week. I decided the day my youngest gets her driver's license, I'm going to look for something to do."

6. Serving as a Role Model

How do your children view you if you've been home since they were born or since they were young? Do they see you as an intellectual being, a warm, loving soul, or even just a servant? How do you want them to view you? One of Vivian's motivations for returning was a desire for her children, especially her daughters, to see that there was a dimension to her life that went beyond running the household. "As I watched my oldest grow into adolescence, I began to think about what kind of an example I was setting for her, and for my other children as well. I wanted them to see that mommies could do more than just be mommies. I wanted them to have a better sense of the possibilities that life holds."

In the March 2005 issue of *Parenting*, Jill Johnson, a mother of three boys returning to work after five years at home, said she wanted them to see that "mommies can go out and earn a living just like daddies can."[6] Lindsay, the chemical engineer, wanted to demonstrate to her three daughters that "you can remake yourself at any point in your life. I wanted to show them that if their lives aren't going the way they want it, they can pick themselves up and reinvent themselves, at any age. I wanted to be a role model for them." The unspoken implication is that if you wait until your children are all grown up before you try to go back to work, your kids will never observe that it's possible to both work and mother.

7. Ambition

You may have been hugely ambitious early in your career, but when you made the decision to stay home, your family commitments combined with, in some cases, diminished confidence may have whittled down your ambition. The Center for Work–Life Policy's "Off-Ramps and On-Ramps" study of more than 2,443 women with high-honors undergraduate degrees, or graduate degrees, found that 39 percent of women aged twenty-eight through forty are "extremely/very ambitious," compared with only 31 percent of women aged forty-one through fifty-five. Among women in business, the "ambition gap" is even wider; 53 percent of younger women in business consider themselves "extremely/very ambitious" versus only 37 percent of older women.[7]

For the relauncher, the difficult part is often balancing reemerging ambition with the reality of daily life at home. Dinner's not the only thing cooking on the back burner; your ambition probably is, too! Recognizing that you have unfulfilled career ambitions is one of the first steps of a successful relaunch. When we tell you that relaunch time is time for you, part of that message is it's time to unleash your stifled ambition. You don't have to announce it to the whole world. The only one who has to know is you.

The "Aha" Moment

The floundering period can go on for some time, as you toss the idea of returning to work back and forth in your head and with your husband, family, and friends. However, in the midst of this, you may experience an "aha" moment, as some of our interviewees did, and that motivates you to explore work alternatives.

Celeste, a social worker before and after her relaunch, summed it up this way: "I never felt cut out for full-time motherhood. When I was running a big fair at the kids' school, another mother called to say that if I couldn't use the school's puppet theater, I could borrow the one she had made for her children. Right then and there I realized I was no match for some of these perfect at-home moms, who set up educational craft projects and other special activities for their kids. When I was working, I had an excuse for not doing these things. Now I had no excuse. I'm also very performance-oriented, and I hated to have a day go by with nothing to show for it, which is so common in the lives of stay-at-home mothers."

"I decided to take a scrapbooking class," Marcia, a former nurse-MBA, told us. "I had boxes of photos around, and that was bothering me. The class was held at someone's house, and there were five or six women of a variety of ages attending. I only wanted to get my photos in the albums! But the other women were into making masterpieces. One woman was spending the whole session on one page creating a beach scene with real sand for her family's beach vacation pictures.

It was beautiful. But sitting there, watching the other women create, I suddenly had this overwhelming reaction. I said it right there. 'I have to go back to work. (a) I can't make this album page, and (b) I don't want to make this album page. I need to go back to work.' It was a turning point for me, and I began a job search in earnest shortly after that."

Take the Relaunch Readiness Quiz

Still floundering? No "aha" moment happened yet? We developed the Relaunch Readiness Quiz as a way of helping you quantify the relaunch decision-making process. Go ahead and take it now to assess your appetite and logistical ability to relaunch. Then read the scoring and interpretation for each section. Or, if you prefer, take it online and let the computer score it for you. Visit www.backonthecareertrack.com and hit the "Relaunch Readiness Quiz" tab.

Part 1. Appetite for Work

1. I miss working . . .

Not at all   Somewhat   A lot

1   2   3   4   5   6   7   8   9   10

2. For the time being, I am very happy being a stay-at-home mother.

Agree strongly   Agree somewhat   Disagree strongly

1   2   3   4   5   6   7   8   9   10

3. I have a hobby or volunteer work that substantively engages me.

Agree strongly   Agree somewhat   Disagree strongly

1   2   3   4   5   6   7   8   9   10

4. I could see myself going back to work in _____ years.

10 9 8 7 6 5 4 3 2 1

1   2   3   4   5   6   7   8   9   (10)

(Circle the number in the second row below the answer you choose in the first row.)

5. The average number of hours per week that I would be willing
    and able to spend working is . . .

0	5	10	15	20	25	30	35	40	40+
1	2	3	4	5	6	(7)	8	9	10

(Circle the number in the second row below the answer you choose in the first
row.)

6. Our family could materially benefit from my earning money.

    Disagree strongly   Agree somewhat   Agree strongly

1	2	3	4	5	6	7	8	9	(10)

Add up all the numbers you circled. This is your score for
   part 1:___53___

Interpretation of Scoring for Part 1

If you score 45 or above, you have a strong desire to relaunch. Even
if your scores for parts 2 and 3 are low, you may wish to explore child
care options to enable you to get back to work in some fashion.

If your score falls between 30 and 45, you currently have a moder-
ate appetite for work. Combined with a high score in parts 2 and 3, you
may decide to give it a go.

If you score less than 30, you're not very motivated to return to
work at this time. Consider investing more time in your hobbies and
volunteer work, particularly those that might open up career options
for you later.

Part 2. Child and Elder Care Responsibilities

For each question, circle the number in the second row below the
number you choose in the first row.

7. Number of children not yet in school:

3+	3	2	1	0
1	2	3	4	10

8. Number of children in preschool:

3+	3	2	1	0
2	3	4	5	10

9. Number of children in elementary school:

3+	3	2	1	0
3	4	(5)	6	10

10. Number of children in high school:

3+	3	2	1	0
4	5	6	7	10

11. Average number of hours per week I spend between 8 AM and 6 PM on weekdays in the care of or related to the care of my children and/or an elderly or ill relative:

50	45	40	35	30	25	20	15	10	5 or less
1	2	3	4	5	6	7	(8)	9	10

Add up all the numbers you circled. This is your score for part 2: ___43___

Interpretation of Scoring for Part 2

If you score 40 or above, you definitely have time to explore relaunching your career. Couple this with a high score in part 1, and you're raring to go.

If you score between 30 and 40, you have reasonably demanding family obligations. If you score high in parts 1 and 3, however, you have the motivation and support for a successful relaunch. A high score in part 1 and a low score in part 3 will make it more difficult, but nothing's impossible.

If you score below 30, you have a lot going on in your household. If you score high on parts 1 and 3, however, don't be discouraged. If you're willing to explore child care options for part of the week, you can still relaunch. This will most likely be necessary if you score low on part 3.

Part 3. Spousal and/or Other Family Support

12. **My husband has some flexibility in his schedule, or I have access to additional unpaid help from a family member.**

Very little   Some   A lot

1   2   3   4   5   6   (7)   8   9   10

13. **My husband or other family members who help me would be supportive of my going back to work.**

Disagree strongly   Agree somewhat   Agree strongly

1   2   3   4   5   6   7   8   9   (10)

14. **My husband or other adult family member would be available to help me an average of _____ hours per week between 8 AM and 6 PM during the week with child-care- or elder-care-related tasks.**

1   2   3   4   5   6   7   (8)   9   10

Add up all the numbers you circled. This is your score for part 3:___25___

Interpretation of Scoring for Part 3

If you scored 20 or above, you have strong spousal or other family support for a relaunch. Couple this with a high score in part 1, and you're off to a strong start, regardless of your score in part 2.

If you score between 15 and 20, you have a reasonable amount of support for a relaunch. Coupled with a high score in parts 1 and 2, your challenge is manageable. If you have a low score in part 2, you may need to engage outside child care resources in order to relaunch.

If you score less than 15, you're not getting much spousal or other familial support for a transition back to work. However, if you scored high in parts 1 and 2, you may not need that much support to pull it off. If you scored low in part 2, you'll almost certainly need to engage outside resources to help you with your child care responsibilities. And you should continue to revisit the relaunch issue with your husband or other close family members to see if you can garner more support. (See Chapter 6: Channel *Family* Support.)

————

Your Relaunch Readiness Quiz score should guide you in determining whether you are ready to relaunch right now. If your scores are high but you're still reticent, lack of confidence may be holding you back. Step 2, Learn Confidence, will show you how to overcome this hurdle.

CHAPTER 2

Learn Confidence

I think that after being out of the workforce taking care of babies, one's work ego sort of turns into a baby itself. It's fragile, vulnerable, with a healthy dose of stranger anxiety. And you go into an interview and have to pass this trembling ego over to some stranger to validate. A pretty painful process! —Pilar

Confidence Lost

In grappling with the issue of whether or not to try to relaunch your career, it's important to separate legitimate reasons why you may not want to relaunch from a fear of relaunching, which usually stems from a lack of confidence or concern about finding the right opportunity. In addition to being concerned about home management issues, you're plagued with concerns about yourself and the work environment: *Will I be able to find rewarding work? What if I'm only available part-time? Do I still have what it takes to succeed? Will anybody hire me?*

Indeed, we believe a lack of confidence, coupled with a lack of vision about opportunities in the marketplace, constitute the greatest hurdles to women considering a relaunch. According to career counselor Mary Lindley Burton, co-author (with Richard A. Wedemeyer) of *In Transition,* the biggest problem among professional women trying to reenter is that they engage in "a highly inappropriate diminution of what they have to offer."[1]

Why do so many full-time moms feel they cannot operate at the same professional level at which they functioned before having children? Part of the answer is that anyone who leaves work for an extended period feels rusty. Carol's husband took a sixteen-month leave of absence from his law firm to work on a political campaign, and he admitted that it took him a few months to get back up to speed. And that was in a situation where the leave involved an intense, fast-paced environment—not exactly the world of at-home motherhood.

Choosing to take extended leave to raise children can make you feel particularly unfit for returning to the job market on several counts. First of all, the demands of full-time motherhood make it difficult for many women to keep up with developments in their fields, as well as with their old colleagues. And while technology has enhanced communication, the flip side of technological advancement is that you can become dated very quickly. And this can kill your confidence. Add to this the speed of change in most industries and many women begin to feel completely *professionally disconnected* within a relatively short time period.

Second, those taking a number of years off are rendered suspect in the eyes of others. "Will she really put her nose to the grindstone after being at home?" Simply giving birth can make people question your postpartum abilities. Katherine Ellison, Pulitzer Prize–winning foreign correspondent and author of *The Mommy Brain: How Motherhood Makes Us Smarter,* related in an interview, "I got a new editor after my second son was born who let me know that he thought I was going to be less productive and that I wouldn't be able to keep my mind in two places at once. He was wrong, of course, but his distrust shook my confidence for a while."[2] There's no question that, try as we might to ignore what other people think, most of us can't help being swayed at least a little bit by the feedback we receive from others, both solicited and unsolicited. And you'll probably find yourself most vulnerable to comments from others when you're first trying to relaunch.

Third, caring for children, while offering many rewards and demanding imagination and creativity, does not provide the same kind of intellectual challenge that many careers offer. Once you settle into the softer world of child care, you often lose the sharpness of mind that enabled you to do quick mental math, design an office building, whip out a marketing plan, make a difficult diagnosis, or write computer code. How do you regain that edge? Can you?

Finally, women's tendency to denigrate themselves in this situation epitomizes a problem women have when they hit career roadblocks of *any* kind. Patricia Chang, a sociology professor at Boston College, noticed in research comparing clergymen and -women that women tended to speak about career disappointments in personal terms whereas men tended to blame supervisors or other institutional systems.[3] If it's true that women tend to internalize career disappointment whereas men externalize the cause of their work problems, then women may have less confidence when approaching the next step in their careers and may be more apt to sell themselves short.

Selling Yourself Short—Literally

In addition to undermining your ability to compete for a job, lack of confidence can also manifest itself in not negotiating for a higher salary or underpricing your services. In *Women Don't Ask: Negotiation and the Gender Divide*, Linda Babcock and Sara Laschever make the case that women (unlike men) tend not to ask for higher starting salaries, higher raises, and better opportunities.[4] Charlene, a brand manager who relaunched as a marketing consultant, experienced this firsthand: "I think the lack of confidence affects me in other ways. In pay, for example. I noticed that another consultant got paid much more than I did on a project. I think if I had marketed myself better, I could have charged more. *I was just grateful to get the work.* One working friend of mine said, 'Charlene, you sound like you think *they're* doing *you* a favor. You've got to believe that *you're* doing *them* a favor.'" Not only did we speak to women who discovered they were charging much lower hourly consulting rates than their male counterparts for the same services, but the women were quicker to discount their rates for a special circumstance. Their lack of confidence led them to question their worth.

Expert Advice

For help in addressing this confidence gap, we sought out Michele Phillips, an authority in the field of self-esteem and peak performance, and the director of Key Seminars, a corporate training company based outside of New York City. Additionally, she is a trainer at the Westchester, New York–based Women's Enterprise Development Center, Inc., and is certified by Jack Canfield (of *Chicken Soup for the Soul* fame) in peak performance training.

Michele advocates a four-pronged approach to boosting your confidence. Most important, and something especially difficult for women, is to understand the difference between confidence and arrogance. According to Michele, *Confidence is being the best you can be. Arrogance is claiming you are better than everybody else.* Women sometimes confuse the two and feel uncomfortable working to make themselves more confident because they think they will be viewed as arrogant. Others desperately want to become more confident, but have trouble figuring out how to take concrete steps to make it happen. If you fall into either category, start by following Michele's suggestions:

- **Take 100 percent responsibility for your reaction to life's events.** Most of the time, you can't control the events you experience, but you can control your reaction to them. A key Canfield principle is E (event) + R (reaction) = O (outcome).[5] You can train yourself to have a different response to events than you have had in the past.
- **Discipline your mind.** Cancel your membership to the *I-did-awful* club. Negative self-talk is one of the factors leading to low self-esteem. Replace negative self-talk with affirmations

of yourself and your abilities. Repeat them, write them down, and post them where you'll see them often so they become your mantra.

Michele's personal affirmations are: "I am radiant. I am in demand. I am courageous. I am a money magnet. I am unstoppable." Even when she has a failure, she picks herself up by focusing on her mantra. She still has times when she loses her confidence, but she bounces back a lot quicker than she did before she adopted this approach. She admitted that it may sound corny to develop these positive statements about yourself and then post them so you can remember them all the time. But it has worked for her personally (and she didn't think she had self-esteem issues to begin with!), and she has seen it work for hundreds of others.

- **Give your mind high-quality "nutrition."** Pay attention to what you read, what you watch on TV, and what you listen to on the radio. Improve the quality of these inputs whenever possible. In addition, surround yourself with winners—with people who you want to become or be like. This doesn't mean only people who are accomplished in material ways, but also those with an approach to life or moral values consistent with yours or worth emulating.
- **Make time to appreciate your accomplishments.** Keep a weekly or monthly "victory log." Write whatever you want in it, but be sure to include a list of accomplishments and goals you have met for the week or the month.[6]

Mommy Dividends

In addition to these tactics, revel in the wisdom you've gained from parenting. In *If You've Raised Kids, You Can Manage Anything*, Ann Crittenden convincingly argued that good management skills are almost synonymous with good parenting skills. Based on interviews with dozens of professionally successful yet tuned-in parents (mostly moth-ers), she identified "four categories of transferable skills" that involved mothers (and fathers) have developed that "cross over and enrich their professional lives." They are: multitasking, interpersonal skills, grow-ing human capabilities, and habits of integrity.[7] Katherine Ellison, in *The Mommy Brain,* described how motherhood enhances brain power in the areas of improved perception, efficiency, resiliency, motivation, and emotional intelligence.[8]

Bottom line: Although your quantitative skills may have slipped while at home with the kids, you've probably grown in other impor-tant ways. You'll handle a disgruntled colleague much more easily than you might have in the past. You'll probably be able to keep more balls in the air than you did pre-baby. The problem is, you can't necessarily describe this growth on your résumé or in a job interview. But that doesn't mean it doesn't exist, nor that it's invisible. Rest assured that, like the aroma of a good home-cooked meal, your "mommy wisdom" will eventually seep out and attract others.

Start Talking

Perhaps the best way to build your confidence is to start talking, first among your comfort circles—close family and friends who are more supportive than judgmental. Then you can try out your descriptions of yourself and your plans among riskier social circles. In chapter 4, we describe the benefits of casual conversations with friends and acquain-tances in building your "elevator story," your quick synopsis of what you're interested in pursuing. The key concept here is *building,* mean-ing that you start with no story and then create one. And the starting point for building a story is to begin talking about it. The by-product of this storytelling process? You'll build your confidence as you build your story.

Carol distinctly remembers when she and Vivian were beginning to formulate the ideas for this book. She was at a party trying to articulate to a male friend the sense of isolation women experience after a number of years away from work. Searching for the right words to properly convey this feeling, she finally stammered out that women in this situation feel "completely professionally disconnected." She realized this phrase perfectly captured many stay-at-home mothers' unsettled emotional state, and it just sort of popped out in the midst of a cocktail-party conversation! In all likelihood, no amount of thinking would have produced it. She never forgot these magic words, and ultimately, they became part of Carol and Vivian's "story" about the book concept they were developing.

Without realizing it at the time, Carol used the same strategy when she began her first relaunch. She wasn't sure what she wanted to do, although she thought it might be something finance-related, since the bulk of her work experience before motherhood was in finance. Every time she spoke with someone, she was aware of what words she was or wasn't using (because sometimes she didn't sound very good at the beginning when she was mired in confusion about what she might do). But sometimes she said something that sounded cogent, and sometimes the person with whom she was speaking responded to her with useful phrases or descriptions. She made mental notes of these exchanges all the time. And when she spoke to someone else, she could begin with choice phrases from prior conversations, then build on them.

Over time, a story was starting to develop, and she started to sound pretty good talking about it! *That's when her confidence took the first little leap.* Soon she ventured out to speak with former colleagues and classmates, and they expressed excitement about the prospect of her returning to work. To them, she was still a consummate professional, based on their memories of her school or work performance. *Their image of her was frozen in time.* Indeed, your old work colleagues and school classmates will probably react positively to the news of your impending return. And their positive reactions will fuel your confidence.

Start Reading

Still, at some point you've got to add some substance to your talk. One day, Carol cracked open an old finance book and leafed through notes from her business school days. She started reviewing the lingo to remember what terms meant and how they worked. Another confidence boost. Finally, she sprang for a subscription to *The Wall Street Journal* so she could get up to speed on company name changes and newfangled financing vehicles. Amazingly, Carol agonized over this decision. She was one of those wives who had a hard time spending money on herself when she wasn't bringing any in. Also, she pictured piles of newspapers gathering dust, because the time she devoted to her children never allowed her the time to read them. And she was afraid she'd feel intimidated or might not understand what she was reading . . . and then she'd feel even worse. Finally, she worried she might somehow discover, through this reading, that she really *couldn't* cut it anymore. But she successfully faced her demons and dialed 1-800-JOURNAL.

Silly as it sounds, signing up for *The Wall Street Journal* represented a major turning point in Carol's confidence-building process. She read here and there, more and more, and began to get a general sense of corporate activity going on at the time. She learned which companies had been taken over and which had failed. At a friend's, she noticed some specialized finance books on her bookshelf and asked to borrow them. All of this took time, but Carol wasn't in a rush.

During this period, Carol attended some social events—not because it was strategic, but just because she was invited to them—where people talked about the markets and the latest financial instruments. This was a problem, because Carol wasn't yet ready to join in these conversations. She wasn't confident enough, and she was afraid she'd have to admit she had no idea what they were discussing. So she did a lot of listening. And bit by bit, she felt she had a better grasp of what these friends were talking about.

As you get closer to going on a real job interview, try out different ways of portraying your background, plans, or expectations at dinner parties, parents' meetings, moms' groups, and family gatherings to see how people respond. As you'll learn later in this book, *these low-stakes and seemingly casual conversations can actually serve as nonthreatening interview rehearsals.*

Build Your Attitude

According to the late Dawn Steel, one of Hollywood's first successful female executives, "If you're filled with self-doubt, your capacity for [a confident] attitude may be dormant, but you can develop it. Don't forget, *it doesn't have to reflect who you really feel you are.* It's a performance. The magic of it is that just doing it turns into a kind of self-fulfilling prophecy. . . . We're talking about the kind of attitude you wear like armor. Attitude helps you dazzle the enemy, dissolves obstacles, and allows you to charge ahead *even while you're still cleaning up the mess that's inside* [italics are our emphasis]."[9] So even if your insides are a bowl of jelly, you can act like a professional and no one needs to know how you really feel.

Although Ms. Steel was not a relauncher, Rachel, a university administrator who relaunched as associate director of an educational foundation, described her first days back at work in strikingly similar terms: "The biggest challenge of going back is gaining internal confidence to match the external confidence I was projecting. I felt like I was just acting the part and [my employer] might discover it. They seemed to have much more confidence in me than I had in myself, but I would never let that on."

As Steel pointed out in her powerful 1993 autobiography, your projected attitude will ultimately lead to increased internal confidence: "Perceived power is a kind of power. Once you've scored a few successes with attitude, the reinforcement of your confidence helps the deeper, gut-rooted strength to emerge. Of course, the best kind of attitude is exuded by a person operating not from perceived but from

real power—from his or her own internal strengths and his or her con-
sciousness of them. But that will come."[10]

Steps to Building Relauncher Attitude

- **Project a positive feeling about your time at home** (even if you
  don't always feel that way about it). If you're embarrassed or defensive about having stayed home with your children, others will
  think you have something to be embarrassed or defensive about.

- **Remind yourself that you're the same person you were before
  you quit—just out of practice.** Like an athlete in the off season,
  you're out of shape, but you know you have it in you to compete.

- **Remember that people's image of you is frozen in time.** When
  you start to contact former colleagues or old friends, they'll picture you as the star performer you were, not as the diminished
  version of yourself you may think you've become after time spent
  in reproductive hibernation.

- **Realize that your maternal experience and perspective are
  major assets**—even if you can't tout them in your résumé.

- **Ditto for your stable life phase.** Most of you are at a more stable phase of life—no more maternity leaves and fewer spousal
  relocations.

- **Don't be afraid to say no.** Remember, this is *your* special time
  now—time to focus on *you*. You've probably spent years devoting
  hours of volunteer time to charitable causes. It's time to say no to
  other people's requests for your time and talents and not feel a
  twinge of guilt for doing so.

- **Don't take no for an answer** advises Persephone Zill,[11] a life
  coach based in Westchester County, New York. The flip side of
  not being afraid to say no is to persevere even if someone else tells
  you no. Whether you're pursuing a loan to start a small business
  or trying to secure a critical informational interview, if you hear
  no from one source and you think you've exhausted all your op-

tions with that person or company, then try again with another source. Be relentless.

• **You are your own spin doctor.** While you certainly want and need to be truthful about your experience, you have the ability to craft your own story. You can position yourself as you wish. The key is deciding *how* you want to position yourself. And before you can do that, you have to figure out what you want to go after.

Assess Your Career Options

Figuring out what you want to do is a problem. It's a vicious circle. You can't figure out what you want to do, because you don't know what's out there. You have to talk to people to find out what's out there. But when you talk to people, they ask you what you want to do. And if you don't know, they think you're an idiot.

—*Susan*

A Job Search Like No Other

A career relaunch differs from your prior job searches. Your early job searches may have been driven by needs for prestige, advancement potential, or résumé building, as well as money. But this time around, although you still may be motivated by financial concerns, you have the chance to do what you really *want* to do rather than what you think you *should* do or what someone else is telling you to do. Back when you were in your twenties looking for your first job, you probably didn't have the wisdom you have now. As Martina related to us, "Your forties are a time for getting rid of all the crap in your life and focusing on the things you really want to do." We think this is good advice for all relaunchers, regardless of their age.

On the other hand, when you first got out of school or were still in the early years of your career, you felt the world was your oyster. All you needed to do was decide what you wanted to do and then go after it. You may have faced some rejections and had to change course, but essentially you felt free to pursue your dreams, with very few constraints. *As a relaunching mother, however, you may face a lot of constraints.* Accustomed to sending your children off to school yourself or greeting them when they come home in the afternoon, you may be loath to give up both those maternal touch points on a regular basis. Even if you decide you're willing to delegate the morning and afternoon hug, or your children are out of the house most of the day, you may not want to travel or put in the number of hours you did in the past. This chapter shows you how to identify career options, given your particular logistical limitations.

The Three C's of a Career Relaunch: Control, Content, and Compensation

Control

Organizational strategists Marcie Schorr Hirsch and Lisa Berman Hills[1] argue that "what women want is not *full time,* but *controlled time.*" Flexibility and control over when and even where work gets done tend to mean more to relaunchers than anything else. Emerging from being home 100 percent of the time, you are used to having your days structured by school hours and bus schedules. It is stress-producing to layer additional, inflexible work schedules on top of this rigid web. It is definitely possible, and many women do it, but if you have a choice in the matter, a schedule with some give in it will reduce the tension that is bound to build when work and domestic schedules collide.

But flexibility and control mean different things to different women, not to mention different employers. Flexible arrangements include flextime, staggered hours, flexible hours, shortened workweeks, compressed workweeks, telecommuting, and job sharing. One woman's ideal schedule may look like the job from hell to someone else. Employed by a small investment management firm, Jessica works from her home in Jackson Hole, Wyoming, one to six hours a week for three weeks, followed by a fourth week in New York for nonstop client meetings and interaction with the markets. Some women would love such a schedule, but others would hate to develop a new child care routine for the fourth week. Vicky, a former teacher, runs an after-school enrichment program out of her home. She takes care of the business side of her business (and her errands) in the morning and opens up her home to fifteen-plus children a day in the afternoon. Again, this works for Vicky, but would it work for you?

Job Content

Probably number two on the wish list for relaunchers, and for many women number one, is appealing job content. If you're opting back into the workforce, you're going to expect to get more out of it, at least on a psychic level, if not financially. According to career counselor Mary Lindley Burton, "Work has to do more for you than before you had a family, because you could be with your children. You have to make certain that you can get excited about going into the office Monday morning."[2]

But again, appealing job content means different things to different women. For many, the job has to be intrinsically interesting. For example, some of the freelance consultants with whom we spoke take a pass on the projects they don't find compelling. For others, it may be a job with prestige and/or lots of responsibility. To still other relaunchers, appealing job content means a job is fun. Vivian has noted that her executive search work reminds her of a treasure hunt. Having great colleagues is paramount to many relaunchers. Some people don't care as much about *what* they're doing as *with whom* they're doing it. Finally, working for an organization that "does good" or has a social action component is a priority for still other relaunchers; thus the appeal of nonprofits to the relaunching pool. In short, and above all, you want work that is worthy of you.

Judy, the former corporate lawyer who had a "traumatic" transition to full-time motherhood, began looking for a job with "more meaningful quality" than her previous corporate work. She relaunched as the full-time legal director of a legal aid society, a position she finds "incredibly rewarding." She supervises other lawyers, works on her own cases, and is a policy advocate. Now, with hindsight, she can say, "I feel really good about what I do. I know people who've been afraid to step off the track because they're afraid of what they'll find later. *I would never be in this job if I had not stepped off the ladder to be home with my kids, and I'm really glad I'm doing what I do.* You never know what the future holds."

Donna, a former loan officer, initially relaunched as a freelance writer and editor, and then retrained to teach English as a second language; she now teaches at an elementary school in Alabama. (See her résumé in "Sample Résumés of Real Relaunchers.") Besides the scheduling benefits of having her workday end at two thirty so she can drive her own kids to their activities, and having the whole summer off so the family can spend an extended period with her parents out of state, she feels she is really making a difference in her students' lives. She's plying her trade in an economically disadvantaged area and believes she's not only imparting language skills, but passing on important cultural adjustment techniques as well.

Compensation

And third, of course, there's compensation. Relaunchers' views on compensation are complicated. In chapter 1, we stated that financial considerations often drive women to relaunch. Yet we have found many women are willing to trade some of their dollars for flexibility and a job they enjoy. Nevertheless, paychecks hold tremendous symbolic power for relaunchers, in addition to their purchasing power. And once you get back in the game and up to speed, many of you will wonder why you should be making any less than others achieving comparable results. We all know that seniority does not necessarily correlate with financial success. The more you think about it, the more you realize you don't want to be taken advantage of in the labor market.

Some women, due primarily to lack of confidence and a dated view (or no clue at all) about market rates for their relaunch field, are caught off guard when they are given an offer. One relauncher, who expanded her role as a business school instructor to include a substantial administrative position as well, had trouble during contract negotiations. "I was such a sucker because they are paying me way under market [for the new expanded job]. I made a strategic error in the negotiations. I had made a point of telling them how much I had been underpaid all along. I was thinking they'd offer me in the high sixties, but then my boss offered me seventy thousand. I immediately said yes to that when I should have recalibrated because it was a first offer and I should have negotiated up from there, but I didn't. I did say I needed the inherent flexibility required as an involved mother, and that is the trade-off in my mind for the lower pay."

Because you are likely to have dated knowledge or no idea of compensation rates for specific positions and industries, please see the resources section at the end of this book.

Trading One C for Another

Although you might long for a job that scores high on all three C's, in practice relaunchers often end up trading one C for another, at least initially. Trading dollars for flexibility is the most common. The business school instructor/administrator quoted above leaves early one day a week to take her twins to gymnastics and rotates school library duty once a month. She even brings the kids to work with her on occasion. As she said, in her mind, this flexibility makes up for the lower pay.

Sometimes the trade-off is between job content and flexibility. Bonnie endured the "corporate equivalent of scrubbing floors" to get a livable schedule. Diane, known by her friends as "the Queen of Contract Work," occasionally takes an assignment that underemploys her, as long as it enables her to control her time.

Finding Your Work Passion

Some women have a pretty good idea of the kind of work they want to do in their second career, either because they want to return to the same career they left, or because they've developed a passion that they want to pursue. For example, Joyce was dead set on returning to her former employer, a large telecom company, and that goal drove her entire job search strategy. Susan knew she wanted to do something to improve public education, even though she had never taught or been in educational administration before.

Most relaunchers are less certain about what they want to do. And that's one of the major problems. Perhaps the only thing you *are* certain of is that you don't want to return to your former job or even your former employer. That's partly because you remember the dreaded parts of your old position and absolutely do not want to put yourself back into the frying pan again. Even if you have mostly fond memories, you may believe that it would be impossible to do what you did before and maintain the level of involvement you have with your family. As Charlene, a former brand manager, said, "I'd love to be a divisional VP at a consumer goods company, but there's no way I could do that and be the kind of mom I want to be."

The other problem is that you don't know what's out there. You're stuck stewing over the jobs you've had or that you know about from your limited circle of acquaintances, and nothing sounds either exciting enough or family-friendly enough to pique your interest.

Self-Assessment Tools

So how are you going to figure out what you want to do? And ultimately, how are you going to figure out a way to get paid for doing it?

The job search gurus divide into two schools. The first and probably the larger school, as exemplified by Richard Bolles's *What Color Is Your Parachute?*, prescribes a battery of exercises and essays to help you figure out your innate occupational interests, values, and skills.[3] Mary Burton's book *In Transition,* a job search manual specifically for people who want to make a career change, asks the reader to write a number of essays analyzing different aspects of her work experience in an effort to figure out what she really enjoys and is good at.[4]

You may have taken tests like the Strong-Campbell Interest Inventory at the end of college or graduate school to help guide you in your initial career choice. These diagnostic approaches are all based on the theory that if you put yourself under a strong enough microscope, you'll figure out what you're most suited to. Today many Internet tools cover the same ground; we have listed some in the resources section.

All of these methods revolve around the concept of identifying your "transferable skills" or "skill set"—organizing data, managing people, communicating in writing, quantitative analysis, and the like. These skills are not necessarily job-specific but can be used in a variety of work situations. A common second step in these approaches is to figure out which tools in your toolbox you enjoy using. If you mastered financial modeling in your old career but have no interest in crunching numbers now, then you shouldn't pursue opportunities where spreadsheet creation dominates the job description. Finally, most of the job gurus in this school help you identify your core work values; these, in turn, help you figure out the type of work environment in which you'll thrive.

Some find career counselors to be a helpful, if sometimes pricey, resource. Connie, a former veteran of high-tech sales and then high-tech executive search, consulted a career counselor while she was still home with her kids, before she was ready to take on a paying job. "She asked me, 'If you could do anything, what would it be?' I told her I would love to make movies. I did acting in high school. I love being part of a production. I love the camaraderie of working on a show. The counselor had a son who was writing in LA. He sent me his script, and I offered to help. He was frustrated from ten years of attempting to get this script turned into a movie. He said nobody has done what they said they would do. Well, I decided to help out. I helped him raise money to get the film made and helped him produce it. Although we haven't sold it yet, it has just been accepted by a prestigious film festival." Connie worked on this as a volunteer project during her time at home. As a result of this experience, she feels she is "done" with high tech and definitely wants to pursue work using her "creative side."

The Opportunistic Approach and the Learn-by-Doing Approach

Whether or not they explicitly say so, many relaunchers follow the other school of thought in the job search world—the opportunistic approach. Under the opportunistic plan, a person has some vague ideas about what she wants to do, and she simply starts to tell people she knows of her interests and experience, hoping somebody will make a referral or a suggestion that strikes her as having potential.

A more recent school of thought, represented by Herminia Ibarra in *Working Identity,* argues that people learn best about themselves— their career strengths and weaknesses—by doing.[5] Her book focuses on dramatic career changes and how to achieve them. She believes that the most successful career changes result from testing out an area of interest and then modifying career goals based on what is learned from that and subsequent work experiments. Although she does not address this philosophy specifically to relaunchers, women considering relaunching their careers are ideal candidates for her methodology. She advocates volunteering, taking courses, or securing freelance assignments in a new field as a way of testing the waters. As a relauncher, you're in a perfect position to experiment your way to a new career. Rachel, the former university administrator who wanted to diversify into higher-level nonprofit work, began her relaunch by enrolling in a part-time MBA program with a public nonprofit emphasis and a number of internships. Donna, who initially pursued a new career in freelance writing and editing, did promotional work on a volunteer basis for the local ballet company. She used a writing sample she produced as a volunteer to successfully compete for her first freelance writing assignment when she decided to relaunch.

In reality, relaunchers probably benefit from both the "look inside yourself" and the "learn by doing" approaches in order to settle on a new direction, because you can't craft work experiments until you've narrowed down your field of interest.

More on Job Content: Job Building Blocks

One way to break the bottleneck of uncertainty and ignorance is to play what we call Job Building Blocks. Break down your old jobs into their component parts (think LEGOs) and see what new jobs or money-making opportunities might be rebuilt from them (see the sample worksheet that follows). For example, if you were an account executive at an advertising agency in one of your old jobs, write that at the top of the worksheet. Then list all the subfunctions of the job—in this case, for example, "meet with clients to determine needs," "work with copywriters and art directors to develop creative elements of campaign," and so on. (Make a separate worksheet for each job, and feel free to use more than one page.) These job subfunctions are the "blocks" that will help you determine what you'd like to pursue next. Go through the same process for all of your former job and volunteer experiences, being sure to include every function, no matter how large or small. After you've broken an old job down into blocks, circle the blocks or components you enjoyed the most, and think about how that brick could become the basis for a new structure—a new job or moneymaking opportunity. For example, if you really liked pitching new business and working with the designers to develop a campaign, maybe you'd like to form your own small ad agency, drawing on a network of freelancers, to go after lower-budget accounts below the radar of most large firms. Or if you enjoyed the research side, maybe you could explore working for a market research firm, perhaps pitching its services to agencies.

Next, create a second list called "New Opportunities." Here, you note the new opportunities that could stem from your past experiences. Finally, after you've brainstormed a number of new money-making structures, write down people or companies to contact to explore these concepts further. If you don't know the names of potentially interesting companies at this stage, just write the type of company you're interested in. Then use the Internet and your own personal network (more on this in chapter 5) to develop specific targets.

When Vivian went through this exercise, she realized that she most enjoyed the recruiting and training she did on one of her former jobs, even though most of her work had been in finance. She also remembered how much she enjoyed writing on all of her jobs. Using the above method, she came up with a variety of alternatives to explore, including joining a big executive search firm; joining a small executive search firm; managing recruiting for a company; running writing seminars for businesses, either as an employee or as a freelancer; and selling training services to corporations.

Following the Job Building Block worksheets, we've suggested a number of potential jobs or moneymaking opportunities by function and/or industry. For example, if the job blocks or components you most enjoyed were in marketing, check out the list for "Marketing and Sales."

JOB BUILDING BLOCK WORKSHEET

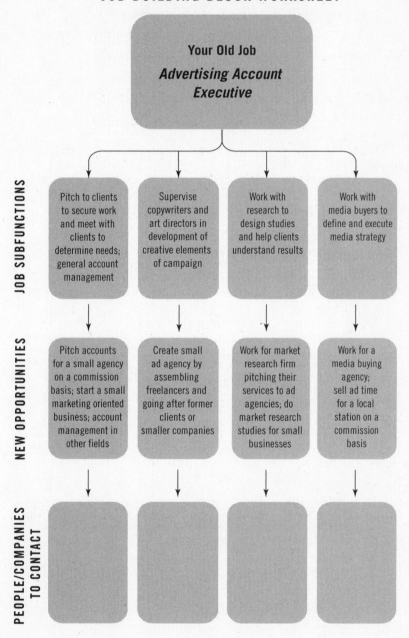

Your Old Job

Advertising Account Executive

JOB SUBFUNCTIONS

Pitch to clients to secure work and meet with clients to determine needs; general account management	Supervise copywriters and art directors in development of creative elements of campaign	Work with research to design studies and help clients understand results	Work with media buyers to define and execute media strategy

NEW OPPORTUNITIES

Pitch accounts for a small agency on a commission basis; start a small marketing oriented business; account management in other fields	Create small ad agency by assembling freelancers and going after former clients or smaller companies	Work for market research firm pitching their services to ad agencies; do market research studies for small businesses	Work for a media buying agency; sell ad time for a local station on a commission basis

PEOPLE/COMPANIES TO CONTACT

JOB BUILDING BLOCK WORKSHEET

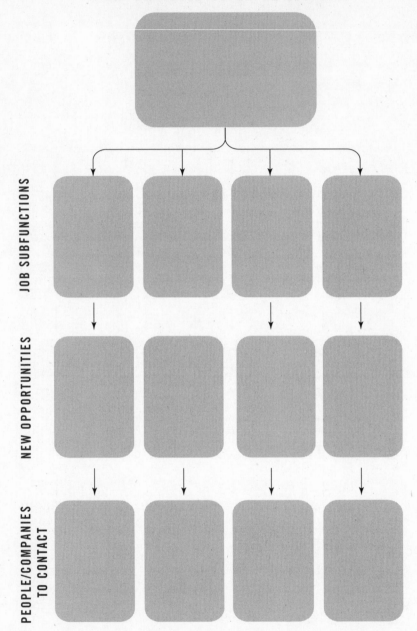

Sample Family-Friendly Jobs Built by Function/Industry

Family-Friendly Finance and Accounting Jobs

CFO at a school or other nonprofit

Financial consultant (stockbroker)

Wealth management professional

Tax consultant for H&R Block or other tax services firm

Bookkeeping/accounting/tax prep for other consultants or small companies

Mortgage broker

Financial adviser to small companies

Business broker

Family-Friendly Marketing and Sales Jobs

Freelance art direction, copywriting, or public relations

Airline booking sales from home

Marketing consulting

Residential real estate brokerage

Media advertising sales

Home and/or Web-based business selling home-produced goods or distributing unusual or hard-to-find products

Assisting an artist or other creative type in marketing his or her business

Many sales positions, ranging from financial instruments, pharmaceuticals, and telecom equipment to clothes and archival scrapbooking materials.

Family-Friendly Human Resource Jobs

Recruiting

Résumé screening and telephone interviewing

Research for recruiting

Training

HR consulting

Family-Friendly General Management Jobs

Buy or start a business

Buy and manage real estate

Open a unique store that fills a niche in your community

Open a franchise

Family-Friendly Legal Jobs

Part-time work at a family-friendly law firm

Teaching law—one class or a few classes

Career services at law schools

Misdemeanor master calendar court

Appeals and training bureau brief writing

Open your own specialized legal practice

Other public sector law jobs—state supreme court

Family-Friendly Jobs in Medicine and Other Health and Science Fields

Per diem physician (usually offered at large HMO clinics)

Locum tenens physician (cover vacations and other longer-term absences)

Part-time physician at a clinic, private practice, or university health service.

School nurse or psychologist

Nursing at a hospital with flexible shift arrangements

Private-duty nursing

Scientific research under a reentry grant

Per diem pharmacist

Family-Friendly Jobs in Education

Teaching English as a second language

Serving as a teacher's assistant

Running your own after-school enrichment program

Private tutoring

University admissions department—reading applications during busy season

University career services department administration

Teaching a single course or multiple courses

Family-Friendly Jobs in the Arts and Other Creative Fields

Freelance writing and editing

Decorating

Interior design

Producing and marketing your own artwork or crafts

Teaching art or music

Video game creation

Web design

More on Control: Focus on Substance, Not Setting

One mistake many women make is thinking that they have to decide in advance whether they want to work full-time, part-time, at home, in an office, for themselves, or for an employer. We advocate that you *focus first on what you want to do,* rather than on the where and the how. In other words, choose the industry and/or the function you want to perform. Don't get bogged down by trying to figure out whether you want to work full-time or part-time. That can be fine-tuned later, once you've found, or developed, the right opportunity. The important thing is not where and how you work, it's what you do, and that can be done through any number of logistical arrangements that may shift over time.

We illustrate this concept with what we call the Relaunch Opportunities Spectrum, pictured below. To preserve your options at the beginning of your job search, it's best to be open-minded about where to situate yourself on the spectrum.

THE RELAUNCH OPPORTUNITIES SPECTRUM

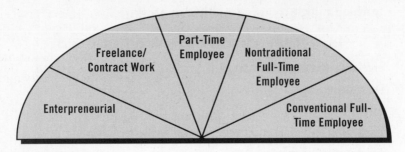

Let's analyze the pros and cons of different points on the spectrum in greater detail.

Full-Time: Conventional and Nontraditional

Full-time jobs usually come with higher pay than other work situations. In addition, most quality full-time jobs include benefits. The downside, of course, is longer hours. And today, those hours are likely to be more than nine to five, especially in any kind of management position. Some full-time jobs can have a flex component, allowing some of the work to be done at home or during nontraditional hours.

If you find yourself gravitating toward full-time opportunities, either at corporations, in nonprofits (including educational institutions), or in government, bear in mind the following considerations.

Corporations

To date, corporations have generally been the most rigid and demanding of all possible workplaces, as well as the least welcoming to relaunchers. On the other hand, nabbing a full-time job in the private sector will probably give you the greatest starting income and benefits, as well as the biggest ego boost and bragging rights. Try to target family-friendly companies, however, by consulting the *Working Mother* magazine "Best Companies" list, studying potential employers' Web sites, and, most importantly, talking to insiders. In particular, consider the culture and average workday of the firm. Do people seem to live at the office, or does the place quiet down after 5 or 6 PM? If you'd rather start early and leave early, focus on companies where the majority of employees keep that schedule. In chapter 10, we profile what some companies are doing to retain women who want more flexibility and to reattach those who have left.

Small Versus Large Companies

If you have impressive credentials, small companies, more than large ones, may be willing to grant you a flexible schedule in order to attract someone with your experience or education. In addition, an unconventional résumé won't necessarily turn them off. They may find a relauncher's background more compatible with their entrepreneurial culture than a big company veteran's.[6] In fact, the Families and Work Institute's *2005 National Study of Employers* indicates that "small employers [defined as organizations with fifty to ninety-nine employees] are significantly more likely to offer flexibility to all or most employees than employers of other sizes."[7]

On the downside, smaller companies or start-ups may not have the resources to hire you full-time or even to pay you decently on a consulting or part-time basis.

Sales

Although sales doesn't occupy its own spot on the Relaunch Opportunities Spectrum, selling is the backbone of any business and can be done at any point on the spectrum on a full-time, part-time, consulting, or entrepreneurial basis. Furthermore, sales can be a great area for relaunchers for several reasons. First of all, although you may be lacking in confidence, your life experience gives you an inborn credibility and gravitas that younger people lack. Most sales positions today are consultative. Customers are looking for someone to help them solve problems. They don't want to receive a canned sales pitch. The consultative sales model takes advantage of the relauncher's strengths—her professional credentials and maturity.

From a flexibility standpoint, sales can be ideal. *You're not supposed to be in the office.* No one has to know that you followed your last sales call with a trip to the pediatrician. In addition, many otherwise corporate environments outfit their sales staffs with home offices and remote equipment and encourage their use. Finally, in sales, results are what count, and results are easily measured. Dollars speak louder than face time. As Sally, a former commercial banker who relaunched as a residential real estate broker, commented, "I have never been in a commission-based business before. *I am surprised by how motivated I am by it.* But the reality is, I can't make the time sacrifice required to be a top producer right now. But I may be able to sometime in the future."

Nonprofits

Not-for-profit institutions typically offer reasonable work schedules (and potentially flexible ones) in order to obtain talent, because they usually can't compete with the for-profit sector on pay. For the same reason, they tend to be more open to candidates with unconventional backgrounds, such as relaunchers. For those seeking a social action role, relaunching into a nonprofit can be a perfect fit. But don't assume that your years on the PTO will weigh any more in your favor with these folks than with the private sector. They're professionals, and very protective of their professional status. In addition to offering generally lower compensation, nonprofits are usually thinly staffed, requiring their employees to handle the mundane as well as the challenging aspects of their jobs.

Government

Government jobs tend to be less demanding in terms of time commitment than their private-sector counterparts, especially in the legal arena. Leslie, who works for the Florida Supreme Court, loves the chance to do interesting, challenging work and still maintain a manageable schedule. For some government jobs, the workday may run from 7 AM to 3 PM, appealing hours for many mothers, who prefer to forgo morning time with their kids in order to be home earlier in the day.

Educational Institutions

Another strategy is to pick a field where the full-time work schedule mirrors that of your children. K–12 teachers, school nurses, and librarians knock off when their kids do and have summers free. Even educational administrators tend to have greater flexibility than managers in the private sector.

Academia

The college level offers even greater flexibility. Although snagging tenure might take you the rest of your life, universities employ lots of talent as nontenured faculty and in administrative capacities. If you can carve out a narrow role for yourself within an institution, such as teaching one class, managing one small area of admissions or career services, or spearheading a specific program, then you've created an interesting, viable part-time or full-time job with flexible parameters. Denise, a former public defender, began her relaunch by teaching one class in legal brief writing at a local law school for "peanuts." After one semester, she told them she needed a big raise. They responded by asking her to serve as assistant dean of students as well and increasing her pay significantly. She still feels she's underpaid, but both part-time jobs add up to an almost full-time commitment with lots of flexibility built in for her to tend to her kids' needs.

As with nonprofits, the pay at educational institutions lags behind the private sector. In addition, competition for good full-time jobs at all levels of academia can be stiff.

Health Care

The health care field, in both the nonprofit and for-profit settings, abounds with opportunity for relaunchers. In certain practices, physicians can schedule specific shifts equal to a full-time position, but broken up in a way that coordinates with children's schedules. Hospital nurses can also work shifts that equal full time, but may be scheduled during unusual hours. In fact, the demand for nurses is so strong that many are able to just name the hours they want to work. Per diem (specific days at specific clinics) and locum tenens (longer-term "substitute" doctors) opportunities offer doctors maximum flexibility in terms of number of hours and length of commitment. Locum tenens agencies offer temporary opportunities, and large HMO clinics offer permanent positions.

We've also seen examples of creative physician opportunities ranging from serving as summer camp physician to the following opportunity spotted in an elementary school newsletter: "Internist needed for house calls practice. Ideal for an at-home mother/physician who is looking for a flexible, but rewarding practice. Contact Sara Smith, MD."

The full-time work schedules of psychologists, speech therapists, occupational therapists, and other health care professionals are also often more family-friendly than those of the corporate world.

Part-Time

Working part-time for a corporation or other organization can satisfy a relauncher's needs to tackle professional issues in a team setting while still allowing for a reasonable amount of time at home. Many of our interviewees reported successful part-time experiences, both before and after their relaunches. But we have a couple of caveats. Don't restrict yourself to supposed part-time opportunities, often a backwater in many corporations. And don't look for part-time jobs by responding only to part-time job ads or announcing to your friends and former associates that you're searching for "something part-time." Can you imagine hiring someone who emphasizes that she wants to work "a little"? How would you view such a person?

Dr. Janet Rowley, one of the biggest names in cytogenetics and a Lasker Award winner (the "most coveted prize in medical science"; many recipients go on to win the Nobel), runs a sizable research lab at the University of Chicago. What is especially notable about her stellar career is that she pursued it part-time for twenty years, while her four children were young, before going full-time. Her first major discoveries occurred when she was still part-time and was observing photos of chromosomes laid out on her dining room table. She advises women who want to return to scientific research to *volunteer* in a lab, "so people can get to know you and see your competencies."[8]

As we've discussed, the goal is to pursue opportunities in your field of interest and expertise. Then, once you've piqued an employer's interest, you can propose ways to make the job work in terms of your schedule—say, part-time or a couple of days a week out of a home office. Corinne, a former magazine ad salesperson, answered a classified ad for a full-time job at a competitor of her former employer. The ad attracted her because the office was in the suburbs, close to her home, rather than in the city. During the interview, sensing that she was a strong candidate, she asked whether they'd consider a reduced hour schedule. "'For the right person,' they told me, 'we would.'" Not only did Corinne get the job, but after learning the ropes she now works mostly from home on a family-friendly schedule. And the best part is that her sales numbers rival those of her full-time colleagues.

Carving out a great part-time job can be one way to get a challenging opportunity with flexibility. Carol had considered a full-time position managing the launch of an umbrella of health care initiatives for low-income families. If she had wanted to pursue something equally challenging and meaningful, but less daunting in terms of time and scope, she might have proposed to management that she undertake running just one of those initiatives, reporting to someone else overseeing the launch of the whole project. As described above under "Job Building Blocks," break down a potential job into its component parts and bid on one of them.

The bottom line: Don't sell yourself short by begging for crummy part-time positions. Go after a good job, then negotiate a workable schedule. Don't assume it's impossible until you've asked, tried to persuade, and been turned down.

Of course, if you want a part-time schedule, you're going to have to accept lower pay. But here's the rub: Companies often try to pay part-timers less than their pro rata share. They argue that if someone's only working 75 percent time, she's worth less than 75 percent of the pay of a full-time employee. Those of us who have worked part-time, however, strongly disagree, noting that we often pull longer hours than those officially negotiated. We still have a strong work ethic that drives us to do whatever it takes to get the job done. So some part-timers have successfully argued that they deserve *at least* their pro rata share, if not more. If you go the part-time route, make sure you revisit the pay-versus-hours issue with your management on at least a semiannual basis.

Finally, benefits are usually not part of the part-timer's compensation package. Indeed, part-timers are more attractive to many employers specifically because they are significantly cheaper hires with no benefits attached. Some companies offer prorated benefits, but this is not yet the norm.

Consulting, Freelance, and Contract Work

In the 1980s and early to mid-1990s, these three words on a résumé were euphemisms for "can't find a real job." But since the late 1990s, the number of people going solo by choice has grown astronomically. In his entertaining opus *Free Agent Nation,* Daniel H. Pink conservatively estimated that there are about sixteen and a half million soloists working in the United States today. (This number does not include temps and microbusiness owners, whom he counted separately.)[9]

Consulting, in any of its various forms, can be an ideal way for women to wade back into the workforce. One of the challenges of consulting, however, is that you constantly have to market yourself (or become dangerously dependent on one or two clients). Another is figuring out how to price your services. We'll delve into how to secure, manage, market, and price consulting assignments in greater detail in chapter 5.

A less obvious drawback is loneliness. Isabelle did a number of consulting projects looking at new brand strategy for toy companies, but found it "way too isolating." Indeed, if one of your goals in relaunching is spending more time with adults, consulting may not be the answer for you. But even this problem has a solution: a partner. In fact, some relaunchers advocate finding a partner first—someone with whom you enjoy spending time and who has complementary skills—then, together, figuring out what kind of work you'd like to do. But beware. Don't assume your best friend will make the best business partner. (More on partners in chapter 5.)

Creative Careers

Creative careers, which are usually, but not always, practiced on a freelance basis, can offer incredible flexibility. Freelance journalism, writing books, even writing ad copy can provide *the crucial high flexibility (control) + high interest level (content) equation* that works for many moms with kids at home. Design is a particularly hot field today. Product design, interior design, Web site design, and graphic design are all creative careers that offer flexible work-from-home possibilities. Professionalize your innate talents by taking a course or two to help you compete for jobs or assignments in this sector.

Entrepreneurial Ventures

Starting a business can be an ideal way to relaunch and have more control over your schedule. You may end up launching a business almost accidentally. It may grow out of a hobby or volunteer assignment, or because you get rejected for more conventional opportunities.

Despite many positives, including more control over your schedule and the opportunity to build significant wealth, launching an entrepreneurial venture poses major challenges, not the least of which is the need, in many cases, to raise capital. However, even women who work full-time on their businesses report that they have greater flexibility than they did when they worked for someone else. Alternatively, some of the entrepreneurs with whom we spoke consciously slowed their business growth rate to preserve their family time, with the intention of revving up their ventures as their kids grow older.

Starting with a Small Home-Based Business

Dawn Oldham, Creative Memories' highest-earning salesperson since 1997, is responsible for fifteen million dollars in annual Creative Memories revenues. The homeschooling mother of five was profiled in a January 2005 *New York Times* article about her entrepreneurial success with the scrapbooking company. After hearing Creative Memories founder Rhonda Anderson interviewed on the radio, Dawn thought she had finally found a source for an acid-free photo album for which she had been searching. The distinguishing feature was being able to write on the photo page. But she couldn't find a Creative Memories representative in Orlando where she lived. So she called the company and ended up buying not just an album, but also the $165 start-up kit. She decided to hold a "crop," where invited guests gather in a rep's house to purchase the supplies and create the albums. Some close friends and her sister attended, netting seventy-five dollars in sales. Gradually, this grew into a few hundred dollars a month. Now she earns more than thirty thousand dollars a month, plus another hundred thousand in annual gifts of trips, jewelry, and cash bonuses, from commissions on sales made by other representatives she has recruited. As of January 2005, she had recruited seventy-six representatives since her humble start in 1990. How does she run this large business and homeschool and care for her kids? Her success enabled her husband to quit his job. He now helps with the children and her business.[10]

Opening a Franchise

If the word *franchising* makes you think *McDonald's,* think again. In addition to fast-food restaurants, a whole host of new franchise concepts have been developed in the last ten years, some of which may help you leverage your skills without having to start from scratch. For example, there are franchises for telecom consulting services, computer services, and more.

One of the hottest new franchises, with particular appeal to women, is iSold It, a nationwide chain of drop-off stores that's now the number one seller on eBay. People with an item to sell bring it to iSold It's local store. iSold It sells the item on eBay and takes a percentage of the price as commission. The company was founded by Elise Wetzel, a former marketing executive at Unilever. In 2002, having just decided to stay home with her two kids, she volunteered to raise funds for her children's preschool playground by holding a virtual garage sale. But when she started trying to list the castoffs on eBay, "it quickly became apparent that it was a lot easier to buy things on eBay than it was to sell them." So she looked for a local drop-off center that would handle eBay sales. No such store existed. And so her idea for iSold It was born. "The idea went through me like a lightning bolt," Wetzel recalled. "I couldn't believe there wasn't already something like this out there." She opened her first iSold It store in Pasadena at the end of 2003. As of October 2005, the company had more than 140 franchise stores open, with 600 under contract.[11]

Gail, a former marketer for Frito-Lay and mother of two, was looking for a business she could own and run herself but that would eventually generate enough income to allow her husband to quit his job and join her. Having bought and sold on eBay, she knew she had found the perfect business opportunity when she spotted an article about iSold It in a May 2004 issue of *USA Today*. Within a year, her store was up and running. Although managing her own business is a bit "like having a third child," she's able to spend afternoons with her two kids by putting her brother in charge of the store. "I'd like to be able to spend more time on marketing and less time on operations," she added. "But I expect that will happen when we get a bit bigger."

If the idea of opening an iSold It franchise sounds overwhelming, you could test the waters by holding your own virtual garage sale on eBay and, if you enjoy the process, marketing yourself as an eBay trading assistant, selling other people's and businesses' unwanted goods online. According to *Business Week*, "Upwards of 430,000 people in the US alone—more than are employed worldwide by General Electric and Procter & Gamble combined—earn a full- or part-time living on eBay."[12]

A Shifting Spectrum of Opportunities

In addition to full-time, part-time, consulting, and entrepreneurship, there's also telecommuting, job sharing, temping, interim assignments—a veritable rainbow of work arrangements. And the categories overlap. Some consulting work could be considered entrepreneurship, and vice versa. More importantly, we've seen women relaunch at one point on the spectrum and migrate to another as their family situation changes and/or additional professional opportunities emerge.

Donna, formerly a commercial loan officer, got her first writing job for a newspaper by responding to an ad for freelance writers. As a writing sample, she sent them a press release she had written as a *volunteer* for a city ballet fund-raiser. They liked it and began giving her contract work, paying her per piece. This experience led to bigger and better opportunities in the publishing world. After her initial work freelance writing, she got some work as a photostylist for the same paper, for which she was paid on an hourly basis. In this capacity, she could accept or reject jobs based on her availability. She also worked as a proofreader for entire editions of a home decor magazine published periodically by the newspaper. Ultimately, she worked exclusively for the home decor magazine. After developing a close relationship with the editor, she was appointed assistant editor for special issues, which she liked because the hours were very flexible and she did not have short-term deadline pressure.

More on Compensation: Taking a Step Back and/or Starting Small

If you had a hotshot job before you opted out, your ego may weigh in on the issue of what's an acceptable opportunity for your return. You might not mind taking a small step down the promotional ladder from where you left off, or pursuing an opportunity a notch beneath your ability, partly because you know you have a learning curve to contend with and partly because you may not be ready to jump with both feet into a job with as much pressure and stress as the one you left. But what about the concept of taking a *really big step back* or starting *really small*? As in taking a thirty-dollar-per-hour job as part-time assistant to an executive recruiter when you used to run human resources for a high-growth company and recruiting reported to you? As in taking a twenty-five-thousand-dollar-a-year job as a research assistant to a big-name business school professor when you graduated as an MBA from that school and you used to be an investment banker? As in taking a teaching assistant position in an elementary school reading program when you used to be a one-in-a-million inspirational middle school teacher? As in taking a job as an elementary school nurse when you used to be the chief operating room nurse nicknamed "the Trauma Hawk"?

Let's think about what's at stake here. First and foremost, your ego. Already in fragile condition, it may be too bruised even to consider what seems to be a move into a menial position. Second, what other people think about you. As much as we are counseled not to care, some of us still can't get away from other people's view of us. This is especially touchy when dealing with self-image as it relates to our careers. For many of us, our identity was so wrapped up in our profession that it took months, if not years, to get comfortable with our new at-home self when we first stopped working. At the beginning of this chapter, we noted that most of us want work that is "worthy" of us. Some of these entry-level and lower-paid positions do not seem worthy, especially if viewed as ends unto themselves rather than as stepping-stones to greater opportunities.

Starting with a Job You Perceive as Beneath You

If you had a borderline score on part 2 and/or part 3 of the Relaunch Readiness Quiz—that is, if you face a demanding routine with little support at home—you may want to start with a job that is beneath you, so to speak, but a good transitional step. Even if you barely break even financially after accounting for child care, transportation, and wardrobe expenses, you should consider the opportunity if the job content or control parameters appeal to you. *Think of it as an investment in your future.* You'll develop contacts and skills you can build on when you're ready to take on more responsibility. And you'll gain current experience to put on your résumé.

Interestingly, for many relaunchers, taking a big step back or starting small can result in either unexpected job satisfaction or surprising financial success. Audrey worked full-time as an operating room nurse in a major teaching hospital until her kids were born. Known as the Trauma Hawk, she could always be counted on to handle the most complicated cases. After her daughter was born she reduced her time from five to two days a week. Even at fewer days, though, she found that her energy level and mental commitment were compromised after having a child. Then her son was born. Audrey realized she couldn't keep up with everything. The worst part was that even though she was working only two days a week, she had problems leaving at the end of the day. Technically her shift ended at 5 PM, but she would be holding a heart in the middle of an operation and be informed there was no coverage for her on the next shift, so she'd end up staying until 11 PM. She'd come home to a note from her daughter, who was then in elementary school: "I have a project and Beverly [the babysitter/housekeeper] doesn't know what to do. Why do you do this to me?"

Although she loved being in a leadership position in a high-profile operating room and the challenges of cardiac nursing, she eventually left completely for a few years. One year she tried to go back by working 10 AM to 2 PM three days a week, but she found she could only set up tables and stock the operating rooms during these hours; she could not do the high-powered stuff she'd thrived on before. This was frustrating and disappointing.

Then Audrey decided to apply for a school nurse position. She thought it would be menial and depressing. She thought she would be jealous of her previous life in a more exciting field of nursing. She did like the idea that her hours and calendar schedule would be the same as those of her kids. To her surprise, the job is a lot better than she'd expected in terms of work content, because kids are at school with some pretty serious situations that she has to monitor. She thinks she can sustain this for a while, at least until her younger child graduates from elementary school.

Vivian took a job as assistant to an executive recruiter, a neighbor who had his own executive search business, at a low hourly rate. Her youngest of five children had just started nursery school, and she was desperate to "do something" but, ideally, she wanted to stay close to home. "I didn't think I could take on a big job, because I was unwilling to hire a lot of child care and, besides, I had zero confidence in my ability to *get* a big job. I was intrigued by executive search, however, since I had enjoyed the recruiting work I had done at my last job, and I sensed it might lead to something more. But the money was hard to swallow. Fortunately, my neighbor was great to work with and really taught me the business. And when I finally got up the gumption to ask him for more money, he paid it willingly. Within two years, I had my own clients and pulled in significant fees. And by my fourth year, I was so busy I had to hire someone to work with me." According to the neighbor who hired her, "A woman returning to the workplace is in a situation similar to any proven player who makes a career change. They need to prove themselves in their new environment. The key difference is that the talent and prior experience become quickly apparent, reducing the learning curve and testing time to a fraction of what it would be for someone totally new."

———

In this chapter, we've tossed out a number of different relaunch possibilities against a range of job functions. Whatever you decide to pursue, before you can market yourself, you must make sure your skill set is up to snuff. Our next chapter tells you how to make this happen.

Update Your Professional and Job Search Skills, and Prepare for the Interview

Summer Job for Middle or High School Student: *Summer job to help computer-illiterate mom. Student wanted for the month of August to teach local mom the ins and outs of computer use. A great job for a student who wants to earn a little spending money. Call Shawnee (mother of elementary and middle school students) at _____. Patience and compassion required!*
    —*From the classified ads section of a middle school newsletter*

You've figured out your field of interest and you may even have started exploring some options. If you haven't already, you now need to update your skills, write your résumé, and prepare for interviews. As you do this, it's important to continue talking with friends and acquaintances who are familiar with your desired field. Even casual conversations can be really helpful during this stage.

Back to School

Many women wonder whether they should take classes before they try to return to the workforce after a long absence. From what we've seen, and from the experts we've consulted, there are arguments to be made on both sides. According to Mary Lindley Burton, who counsels primarily professional men and women, "Unless you're pursuing very technical opportunities, skills are rarely the issue."[1] On the other hand, if refreshing your skills will boost your confidence, by all means take a class or two. Just having to show up somewhere and complete assignments will help condition you for your relaunch. In some professional fields, updating skills *requires* taking courses. Examples include continuing medical education credits, accounting accreditations, and teacher certifications. Whether or not you meet professional requirements in your field, updating skills and knowledge through course work can demonstrate to your spouse, children, and prospective employers a level of seriousness about your desire to return to work. The opportunity to network with professors and other students also weighs in favor of taking some classes. Most importantly, if you want to relaunch in a radically new direction, you may need additional professional training. Finally, most professional schools offer career placement advice and services that can be very helpful to the relauncher. So if you want to make the transition slowly, or make a big change, go register.

Enrolling in a Degree Program

If you're contemplating a major career change, you may well have to get an additional degree. This can be expensive and time-consuming, but the payoff—in terms of increasing your marketability, lifetime earning potential, and long-term job satisfaction—often justifies the investment. And don't feel like you're necessarily starting out from scratch. Your old skills will probably come into play in ways you can't necessarily predict and will distinguish you from your twenty-something classmates when you graduate.

Tammy, formerly a PhD teacher of English literature, loved teaching but disliked dealing with the politics of the educational establishment. When the mother of two young boys contemplated a relaunch years later in another city, she started thinking about changing careers to something computer-related. She did some research and found a local university that offered a master's in systems management. The program targeted military officers, but civilians could also apply. Application requirements included taking the GRE.

"Taking the GRE was a huge turning point for me and, in the end, an enormous confidence booster. My degrees were in English, and I had had no math since high school. I got some GRE self-study books and studied for eight weeks. It paid off; I scored a 770 on the math and a 790 on the verbal. It made me feel so smart! I was then able to enter the program with a lot of confidence in my own intellect."

She was accepted and decided to take the technically hardest course first to see if she could cut it and whether or not she liked it. She was so good at this first class, she was asked to be a research assistant to the teacher. For two years, she went two nights a week, from 6 to 10 PM. And she loved it. Everyone else in the program was in the military or a defense contractor. Out of 250 students, there were only two women. Tammy was the only one in the program paying her own way—although in her second year, she won a fellowship through a state grant for women returning to school after being home with kids.

Following graduation, Tammy took a nine-to-three job developing computer training programs for a small company that couldn't afford to hire someone full-time. After a year and a half, the company folded, but she secured a full-time position elsewhere. Although she had applied for a systems analyst job, she ended up in training. She wrote instruction manuals for computer systems, combining her experience in teaching with her newly acquired technical expertise. A few years later, she was transferred to quality assurance, which turned out to be the perfect field for her. Now she's at the VP level.

Getting an MBA

If you're interested in business and don't already have an MBA, getting this master's can be a great way to increase your marketability and ease the transition from home to work. With a range of programs to choose from, including executive, part-time, not-for-profit-oriented, and online options, make sure you pick one that is geared to your needs and interests.

Rachel, whose last job had been as associate dean of students at Seattle University, knew she didn't want to return to the high-stress environment of university administration, where she had to carry a beeper and never knew when she might be called to extricate some hapless student from jail. But she wanted to stay in the nonprofit world. During her second year home with her one- and six-year-old, she began to think about going back to school. "I liked that I'd be intellectually engaged and make professional connections, but I was concerned about whether there would be enough flexibility to accommodate my children's schedules. In the past, I'd thought about a PhD program, but decided I couldn't handle the dissertation process—it was way too isolating."

She started assessing her strengths. She considered herself a counseling/social work type, but when she met others with this profile, she felt that none had any management skills. She believed she had superb management skills as well as social work skills, and she wanted to use both. She began looking at MBA programs so she could further develop her management and quantitative skills, and she was accepted at one in her city that was part-time and had a public nonprofit emphasis option.

Rachel had always negotiated special situations in her career. Now she was going to negotiate one at this university. At thirty-eight, she was not only the oldest student in the program, but also the only mother with young kids. Everyone else was twenty-four to thirty-two, worked during the day, and took their courses at night. She convinced the dean to let her take most of her classes during the day while her kids were in school; she attended classes requiring teamwork at night.

"I loved being back at school—from the energized urban campus to the compelling class discussions. At first I didn't tell anyone I was a stay-at-home mom, because I was afraid I'd be viewed negatively.

But in fact, my teammates were more than willing to accommodate my scheduling needs [when setting up outside class meetings] because they were so in awe of my participating in this program as a mom."

In order to pursue the MBA, Rachel upped her two-and-a-half-year-old's time in preschool from two mornings a week to two full days and enrolled her second-grader in an extended-day program two days a week at her elementary school. Initially, she felt guilty about the changes to her younger daughter's schedule, but gradually she began to feel like she was a good role model for her children, especially as she saw them becoming more independent and responsible.

In addition to the stimulating academic environment, she relished the contacts she was making, because "I could not imagine cold-calling for informational interviews to parlay my way into a job." In her non-profit concentration, she got to know faculty and alums who helped her out with connections.

After six years, including several internships with nonprofits, she secured what she calls a "dream job" as assistant director of an educational foundation that funds new education initiatives. She manages the grant review process and plans huge events where precommitted donors meet with grant finalists.

Rachel works about thirty hours a week, three days a week in the office and two from home. With flexibility of paramount importance to her, she asked to be paid on an hourly basis so she wouldn't feel she was shortchanging the organization if she needed to work less than her agreed-upon hours during the summer or at some other personally busy time. "I keep the line between work and home really solid. I try to preserve the after-school time to be there for my kids. I've had to miss a couple of the kids' events, but I've always managed to get some other special adult to attend in my place. My personal time is gone. But that's an okay trade-off for me right now."

Enrolling in a Certificate Program

If Tammy's and Rachel's stories seem a little daunting, don't despair. A low-stakes way to dip your toe in the water is to participate in a postbaccalaureate certificate program, even if you already have an advanced degree.

These programs emphasize academic updating. For example, a university postbaccalaureate certificate program in the sciences is designed for people who need to update or acquire new knowledge because they were liberal arts majors who have now decided to apply to medical school, because their job requires a major update of scientific research developments in a hurry, or because they need to update an old degree in anticipation of a career change or reentry.

A director of a state university postbaccalaureate certificate program in biotechnology told us that a number of students in the program have twenty-plus-year-old degrees. "All the big developments in molecular biology have occurred in the last twenty years. So if a person applied who had a twenty-year-old biochemistry degree, we might recommend that she take two semesters of molecular biology concurrently with the certificate program requirements." The parameters of these programs vary, but most involve two or three semesters of classes that are offered both day and night, in some cases followed by a lab placement for a few months. A Web search for "postbaccalaureate certificate programs" will give you a sampling of what's out there.

Technical Certificate Programs

Today there are also many targeted certificate programs, in everything from Web design to real estate appraisal. These will prepare you for a specific trade, include networking opportunities, and often provide job placement assistance as well.

Kim, a city planner who was an active volunteer fund-raiser during her years at home, relaunched after completing a fund-raising and development certificate program. "It was an eighteen-month program, and the courses were very high quality. I got two major things out of it.

First, I was in a classroom of fund-raising professionals and I realized I knew as much as, or in some cases more than, anyone else. I measured up. Second, I learned the language of fund-raising—all the buzzwords, plus some of the technical stuff that cutting-edge development people use in the twenty-first century."

Reentry Scholarships and Grants

If the cost of tuition is keeping you out of school, check to see whether your state, university, professional organization, or particular educational program offers any kind of reentry scholarship. In researching this book, we found a Web search of "reentry scholarships" to be much more fruitful than "reentry grants," which is mostly a listing of reentry programs for prisoners and juvenile offenders. What's important to realize is that these scholarships are specifically for you, the relauncher! Research them, be aware of them, and, most importantly, apply for them. Like Tammy, you may surprise yourself with unexpected funding for your prelaunch course work. It's not bad résumé material either. As you can see from the sampling listed in the resources section, available scholarships cover a broad geographic and academic range.

Technological Skills

Even if you decide to forgo a full professional training program, you may want to address certain weaknesses with a continuing ed course or even a private tutorial. The most common weakness among relaunchers is computer skills. Just about every decent job these days requires competency in e-mail, Internet search, Word, Excel, and PowerPoint. If you're not comfortable with these programs, either take the time to figure them out, sign up for a course, pay your teenager to teach you, or find a tutor. Good tutors might include computer teachers at your local high school, community college, or local community education program.

Relaunch Seminars

As relaunchers proliferate, seminars to serve them have popped up across the country, offered by universities, nonprofits, and even for-profit firms. These tend to feature a mix of skills updates, networking, and job-hunting techniques. For a list of providers, see the resources section.

Self-Study

If you decide to forgo formal training, or to supplement it, do take the time to create a program of self-study to update yourself on your target industry. Can you imagine putting a house on the market without sprucing it up a bit? Competing for jobs or clients with no preparation will likely be just as unsuccessful. That's why Carol read *The Wall Street Journal* for months before she began interviewing. "My big fear was that I would start talking about a company that no longer existed, either because it had been acquired or because it had gone bankrupt. I knew this would make me look either stupid or dated, both highly undesirable!"

Review old notes or texts on your field's fundamentals. Familiarize yourself with the projects you undertook in your old jobs. Spend time in the library, online, or both, looking at industry publications and Web sites to get a feel for what's going on. Your college or graduate school may have pre-identified valuable resources in particular fields.

Join an industry or professional association and start attending meetings or conferences. Do these things not just to network for jobs, but to get yourself current and increase your marketability. You'd be surprised how much you can pick up in just a few days of intensive research. Remember, those who are working full-time rarely or never get the chance to kick back and survey the landscape. Your out-of-the-fray perspective, coupled with a review of the latest industry news, might actually give you some insights those stuck in the day-to-day grind don't have. "I had much more time to keep up with the medical literature when I was home with my young children than when I was working nonstop," a relauncher physician noted.

All of this can be done concurrently with your self-assessment and early explorations. Don't feel you have to be a PowerPoint guru before you go on an informational interview. The fact is, no number of classes will prepare you for your first real assignment. You'll undoubtedly learn more in a trial by fire on the job than you possibly can prepare for in advance.

The Elevator Story

Critical to how you present yourself to potential referral sources, employers, or clients is your "elevator story"—your ability to describe the kind of opportunity you're looking for succinctly and in a way that galvanizes your listener. According to Pam Lassiter in *The New Job Security,* "The Elevator Story refers to the answer you would give a potential employer [or client] if you were asked, 'What do you want to do?' while on an elevator ride."[2] To do this most effectively (and concisely), Lassiter suggested an elevator story formula; we've adapted this from her book and a presentation she gave at the Harvard Business School seminar Vivian attended for women seeking to reenter the workforce.

- **The introductory sentence.** Say something that both summarizes who you are and grabs your interlocutor's attention. If you've only been out of the workforce for a couple of years but had substantial experience in your target field before, you might lead with, "I have more than _____ years of experience in _____." With less than five years' experience in your target field, say you have "in-depth" or "extensive" experience.

    If your experience is ancient or not relevant to your new chosen arena, start with, "I'm exploring the field of _____ " or "taking courses in _____," whichever applies.
- **Three skills.** In your second sentence, pick three skills that you

know are relevant to your target field and develop a phrase for each. Make sure you use a little humor so you don't sound like a self-promoter on autopilot. If you're interested in consumer marketing, for example, you might say something like, "I particularly enjoy figuring out what makes me and the other mothers I run into in the supermarket buy what we buy and, more importantly, what would make us buy more. Then, once I've come up with an idea, and properly tested it, of course, I like to convince others to give it a try."

- **Two results.** Ideally, give two examples of results you achieved using the skills you mentioned above. *Feel free to draw from your volunteer experience as well as from your professional experience.* For instance, to continue with the above elevator story, you might say, "When I was assistant brand manager at General Foods, I noticed that women tended to buy cereals that featured some kind of popular character on the box. It may seem rather obvious now, but it wasn't that common at the time. So I persuaded my boss and the rest of the team to change the packaging, and our sales increased 20 percent! More recently, when I chaired the benefit auction at my kids' school, I came up with the idea of auctioning off certain services, like a personal shopper, a home organizer, and a life coach—things that I knew would appeal to the mothers in the audience—and we raised 30 percent more than we had the year before."

- **Question.** Now that you've differentiated yourself with some entertaining stories that tout your relevant skills, draw in your conversational partner with a question. But, warns Lassiter, *don't ask him if he knows of any jobs in your field.* Almost nobody knows of real live openings off the top of his head. You'll just get a no, and that will be that. Nor should you ask something like "Do you know of any jobs for a person like me?" or "for a person with my skills?" It's even worse than asking someone if he knows of any jobs in your field, because you're asking him to figure out where you fit. That's not his job, that's yours! Ask him, instead, a less pointed question that will encourage him to suggest names of companies to explore or people to contact. To complete the above elevator story, for example, you might ask: "Are you aware of any marketing companies that want to improve their consumer initiatives or marketing consultancies that focus on the consumer?" More than likely, you'll get a useful response, or at least a willingness to spend some additional time with you to brainstorm.

Once you've composed your elevator story, try it out on your family and friends to refine its content and delivery. You'll be using it over and over, and potentially adapting it slightly, depending upon the audience. In a job interview, for instance, your elevator story answers the ubiquitous "Tell me about yourself." But instead of closing with your open-ended question, you'll ask, "Is this the kind of background you're looking for?" If you're exploring a couple of very different fields, you may want to develop more than one elevator story, with each tailored to the appropriate audience.[3]

The Elevator Story for a Low-Rise

If you find the self-promotional second and third sections of the elevator story too long or too hard to deliver, craft a good summary of what you're looking for with an intelligent question at the end. Or adapt the second and third sections to a format you're comfortable with. At the very least, you need to be prepared to answer the question "What are you looking for?" in a concise and compelling way. For example, the fictional relauncher described above might have said, "I'm looking to leverage my consumer marketing skills either for a consumer marketing company or as a consultant." This sound bite may well be your most important marketing tool.

The Résumé

Probably nothing sends more relaunchers into a panic than the thought of having to write a résumé. It shouldn't. The résumé should be only one of the many ways a prospective employer or client will get to know you. If you can't bear to create one yourself, you can always hire a résumé writing service, for a nominal fee, to do it for you.

First, and perhaps most important, a few words about the length of your résumé. Keep it brief. Think of your résumé as your business card or a brief profile of your professional and educational experiences. It's not intended to tell people everything about you, but rather to give the important highlights and pique their interest so they'll want to meet you. According to a vice president of human resources at Citigroup in New York, a résumé should present your accomplishments. It's not supposed to be a stack of job descriptions. The optimal length is always one page. As a general rule, if you've worked less than seven years or spent most of your career at the same company, one page should suffice. If you worked longer than seven years, or worked in a number of different environments, going over a page is fine. Under almost no circumstances should a résumé be longer than two pages.

If your résumé extends beyond two pages, you may be including too much detail, exhibiting a lack of efficiency and organizational skills and disregarding the reader's time. However, always be prepared to tailor your résumé for a specific audience or opportunity. In those unique situations requiring a more in-depth résumé, it's probably preferable to use a readable font size, preserve some white space, and run to three pages rather than require a recruiter to take out a magnifying glass to read two densely packed pages. (A medical or scientific CV that lists publications and research grants is an exception to the one- or two-page rule.)

Take a look at the sample résumés in the resources section. You can use these as models when you write your own. Although these résumés may cover fields very different from yours, the structure and language should still be helpful to you. Keep reading, too, for a question-and-answer section that should guide you in preparing an effective résumé.

If I've been out of the workforce for a long time, would I be better off writing a functional rather than a chronological résumé?

Most résumés list employment history in reverse chronological order, followed by a paragraph or a set of bullet points under each. A functional résumé summarizes your experience in four or five different functional paragraphs, such as management, marketing, negotiating, and so on, followed by a bare-bones list of your jobs at the bottom.

We're not big fans of functional résumés. They can be confusing, often leaving the reader with questions about the candidate's actual professional skill set. They're also nonstandard and may suggest that the résumé writer has something to hide or is offering smoke and mirrors rather than tangible and specific work experience.

Should I include an objectives paragraph at the top?

If you're focused on a specific professional goal or path, feature it at the top of your résumé and try to do so in no more than one sentence. If you're uncertain about a specific career path or don't want to limit your opportunities, we don't advocate including an objectives section, unless you are able to articulate it in a neutral and flexible manner. If you aren't tied to one career direction, you don't want to limit the scope of your ambition to one sentence. You could craft different objectives for different purposes, but often your résumé will get passed around, and you don't want to be pigeonholed by what you wrote for one particular recipient. Also, narrow objectives, such as "to find a position in magazine advertising sales," are too limiting, and broad objectives, such as "to find a challenging, growth-oriented opportunity," are too catchall and sound clichéd. So unless you have a clear, narrow objective, save space and time and eliminate it. You can always describe your objectives in a cover letter.

Should I include a brief summary of myself?

Michelle, who once did basic biology research and desperately wants to return to the same field, noted that she has one unusual but highly valuable professional strength: "Any experiment I perform, I can make work the first time. Not everyone can do that. It is a skill people sought me out for. Some people have a fear of actually doing the experiment so they procrastinate and never really do it. Some people are careless in measurement or another aspect of the experiment. I remember I was eight and a half months pregnant and something had to be sequenced. It had to be done right the first time. So they called me over to do it, and I did." Carol urged her to put an eloquent version of this—something about "superb clinical research skills"—in bold print at the top of her résumé. This will be meaningful to a lab director who's lacking an experiment guru, or in a for-profit setting where Michelle's accuracy could save her employer money. (If she can quantify potential savings from her special skill, she should do so.)

A summary can also be a good way of positioning yourself if your résumé seems to be all over the map. But for most people, we think a summary, like an objective, can be either too narrowing or too clichéd. Your goal is to entice the recruiter into calling you, not to tell her everything about you so she doesn't have to bother.

Should I put my education first or my work experience?

There is no hard-and-fast rule, but generally the farther out you are from your education, the less focus it should receive, and therefore the farther down your résumé it belongs. If you're fresh out of a degree program, or attended a prestigious school, you may prefer to lead with your education.

What should I include in the education section?

List your alma maters, in reverse chronological order, including degrees earned, majors, year of graduation, and any academic honors such as magna cum laude or Phi Beta Kappa. Leaving off the year of your degree is a disingenuous way of trying to mask your age, and recruiters are liable to assume you're older than you are and resent the fact that you dismiss their ability to see past this aspect of who you are. Besides, someone may want to verify your credentials, making dates critical. Employers have a right to ask when you graduated, so you might as well include the information and spare them the inconvenience. Be sure to include significant athletic or extracurricular accomplishments. If your GPA was 3.5 or above, you may want to include it as well. All these additions mark you as a high performer.

How should I describe my prior jobs?

Make sure you briefly describe the company and include the name of the successor company if your old employer was acquired.

Remember to focus on accomplishments, rather than simply regurgitating your job description. Wherever possible, quantify results and highlight how you added value to your employer. Try to substitute words such as *managed* or *administered* for *responsible for*. If you did something as part of a team, add that qualifier. No one expects you to have done everything yourself. Everyone is looking for good team players. In contrast, during the interview phase of the process, focusing on *I* and your individual accomplishments takes priority; most hiring managers and recruiters want to know about your specific contributions. If you led a team, say so. Take credit for your innovations. Use words like *initiated, spearheaded*. Get out that thesaurus. A well-written résumé with colorful but accurate diction will demonstrate that you're a great communicator.

If the jobs you held differ greatly from the kind you hope to relaunch into, make sure you emphasize the Job Building Blocks in common with your target career. For example, Vivian highlighted her roles in recruiting and human resources at the consulting firm where she had last worked, because that was the direction in which she hoped to relaunch.

What do I do about the employment gap in my résumé?

We know you haven't been sitting around eating bonbons, but how do you make your time off sound like something more than an extended vacation? Full-time working people often have misconceptions about how full-time moms spend their time. The fact is, most employers still don't understand how transferable household management and child-rearing skills are to the workplace. As a result, phrasing such as "managed three children, home finances, and contractors" will likely turn off most résumé readers. One of the editors to whom we pitched our book, a twenty-something who was pregnant with her first child, sniffed: "I hope you're not going to try to argue that being at home is the perfect training ground for the workplace." That convinced us that touting your mommy skills in a résumé risks making you look foolish and naive (the same goes for the interview). It's also insulting to full-time working mothers who hold down job responsibilities *in addition to* creating nurturing homes. Finally, it pegs you as a member of the leisured class who either doesn't need the work or won't produce when the chips are down. Someday women may proudly insert paragraphs about what they accomplished as a mother into their résumés, but we don't think that day has come . . . yet.

So if you haven't done much besides cooking, carpooling, and laundry, you have a couple of choices. You can leave the gap as is and state that you've been a full-time mother in a cover letter; you can leave the gap as a gap and say nothing about it in a cover letter; you can put "Mother of __ children" in a "Personal" category at the bottom of the résumé; or you can list the dates you've been out of the workforce on the résumé and indicate that you've been home full-time raising your children. For example:

11/98–Present
Mother: Three children born 4/98–8/02. Current ages are 5–9. At home full-time since 7/00.

One approach isn't necessarily better than another. While some women may prefer to be up front about the fact that they have been full-time mothers for a certain number of years, others may feel more comfortable not including this information in their résumés. Carol took the former approach, while Vivian left motherhood off her résumé. She was afraid (rightly or wrongly) that if potential employers or clients knew she had five children, they would assume she wouldn't be able to handle demanding work on top of her maternal obligations. The fact is, if your volunteer work includes school-based positions, anyone carefully reading your résumé is going to assume you're a mother. Nevertheless, remember you're not required to tell anyone whether or not you're married and/or whether or not you have children, either on a résumé or in an interview (more on this later).

Should I list volunteer work?

Unlike motherhood, volunteer work definitely belongs on your résumé. And most women who've been home for more than a year have extensive volunteer credentials. So in addition to "Work Experience" and "Education," you should have a section for "Volunteer Work" or "Volunteer Experience" or "Community Service," whatever you prefer to call it. Describe these positions as you would a job, quantifying results wherever possible. In Carol's résumé, for example (see "Sample Résumés of Real Relaunchers" at the back of this book), her description of her work as co-president of the John Ward Elementary School PTO sounds like something she could have written if she were a corporate department head, using strong active verbs such as *created, managed,* and *established.*

Carol also quantified her results by stating, "Proposal was awarded $10,000 by Newton Schools Foundation (NSF), one of the largest single-school grants ever made by the NSF to an elementary school. Increased school volunteer force by 25%."

Philippa, a mother of three and former management consultant who relaunched by accepting a consulting assignment with her old employer, similarly quantified her involvement with the Junior League of St. Louis, highlighting her people management skills as follows: "Responsible for all league projects covering over 5,000 volunteer hours and 130 active members. Previous leadership appointments include community impact co-chair—co-led team of 40 in contributing 1,380 volunteer hours."

Although your volunteer work may have been as substantive and demanding as any paying job (and perhaps more so), we generally don't advise that you try to fudge the line between paid and unpaid experience. You don't want to look like you're trying to put something over on anyone or imply that you were paid for work you did on a volunteer basis. But there may be exceptions to this advice. If you provided professional services on a pro bono basis, you could list your involvement under "Pro Bono Work." And if you received an honorarium, you can call it consulting.

Leslie, an attorney, volunteered at the Florida Victim Assistance Office. As part of this job, she made a major presentation, for which she was later issued a courtesy check for a thousand dollars. So she listed this job under the "Legal Employment" section of her résumé as "consultant." Also, if your volunteer work directly relates to the field you're targeting, you might categorize these accomplishments under "Relevant Experience."

Should I list references?

Of course you'll provide references to anyone who is seriously interested in you. But there is no expectation that you list them on your résumé. You don't want to anger your mentors by having them receive unprompted and unnecessary calls. No prospective employer should be contacting your references without first obtaining your consent and approval, usually at the point of making an offer of employment.

Should I list software, computer languages, industry certifications, or foreign languages?

If you have specialized computer programming or other advanced skills or credentials, include this information on your résumé. Possible section headings include "Certifications," "Other," or "Computer Skills." Don't bother listing working knowledge of common programs such as Word or Excel; in today's world, these skills are a given. Nicky, whose résumé was plucked off Monster.com by a large Wall Street firm despite a three-year gap, credits the Series 16 designation she displayed prominently for catching their attention.

Knowledge of foreign languages should also always be included, even if you don't think it's germane. You never know who may find it useful. On one of Vivian's executive searches for the US subsidiary of a German company, candidates with knowledge of German had an edge.

Should I include interests and hobbies and/or other personal information?

As we discussed above, you're not required to inform potential employers of your marital and maternal status. Nevertheless, many relaunchers put "mother of ___" and the children's ages under a "Personal" heading at the bottom of their résumé. Although it's wonderful to be up front, be aware that if you include "mother of four" on your résumé, some employers may worry about your ability to deliver on the job. This is especially the case in certain industries that require intense time commitments. Again, if you've listed school-related volunteer experiences, you're not hiding your children. You're just not drawing attention to them. You can always tell people about your family later, after they've gotten to know (and hopefully like) your professional persona. Why make "mother of four" be the way they define you? According to one employment lawyer we consulted, "Listing any type of personal information on your résumé calls attention to a personal attribute that may not define you in total; thus it's best to leave it off unless you believe it relevant to how a prospective employer may benefit from this knowledge." Bottom line: It's your call.

Listing interests or hobbies is also somewhat controversial. They can be a good conversation starter, as well as a way to distinguish you from others. But only list those hobbies or activities in which you are substantially engaged. In other words, don't include skiing if you hit the bunny slopes once five years ago. Intellectually or physically demanding hobbies, such as chess or marathon running, imply high intellect or energy. Some prospective employers will view these positively, although others might consider your including them on a résumé irrelevant.

The Bio

If you decide to pursue consulting work or an entrepreneurial opportunity, you'll need to prepare a bio to use in your marketing materials. If you're not familiar with this kind of personal presentation, look at the executive biographies on any corporate Web site to get a feel for them. They summarize a manager's experience and accomplishments in the third person. They're a boon to relaunchers, because they typically dispense with dates and other annoying details. The form also offers almost limitless positioning potential. Unless your time as a full-time mom adds to your credibility—if you're trying to drum up work as a relaunch coach, for example—there's no need to mention your years at home in the bio, and no corresponding black hole to cover.

Here's the bio Vivian put on her executive search firm's Web site:

> **Vivian Rabin** is vice president for US operations for Salovey & Associates. Vivian has over twelve years of diverse business experience, including increasing leadership roles in finance and human resources, in the media, financial services, and consulting industries. Prior to joining Salovey & Associates, Vivian was director of recruitment and personnel for The Advisory Board

Company, a publishing and consulting concern in Washington, DC, where she initiated an MBA recruitment program, established an HR infrastructure, and provided senior management training. Vivian holds a BA and an MBA from Harvard University.

Here's the bio kids' marketer Marla Libraty uses to pursue consulting assignments:

Kids' marketer **Marla Libraty** brings over fifteen years of creative strategic experience to any kids' marketing challenge. As a board member for Step Into Art, a nonprofit organization that provides dynamic, content-rich art programs for kids, Marla provides guidance on programming, marketing, and organizational development. Armed with an MBA from UCLA, Marla helped launch Mattel Toys' Becky, the first-ever fashion doll in a wheelchair. The doll, a close friend of Barbie, was cited as garnering the most press of any product Mattel had ever launched, as well as accolades from affiliated organizations and kids around the world. Marla's experience with international brands with kid appeal includes the initial development of the Eveready Battery Company's Energizer Bunny sales promotion materials leveraging the ad campaign's widespread success. Always up for an adventure, Marla and her husband lived in Bangkok, Thailand, for more than four years with their three children. While in Thailand, she initiated and structured the Pizza Company (formerly Pizza Hut, Thailand's largest fast-food pizza company) Birthday Party Program. Currently, Marla is engaged in a variety of projects, including a new business concept that would support kids' exploration of future careers. Marla is available to consult on kids' marketing issues and new products and services.

The Interview

Whether you end up taking a job within an organization, consulting, or starting your own business, you're likely to find yourself in an interview situation at some point in the relaunch process. Good interview skills can highlight your qualifications. Similarly, poor interviewing skills can diminish an otherwise strong work history. Let's take a look at preparing for this process.

The Informational Interview

An informational interview is a meeting with someone in your field of interest to learn more about the industry, company, or job function. *It should not be a thinly disguised attempt to get a job.* To obtain an informational interview, e-mail, write, or call (depending upon your level of closeness to the target individual) someone who does work you think might be of interest to you, or who works in a company in which you're interested. Alternatively, call someone you know who may be able to facilitate setting up the informational interview for you. Some of the names you scribbled on your Job Building Blocks worksheet in chapter 3 might fit the bill. Your informational interview targets should be peers. You're trying to gather information, rather than sell yourself. Tell your contact that you're trying to learn more about the field, function, or company, and ask if you could speak with him for twenty minutes or so, either on the phone or in person. Do not say, "I am looking for a job in the _____ field" or "at the _____ company and wanted to see if you could help me." Most people don't have jobs to offer (or don't think they have jobs to offer) and will try to decline your request. Don't ask for an "informational interview." That sounds too formal and is off-putting.

Even meetings with friends should be treated as opportunities to pick up valuable information about their field as well as letting them see you in a different light. Come prepared with a notebook, a pen, and a list of questions. Solicit their feedback on your résumé. Be on

time and don't overstay your welcome. If you asked for twenty minutes, make sure you keep to that limit, monitoring your list of questions to make sure you cover everything of importance to you. Always
ask for referrals to additional people you might talk to for information, and/or for referrals to anyone in the field or at the company who
may be hiring or need more help. Then contact those people, saying,
"_____ suggested I contact you."

Thank everyone with whom you speak along the way—a quick
e-mail is fine—and feel free to periodically update people by e-mail.
Although the purpose of an informational interview is not specifically
to practice for a real interview, it does give you a chance to test your
elevator story as well as increase your comfort in an interview setting.
Also, the more you substantively engage people in these discussions,
the more they are apt to help you.

The Mock Interview

If you have a real interview set up, let a good friend, preferably someone who is working, conduct a mock interview with you. Try to simu-
late actual interview conditions. Don't let yourself burst out laughing
when you mess up. Take it seriously and you'll be much better prepared
for the real thing. University recruiting services may offer videotaped
interview sessions, often free to alums. Even if you live far from your
alma mater, check to see if they have reciprocity arrangements with a
university near you. This may give you access to their services. Take
advantage of these if they're available to you.

The Telephone Interview

Both executive recruiters and in-house hiring managers increasingly
rely on a telephone screen to whittle down the list of candidates.
Don't denigrate such an interview's importance just because it's taking place over the phone. In fact, you can use the phone interview
to your advantage as a means of giving a voice to the details of your
résumé or profile. A telephone interview is every bit as important as

an in-person meeting. And because so much business is done over the phone, employers want to assess your phone manner as much as anything else.

If someone reaches you at a bad time, don't feel compelled to continue the discussion because you're afraid the caller may never make time for you again. Inform the caller that you're currently unavailable but eager to discuss the opportunity (no need to tell her that your four-year-old is screaming for you from the bathroom) and ask to set up a mutually convenient time. Then prepare for the call as you would for an in-person interview. Remember, each and every contact you make with a prospective employer is part of the interview process. Make it count.

The In-Person Interview

Real interviews require intense and meaningful preparation. Although they eclipse résumés in terms of importance, most people spend far less time gearing up for interviews than putting together their résumés. Construct a five-minute thumbnail sketch of your work history, emphasizing what you think is most relevant for the particular interview, and practice delivering it out loud—in front of a mirror, if possible. This can be a modified version of your elevator story. It shouldn't sound word-for-word memorized, but you should be comfortable enough with your story that you can tell it with relative ease. Make sure you know what you'll say to any obvious questions your résumé might prompt, such as, "Why did you leave _____ company?"

Also, make sure you know what you're going to say about your years out of the workforce. Although prospective employers are not allowed to ask you about your marital or family status, many will inquire indirectly anyway. This does not mean that they're trying to screen mothers out. They may simply be ignorant of the law and/or curious about you. Don't assume the worst and get defensive or scold them for asking you a possibly illegal question. That's a surefire way of antagonizing your interviewer. No one is going to want to hire someone who's that prickly or even litigious. Furthermore, interviewers *are* permitted to probe gaps on your résumé, so you may well end up sharing some details about your personal life. Be brief, straightforward, non-judgmental, and nondefensive in describing your situation, bearing in mind that your interviewer may have strong feelings about this issue. Don't say, "I stayed home with my kids because I wanted to be a *good* mother." This implies that mothers who didn't take time out are *bad* mothers, a suggestion that is not only false, but that many interviewers (both male and female) will find highly offensive. One possible line: "I took time off to be with my children, but have been eager to return to work." Be prepared for any sort of reaction. One woman told us that her male interviewer replied, "My wife can barely manage taking care of our kids, let alone working. How are you going to manage?" She shot back, "I have plenty of help. It's not a problem for me." Respond with confidence, not defensiveness.

And here's one of our all-time favorite responses to the "How are you going to manage?" question. Laura, who relaunched by applying to rabbinical school, was asked by the interview committee: "You have three young children. This is an intensive full-time program. How can you do this?" Her answer: "There are lots of busy women in the world who do lots of things, and I plan to be one of them."

Do Your Interview Homework

Knowing the industry and the company will always give you a competitive advantage. Crawl all over the Web site. Talk to friends in the industry or at your target company. Don't feel you have to name-drop your knowledge—it comes across as obnoxious. Interviewers can tell in a minute who's done their homework and who hasn't by how a candidate speaks about the industry and the company. A perceptive question can be a more powerful selling tool than a long-winded answer. Whenever possible, draw connections between what you've done and how you can use that knowledge, experience, or network for the company. Try not to relate items back to parenthood, but rather to your prior professional experience or relevant volunteer work. Although your last job may have been years ago, demonstrate your comfort level with at least one aspect of the job or the company by showing that you have something to contribute in a particular area. Make sure a strong business vocabulary replaces mommy-speak.

Although in a formal interview the spotlight is clearly on the interviewee, the best interviews sound more like a conversation than an inquisition. Treat this as an opportunity for you to learn more about the job; the working conditions, including your prospective boss; the company; and even the industry. Many companies have prospective employees meet with several members of a department or team, so use each interview as a way to gather information for the next. Throughout each meeting, take mental notes of the conversation. Use this information later in crafting a detailed thank-you letter.

Handling the Tough Questions

Case-study questions have become more common in interviews. In this type of question, the interviewer describes a hypothetical problem, and then asks you what you would do or how you would think through the situation. The key to successfully answering these questions is to realize that you're not necessarily being tested solely on your technical knowledge, but also on how you think through problems. Don't feel obligated to shoot back the perfect answer. Take a moment to digest what you've just been told. Ask good clarifying questions. Even if you don't know much about the issue described, don't digress from the question. Use your general business knowledge to articulate some assumptions and talk through the problem. The substance of your answer is less important than the fact that you confidently navigated your way through an intense question.

In one interview, for example, Tanya was asked, "How many police officers do you think are deployed in Manhattan?" Instead of saying, "I have no idea," she talked the problem through: "Assuming there are about two hundred east–west streets and fifteen north–south avenues, or a total of three thousand blocks, let's say there's one for every five blocks, so that comes out to about six hundred." Even if she's wrong, she's given a good answer because she exhibited her ability to analyze and think through a problem or question.

If after the interview you reflect on a more complete or better answer to the question, it can't hurt to e-mail the specific interviewers and let them know. Carol did this and found out later it was a factor in her clinching her relaunch job.

Dressing for the Job You Want and Not the Job You Have

Make sure you look professional and put together when you interview. If all you've bought in the last five years is sweatpants or date-night dresses, spring for a new outfit that makes you look current and feel confident. Ideally, try to get a sense of the dress code where you'll be interviewing and choose your clothes accordingly. You might even want to ask someone who's working for the type of employer you are targeting to give you some wardrobe advice. If you're not certain, it's generally better to be a little overdressed for a first interview than to appear too casual.

Project Confidence (Even if You Have to Pretend a Little)

Probably the best advice we could give is that, no matter how nervous you feel, try to appear relaxed. No matter how desperately you need a certain job or consulting assignment, don't let on. Appearing desperate or timid turns people off. You've got to trust that you have the ability to make the right opportunity jell. Diane, the Queen of Contract Work, thinks that "when you're not financially driven, you end up more in demand because you're a little more cavalier. This makes you more appealing in your presentation to others. Knowing it's okay if something doesn't work out makes you more relaxed in your business interactions." And, we might add, more successful.

Some people find they interview better if they can convince themselves they have no chance. They become more relaxed and can give their honest reactions and thoughts without a lot of tension getting in the way. As Conan O'Brien told the Harvard graduating class of 2000 about the ups and downs of his career: "And then an insane, inexplicable opportunity came my way, a chance to audition for host of the new *Late Night* show. I took the opportunity very seriously, but at the same time—I have to be honest—I had the relaxed confidence of someone who knew he had no real shot, so I couldn't fear losing a great job that I could never hope to have. And I think that actually that attitude made the difference."[4]

On her way to an interview with a clinic down the street from her old hospital, Shelly, a physician, told herself to stay calm and focused. "I knew I had this intellectual dimension. I just had to polish it up and beam it on everyone. My strategy was to go in there and present myself as a high-powered professional. A male friend had recently said to me: 'You're a doctor. No one can take that away from you.' That gave me confidence. Then, on the way to the interview, I saw a taxi with one of those Monster.com advertisements on top that said in big letters: YOU'RE HIRED. I took it as a good omen. When the interviewer told me that it would take at least two years for me to build up a brand-new practice and that this would be a big investment for them, I told them I thought they weren't analyzing this correctly. I said, 'I already have a practice here [because before she'd left to stay home with her kids, she'd worked in the same neighborhood]. I think when word gets out that I'm back, my clinic patients will come back to me.' I got the job, and they paid me 25 percent more than the original salary range."

Dealing with Rejection

Since many relaunchers begin their search with a diminished view of themselves, they're more vulnerable than most to rejection. Rejection can occur across the Relaunch Opportunities Spectrum: You don't get a second-round interview for a full-time job; a prospective client decides not to move forward with a proposed project; a coveted distributor refuses to stock your product. No matter the form, it hurts. If you're rejected, don't take it personally. It doesn't mean the employers or clients think you're a loser. It just means they don't think you're a fit for the particular opportunity under consideration. In fact, you may have more success with another department or manager at the same company. Furthermore, as with many painful experiences, *a relaunch rejection can morph into a growth experience.*

The Benefits of Rejection

- **Rejection helps you realize what *won't* work, at least not as a first step, and lets you refocus.** After failing to find the kind of substantive part-time marketing job she had enjoyed earlier in her career, Charlene realized she had to shift her focus to consulting rather than corporate employment. Maxine interviewed extensively for corporate real estate jobs. But rather than continuing to beat her head against a brick wall, she turned to pursuing graduate teaching and consulting opportunities. If your efforts in one direction seem to fail, don't give up entirely—refocus.

- **Rejection helps you learn more about yourself and organizations.** Early in her relaunch, Vivian secured an in-person interview for a sales position with a high-end corporate training company. Although she thought she was eager for the job, "Between getting my five kids to school and taking two commuter trains, I barely managed to get to the interview on time. When I didn't make it to a second round, I was actually relieved. I realized I just wasn't ready for a full-time job in the city. If I had to struggle to get to the interview, how was I ever going to do this every day?" Kim, the former city planner who wanted to relaunch as a professional fund-raiser, thought all her years as a volunteer for Catholic charities would make her a shoo-in for a paid job at one of these organizations. But even with professional fund-raising courses under her belt, these nonprofits wouldn't take her seriously. After several rejections, she realized she should target organizations that *didn't* know her as a volunteer. She ended up relaunching as director of development for an agency that assists the homeless.

- **Rejection teaches you that you can take it and won't fall apart.** This may be really cold comfort, but it's true that surviving rejection makes you stronger in the long run. Anyone who's experienced only success probably harbors an abnormal fear of failure. And we all know how crippling that can be.

- **Rejection gives you practice. And practice makes perfect.** With each interview or consulting pitch, your presentation will improve.

But let's not dwell on rejection. With preparation, persistence, and the networking strategies we outline in our next chapter, you should be able to discover or develop an opportunity that works for you.

CHAPTER 5

Network, Market Yourself, and Clinch the Opportunity

I'm going to get hired by either a friend, or a friend of a friend.

—*Carol*

By now you should have decided that you really do want to work for pay. You've figured out the field you're interested in and researched it in the library and online, as well as by speaking to those close to you who know something about it. You've developed an elevator story and a solid draft of your résumé and/or bio. You've taken or are taking a class or two or are otherwise addressing any holes in your skill set. You're now ready to begin marketing yourself in earnest.

Note that, as with any attempt to describe a fluid process like a job search, the particular steps may overlap or occur in a different sequence for different people. In an effort to develop a framework for your relaunch, we've enumerated steps that may in fact occur simultaneously or in a slightly different order. Don't worry about this.

Jumping into the Job Market

Employment Ads and Search Firms

According to Richard Nelson Bolles in *What Color Is Your Parachute?*, using the Internet alone to search for jobs results in success about 4 percent of the time. Focusing on classified ads in newspapers works 5 to 25 percent of the time, depending upon the level of compensation you're looking for. The higher paying the job, the less likely you are to find it by answering a classified ad.[1] That doesn't mean you should never answer an ad. Responding to postings on your college or graduate school Web site can be quite productive, because employers are specifically seeking someone with your degree. Also, if your experience exactly matches the specified job requirements and the field is highly specialized, then your bid might be successful.

Just be aware that if you *only* answer ads, you may never find an opportunity. First of all, many screeners will automatically put you into the slush pile because of the gap in your résumé. More importantly, many companies don't advertise openings. Department heads often recognize a human resource need and fill it with someone a colleague recommends before an ad ever gets written. Only through networking will you discover such opportunities. Finally, answering a classified ad in the usual fashion won't net you consulting work or an entrepreneurial opportunity. (You may be able to use ads to identify needs in the marketplace, but you'll have to respond to them differently than you would if you're simply seeking a job. More on this in "The consulting Relaunch" section later in this chapter.)

Headhunters aren't likely to be much help, either. Companies usually engage search firms to find employees who have very specific, cutting-edge qualifications. Relaunchers are not likely to be seen as up-to-date experts in their fields. Also, search firms are paid by employers, not employees, so they have no incentive to help you per se. There's nothing wrong with sending your résumé to a search firm, just don't expect the phone to ring as a result.

Staffing Firms

Staffing firms, such as Robert Half, are also paid by the employer. But they handle a much larger volume of assignments than search firms, and usually those at lower salary levels than positions filled by search firms. Staffing firms no longer provide only administrative assistants. They now operate in virtually every arena and for almost any function, including financial, legal, and medical personnel. They place people in both short-term and long-term assignments. In addition, staffing agencies constantly try to build their pipeline of candidates and will be much more open to people with different backgrounds. If you're not sure what you want to do, signing up with a staffing firm can be a good way to play the field and put some current experience on your résumé. Many staffing firms offer training and benefits, as well. Finally, if you land in a company and/or job you like, you've got a good chance of staying there beyond the term of the staffing firm contract. The downside is that, depending upon which agency you sign with and the terms of the arrangement, you may have limited choice in assignments.

Career Counselors

Career counselors can be helpful. *You* pay them—usually by the hour—so they presumably have your best interests at heart. But like therapists and personal trainers, they vary in quality. More importantly, you get out of them what you put in. They'll give you homework to do to help you discover your work passions, to target industries, and so forth. They'll help you build your confidence and develop action plans and timelines. They'll assist you with your résumé and advise you on networking calls. But ultimately, you have to do the hard work yourself. If you're interested in using a career counselor, ask friends for referrals, or choose from those listed on various Web sites. Most Web sites include the counselors' bios. Make sure you choose one with experience helping relaunchers and people in your target industry and/or function. See the resources section for Web sites that provide lists of career counselors.

Relaunch Matchmakers

As we noted in the "Back to School" section of the last chapter, a cottage industry of vendors has sprung up specifically to serve relaunchers.

Their services range from individual career counseling to back-to-work seminars to Web sites with job postings specifically geared toward reentering women. (See the resources section for a listing.) Some focus on matching currently benched talent with corporations looking for flexible or temporary experts for specific projects. As one element in your marketing campaign, they're certainly worth exploring. As with the resources discussed above, however, all the usual caveats about cost, quality, and who is the paying customer apply. Keep your eye on www.backonthecareertrack.com (our Web site) for developments in this arena.

Cold-Calling (or Writing) Small Companies

Bolles didn't rate this method specifically in *Parachute*, but he did rate similar methods. He claimed 47 percent of people can get a job by "knocking on the door of any employer, factory or office that interests you," and that 69 percent get jobs by using the yellow pages to call employers in their field and ask if they're hiring people with their skills. Nevertheless, we're skeptical that these techniques will work for relaunchers who are looking for professional or management-level assignments. Nor do we think most gun-shy relaunchers would be willing to try them. We do, however, recommend a slightly different strategy: Write to the principals of small, under-the-radar firms in which you have an interest and propose ways in which you might be able to help them grow or be more productive. Then place a follow-up call.

Cruising the Web site of *Fast Company*, a business magazine, Vivian spotted a small firm in her area that offers writing seminars to businesses. After studying its Web site, she wrote the top executives a carefully crafted letter outlining what she felt she could do for them, and enclosed her résumé. To her delight, when she placed a follow-up call, they invited her in for a meeting, asking her to prepare and deliver a brief writing seminar so they could assess her skills. She invested a lot of unpaid time into this presentation, but the effort was definitely worthwhile. The company proposed several different ways she might work with them on a freelance basis. Although she ended up sticking with her executive search business, the experience was a major confidence builder. It also introduced her to this very powerful job search technique.

Networking

Research shows that more people get jobs through personal connections than by any other means.[2] But how do you make such connections and, once you have them, how do you use them without seeming blatantly opportunistic? The answer is networking. Networking allows you to strengthen old ties while making new connections. It enables you to build relationships that pay off now, or ten years into the future. Networks can help you land a job, a client, an IT consultant for your entrepreneurial venture, or a summer internship for your kid.

Before we show you how to build, or resuscitate, your network, let's discuss what networking is and isn't. It isn't entering a room full of strangers and passing out your business card to everyone in sight. It isn't contacting people you barely know and asking them if they know of any jobs in their field. Networking, done properly, shouldn't be called networking. *Networking, at its best, relies on one basic principle— developing a mutually beneficial relationship.*

Nobody likes to feel used. You never want someone to think, *She's just talking to me because I know so-and-so or because I work at ___ company.* If that is the only reason you're approaching someone, you have no right to do so. You've got to develop and show some interest in other people's lives and problems to be an effective networker. In *The 7 Habits of Highly Effective People*, Stephen Covey described all relationships as having an emotional bank account.[3] If you do for others—if you make deposits in your account with them, so to speak—they'll want to even out the score and do for you. This doesn't mean that you only do for others in expectation of making a return. Nor does it mean that you can't ask others for help without doing something for them first. It simply means you understand the way the system works and draw on this understanding in all your interactions.

"But What Do I Have to Offer?"

You're probably thinking: *I've been out of the workplace for ___ years; I'm just a boring old stay-at-home mom. What can I possibly offer anybody?* Don't cross yourself off so fast. You have a lot to offer:

- **Psychic value.** Don't discount people's genuine interest in hearing from an old friend or colleague. If you do it with confidence and warmth, it triggers fond memories, which will rub off on you. Also, approaching someone as the expert is flattering. No matter how successful people are, they want to be acknowledged for it.
- **Volunteer connections.** You may think your volunteer work is no big deal. But if you're an involved parent at your child's school or a board member of a charity, that may be a big deal to your contact. Ask him about his family so you can figure out how you might be of service.
- **Nonprofessional expertise.** Following on the last idea, all sorts of "mom knowledge" may be valuable. Remember, your professional contacts have *lives* as well as *jobs.* Almost everybody needs a good babysitter, tutor, contractor, decorator, doctor, real estate broker, or insurance agent at some point in their life, or advice about dealing with same. As you get to know your contacts, you can use your mom knowledge as currency in exchange for their market data.

Even More to Offer: Meeting Employer, Client, and Customer Needs

As you start to speak to and meet with your contacts and with those to whom they refer you, ask questions to clarify their problems and needs. Use your research and the information you pick up in other conversations to craft questions that will help you uncover potential opportunities. Don't ask people outright, "What's your biggest problem?" or state, "I've heard your ___ Division is a mess." According to Pam Lassiter, whose book *The New Job Security* details this process, "Companies, or people, rarely like to openly admit to problems."[4] Even "What keeps you up at night?" or "Where's your pain?" have become old hat. Try to put a new spin on the question. Maybe: "What do you see as your biggest challenge?" or "What would you like to accomplish that you and your staff haven't been able to?" If you have some specific knowledge, design a question around that. For example, "I get the sense that the division might benefit from having someone develop more relationships with research directors at pharmaceutical companies. Is that the case?" Once you've discovered a need, explain how you and your skills might be able to help: "When I was at ___ Consulting, I did a huge survey of pharmaceutical research directors, so I'm familiar with their issues and with a lot of the players. Would you be interested in exploring this further?"

Notice that this "nugget of need" that you've uncovered could be the nucleus of a full-time job, a part-time job, or a consulting project. See how your contact responds. Then you can inch it forward in the direction that suits you best, but always phrasing your thinking in terms of how it meets the contact's needs. For example, if you really like the company and would love to work there full-time, keep pushing to figure out other projects you might be able to successfully undertake. Then you could say something like, "It seems there are a lot of areas where I could add value. I'd love to come in and dig in. If I come in full-time, I'll be able to get up to speed quickly, work more closely with everybody, and therefore get better execution. How does that sound to you?" If you're still checking out alternatives or want the flexibility of consulting, you might say: "This sounds like something I could do as a consulting project. That way you could get a feel for my work without having to make a long-term commitment. Can we talk a bit about how I might approach the project?" As we've done here, end with a question to gauge your contact's response. And again, most importantly, always try to phrase *your* requirements in terms of *their* needs.[5]

Networking Breadth and Depth

In building and tapping your network, you need breadth and depth. Breadth will get you beyond your small circle of acquaintances to where opportunities exist that you might not otherwise hear about; depth means people who really know and care about you and are willing to go to bat for you when you need it.

More than twenty-five years ago, a sociologist discovered that most people get their jobs through personal connections, but not necessarily through people they know well. This is the "strength of weak ties" principle, and this is why you need breadth in your network.[6] Although your family and close friends may be your biggest cheerleaders, they are unlikely to provide you with any new market information you can't access yourself. You frequent the same places. You speak to the same people. Any opportunities they know about, you probably know about, too. You need to get beyond that circle to learn new information. For example, while Judy, the former lawyer we described in chapter 1, was teaching a course at a local law school, she bumped into a law school classmate whom she hadn't seen in over fifteen years. This acquaintance worked at a legal nonprofit that Judy was very interested in. As a result of her acquaintance's introduction, Judy became the legal director of the organization.

Still . . . while weak ties are great, you can't expect peripheral connections to spend lots of time helping you relaunch. Clearly, you need some solid muscle in your corner as well. You need what career counselor Mary Lindley Burton calls a "board of directors"—a group of people you can turn to for advice and assistance.[7] These are people you can ask to review your résumé and cover letters, brainstorm with you about consulting opportunities, and console you after a bad interview. You don't need to gather them together around a mahogany table. You don't even need to offer them a seat. You've simply identified them in your mind as people you want on your side (and you of course try to help them in any way you can). As you review the networking sources below, keep your antennae up for the savviest and most helpful people you know in each of these environments. These are the people you'll turn to as your board of directors. Ideally, some of these people work in your field of interest or at least have some connections to it.

Networking Contact Pools

Before you protest that you have no connections, we're going to show you just how many you have. Everybody has connections—old friends, former colleagues, neighbors, fellow church members, and so on. Anybody you've ever known (and more) is in fact part of your network and therefore a potential connection to a new opportunity. As you'll see depicted in the following chart, your network contains three basic contact pools: people from your past, those from your present, and those from your future. These are people you can call either to obtain more information about a particular field or company and/or as a source of referrals to others who may be able to help you. As you read through these pages, make a list of all the people whom you might want to approach for information and/or potential referrals. Even if their connection to you or your chosen field seems tenuous, write them down for now. You don't ever have to contact them if you later decide it doesn't make sense. Star anyone connected to one of the Job Building Blocks you identified in chapter 3. These are people you most likely will want to approach.

CONTACT POOLS

People from Your Past	People from Your Present	People from Your Future
College or grad school classmates	Friends	Create a college or grad school alumni network
College or grad school profs	Neighbors	Create a corporate alumni network
People from prior jobs: clients, vendors, competitors, advisers, junior colleagues, corporate alumni groups	Church/synagogue volunteer co-workers	Create a Relaunch Circle
	Volunteers' spouses	Find a Relaunch Buddy
	People in courses you're taking	

People from Your Past: The Beauty of Being Frozen in Time

College or Graduate School Classmates and Friends

Even if you haven't been in touch with them for years, your classmates can be a great resource. Many universities have alumni databases. Use these to search for alumni who might be able to assist you. Start by focusing on your class, then broaden your list to include alumni who graduated within a couple of years, ultimately assembling a complete list of alumni whom you may wish to contact.

If you're not already doing so, start reading the alumni notes of your college or graduate school alumni publications. Referencing something a classmate wrote in the alumni notes provides the perfect excuse for initiating e-mail contact with a long-lost acquaintance. Then when you're ready to begin your relaunch in earnest, you have a basis for contacting them without looking purely self-serving. Even if you haven't kept up, if someone is doing something you find interesting, or if you have an idea you think might be helpful, don't be shy about dropping a quick e-mail, then following up with a call.

Finally, drag yourself to alumni club events and alumni reunions. Sadly, we've heard women admit that they purposely steer clear of such venues because they're embarrassed about their current nonprofessional status. Wrong attitude. The more you get out, the more positive interactions you'll have, the more confident you'll feel—and the more likely you are to stumble upon your dream opportunity. An alumni gathering is the perfect way to begin to crawl out of your domestic shell, because you've got built-in commonality and affability.

Whether you reconnect by e-mail, by phone, or in person, remember that your former acquaintances' image of you is frozen in time. Even if your view of yourself has diminished, their view of you has not. To old acquaintances, you are the same bright, talented person you were years ago.

College or Graduate School Professors

Don't forget about professors from your alma mater or in your community. They may know of opportunities or may be able to offer you an opportunity themselves. Recovering from a nasty divorce, Maxine, a former real estate executive, "contacted old colleagues and felt like an idiot. I was twice referred to as a 'legend,' as though I was already dead." After a consulting project here and there, she got in touch with one of her former real estate professors and was invited to teach a class for a semester and develop course materials. The experience was a net loss financially, after factoring in moving expenses, but it led to other more lucrative and compelling consulting assignments. "I started to regain credibility."

People from Prior Jobs

Using your résumé to jog your memory, go through each of your prior jobs, noting people you may want to call for information, referrals, or references. These are not only former fellow employees, but also clients, vendors, competitors and advisers. Rachel, whose experience in a part-time MBA program we described in the previous chapter, credits a stellar reference from her first boss in landing her dream re-launch job with an educational foundation. She had kept in touch with her original boss, and he called back within an hour of her potential employer's calling for a reference. He told them, "Rachel was the best hire of my career." *She hadn't worked for him for fifteen years, and he still said that on her behalf.* That was pretty powerful. She had sought him out at professional meetings and occasionally contacted him by e-mail or phone. Despite the decade-and-a-half time lapse, the relationship remained strong.

But if you haven't kept in touch, don't despair. Resuscitate. (And then don't let those relationships die again.) The frozen-in-time concept applies particularly well in approaching people who were senior to you. Even if you feel like a dinosaur, you're still a bright young thing to the old guy who hired you years ago. He certainly won't view you as too old for the job.

In addition to the "usual suspects"—your former bosses and team members—don't forget:

- **People who used to be junior to you:** These are people whom you mentored, either formally or informally; who reported to you; or whom you just knew. These young guys are now in many cases running the show, or very close to it.

  You can call these contacts cold. If you had solid relationships with them, even ten years ago, they will recall you instantly. If there is any doubt, you can preface your call with a short e-mail to jog their memory. If they enjoyed working for you or if you had a positive influence on them as a mentor, they will be very receptive to helping you get back in, almost as if they owe you one.

- **Corporate alumni groups:** In an effort to maintain relationships with former employees, for business development purposes as well as for potential rehires, many companies have launched corporate alumni Web sites that also enable former employees to keep in touch with one another. Modeled after the university databases noted above, these sites offer a painless way for relaunchers to reconnect. If you haven't visited your former employers' sites recently, make sure you do so. You may be pleasantly surprised by a link designed just for you. Finally, make an effort to attend corporate alumni social functions whenever possible.

People from Your Present

Although you might think all your prized professional connections are lodged in your past, you'd be surprised by what the guy next door—and others currently in your life—might be able to do for you. Just as you went through various contact pools from your past, make a list of your friends, neighbors, church or synagogue acquaintances, and children's friends' parents who work in fields of interest. Call and ask them if you can spend some time on the phone or in person brainstorming possible back-to-work ideas. "I'm thinking about going back to work and would like to talk with you about your industry. Could you spare a few minutes?" is a low-key way to open such a conversation. We'd be surprised if they turned you down.

People You Meet as a Volunteer

Your volunteer connections can be among your most useful, especially if you've done volunteer work in your chosen field. Leslie, the lawyer with the Florida state attorney's office, made a smart strategic move. During her maternity leave, she volunteered to write legal briefs for the Appeals and Training Bureau. The bureau was desperate for this kind of help, and its director loved her brief writing. After a six-month leave, she decided she didn't want to return to the intense schedule of the state attorney's office, so she approached the Appeals Bureau. Knowing the caliber of her work from her volunteer stint, they offered her a three-day-a-week position immediately. The same tactic yielded results again after a lengthier subsequent leave. "I volunteered at the Florida Victim Assistance Office, because a friend of mine was running it. It was a little awkward to be a volunteer when I was more qualified than the paid staff, but it gave me exposure to people I had worked with at the state attorney's office. In fact, as part of my volunteer assignment, I had to make a big presentation to a group that included the state attorney. This was the clincher in my later getting a job with the state supreme court. Because when I applied for a paying job at the court soon afterward, they called the state attorney for a reference. Since he had just seen me make this volunteer presentation, my abilities were fresh in his mind, and I think he probably gave me a really good reference."

What if most of your volunteer work has been for the PTO? Remember to consider the *working spouses* of your fellow PTO volunteers for potential sources of jobs or job leads. The parents with whom you have volunteered know your strengths and will pitch you to their spouses. If those spouses are in jobs related to your previous work experience, ask your PTO co-worker to make an introduction. Virginia was PTO co-president with a woman whose husband was a business professor at a nearby university. Since Virginia, an MBA, was considering academic research as a possible first step in relaunching herself, she asked her PTO co-president to make an introduction. The professor was more than happy to grant Virginia an interview.

People in Current Classes

If you take courses as a first step in your relaunch, professors and university career centers aren't the only resources at your disposal. Your classmates can be a gold mine of information and assistance. This is a perfect example of using newfound contacts in a university program to get job leads.

People from Your Future

In addition to reconnecting with people from your past and putting a professional spin on your current personal network, *you can create your own networks going forward.* To supplement your own contact lists, visit Ziggs (www.ziggs.com), LinkedIn (www.linkedin.com), or other networking sites to connect with those who share your educational or professional background or interests.

Create Your Own College or Grad School Alumni Network

If your college or graduate school doesn't have a local alumni club, start one. Rhonda, a graduate of a small southern women's college, formed an association for women from her alma mater in the Chicago area. This has given her another group of acquaintances with whom to exchange information and seek advice.

Create Your Own Corporate Alumni Network

If your old place of business hasn't started an alumni network and you think it would be of value, start your own. That's what former employees of Enron and Arthur Andersen have done. The Andersen alumni site even charges a fee to recruiters who want to post jobs there. Janet Hanson, who built her career on Wall Street, has taken this idea several steps farther. After she left Goldman Sachs in 1993, she created 85 Broads (a humorous play on Goldman Sachs's headquarters address, 85 Broad Street in New York City) as an independent network for *both* current and former Goldman Sachs women professionals. Today, 85 Broads has grown into a global network community that connects and empowers nearly fifteen thousand members, including women MBAs and undergraduate students from the world's leading graduate business schools, universities, and college campuses. Using her own resources and the technology platform of her money-management company, Milestone Capital, Janet created a password-protected site and a rich Web-accessible database that has given "some of the most incredible women on the planet" an innovative platform for connecting with each other throughout every stage of their careers and lives. Although 85 Broads membership is limited to current and former Goldman Sachs women and students/alumnae from select colleges and universities, its "network best practices" (as cited by women's advocacy group Catalyst) and a new book Janet has written entitled *More Than 85 Broads* are inspiring other women and organizations to start their own networks and discover "the power of the connection."[8]

Create Your Own Relaunch Circle

Perhaps the most useful network you could develop is your own Relaunch Circle. Gather together a small group of currently at-home women who are thinking about relaunching to serve as a mutual support group. Meeting monthly, or at other intervals, you'll be able to critique one another's résumés, discuss the pros and cons of various relaunch options, conduct mock interviews, trade job and consulting leads, and generally boost one another's confidence. As you get to know one another, you'll also exchange advice on work–life balance issues. Vivian has been meeting with a group that she got to know at the Harvard Business School course, described in the introduction, bi-annually for more than three years now, and has found it amazingly helpful. To form a Relaunch Circle, visit our Web site, www.backonthe careertrack.com.

Find a Relaunch Buddy

If forming a group seems impractical or overwhelming, consider finding a Relaunch Buddy. One relauncher wrote us: "I want to build some camaraderie, as well as have someone who is smart and competent give me feedback on directions I'm taking, and on proposal letters for consulting assignments or cover letters. Ideally I'd love to meet or speak on the phone once a week and spend, for example, 45 minutes on her search, and then 45 minutes on mine. And throughout the week it would be great if this person was available to give feedback on stuff I send to them via e-mail." If you're having trouble finding a relaunch partner on your own, visit our Web site, www.backonthecareertrack. com, to look for a local or virtual relaunch partner.

Making Choices and Clinching the Opportunity

As you market yourself, by networking with people in your contact pools and those to whom they refer you, you'll start to uncover potential opportunities: a possible full-time job here, a potential consulting project there, a teaching offer somewhere else. You may be able to do some of these things at the same time in order to test-drive a couple of different options. But in most cases you'll have to choose. And this is the tricky part: deciding which way you want to go and clinching the opportunity. *Don't be afraid to turn down what seem like great leads at the beginning of your search because you're afraid no others will come your way.* You need to make sure you're getting a good match with your strengths and desires at this time in your life. On the other hand, if you keep looking for the perfect fit, you may never relaunch. Something will be wrong with almost any option. Bottom line: Choose a path you think you'll enjoy and can handle today, but that also leads to growth in the future. Below, we highlight the factors that will enable you to clinch the opportunity for an employee, consulting, or entrepreneurial relaunch.

The Employee Relaunch

An *employee relaunch* refers to returning to the work world at an established organization where most employees work on site full-time. In addition to corporations, this includes partnerships (such as law firms), nonprofits, and governmental organizations. Although most women assume they'll have to log long hours if they relaunch in a corporate setting, we've seen an increasing number of people manage to relaunch into good-content jobs on a part-time basis. The key success factors outlined here apply whether you're seeking to work full-time in a conventional setting or in some sort of flexible arrangement.

Get an Inside Sponsor

We hear this over and over again. The bigger and/or the more prestigious the company, the more you need an inside sponsor to champion your cause. That's because it's hard enough to get hired at these places if you're an ordinary qualified candidate. As a relauncher, without a senior person touting you, it can be extremely difficult. Look at the question from the company's point of view. Who would *you* rather hire—a proven insider, a freshly trained eager beaver, or an unknown relauncher? In a competitive situation, you need someone who has clout with your prospective manager to say, "Give her a chance." This makes you a less risky hire.

Joyce, who had her heart set on returning to the large telecom company she had left ten years before, was hitting a brick wall. "When I called the company about coming back, they said it was a bad time. They focused on the gap in my résumé. 'What makes you think you can just walk in here and get your old job back?' one potential colleague asked. Finally, I called Heidi. We had been second-level managers together, and we were promoted to third level at the same time. I knew she could probably help me because of her seniority. I hadn't called upon her directly for help before. But finally I called and made it very clear that I needed her help. She got me interviews with the people who were hiring. She vouched for me."

According to Heidi, with whom we also spoke, "I had to go to bat for Joyce. She was competing against candidates who were then in the company. She had to learn Excel. But she never let it get in her way. She has great interpersonal skills. She knew she'd have to put in extra time and energy to get up to speed. And she did. She was brought in one level lower than where she had been when she left, but within two years she was promoted back to her original level, and she's progressed from there."

A sponsor doesn't always have to be a company executive. An outsider with pull can have the same impact. Sharon, who had spent ten years in the technology lending group of a large San Francisco bank, had targeted a small technology investment bank for her relaunch. She had great skills and a reasonably current Rolodex, having been out of the industry for less than two years. The hitch: She didn't want to work the typical investment banking schedule. The first person she called at the firm, a guy she knew from her old job in commercial lending, said there was "no way" she could get a job there part-time. Then she contacted a friend who was a senior executive at another firm. When she told him how dismissive the first guy had been, he said he knew the head of the firm and would put in a call on her behalf. With that sponsorship, "no way" turned into "three days a week," which she subsequently bumped up to four.

Convince the Decision Makers That You're Committed

Prospective employers are often less concerned about the gap on your résumé per se than about *the potential lack of commitment that the gap implies.* Are you going to show up every day, or will you be calling in sick every time your kids are? Will you stay late on occasion, if necessary, or will you be out the door despite a looming deadline? These (often unspoken) questions lurk in the mind of a potential boss. Convincing your hiring manager that you're committed is often the biggest hurdle that you'll face. Even if you're angling for a flexible arrangement, you've got to make it clear that you can't wait to get back to work and that, while you don't want to hang around until midnight every night, the company can count on you in a pinch.

Negotiate the Tools You Need to Be Successful—the Three C's Revisited

As you get into discussions with a potential employer, there's a lot to be considered and negotiated. In many cases, your ability to negotiate will be limited by strict salary bands or human resource policies. But you won't know whether something is possible *unless you ask.*

When an employer has made you an offer, your stock is high and you have leverage. The employer doesn't want to have to go back to the drawing board with someone else. They've chosen you, and they want it to work out. So politely, confidently, emphasizing how what you're requesting will enable you to do a better job, ask for the compensation, content, and control you need—and try to get as much of it as you can in writing.

Compensation

- **Salary.** If the first offer falls below your expectations, counter. Many employers purposely start low, fully anticipating that candidates will ask for more.
- **Bonus.** If one isn't offered, request one. Ideally, it should be based, as much as possible, on your individual performance. If there's no room to negotiate on salary, a bonus can funnel you more money in the face of an inflexible base pay range.
- **Benefits.** If you don't need them, tell your employer that you'd prefer a higher salary and don't plan to sign up for benefits. Of course, you don't want this to be binding, in case you need benefits at some point in the future.
- **Performance and salary review.** If the company devises an unusual compensation package or career track for you, make sure you ask to revisit the plan every six months. Ideally, you want to mainstream yourself into a more typical career path and compensation plan over time. You don't want to remain a relauncher forever.

Content

- **Job title.** Although many people claim job titles are meaningless, they can be crucial to relaunchers trying to reestablish their credibility. Frances, who was in the final stages of negotiations with a small investment bank, argued that she needed the title *managing director* to be taken seriously by potential clients. On the other hand, Carol didn't care what her title

was as long as she was paid a lot. Decide what is important
to you.

- **Job responsibilities.** Don't think of your job description as
  ironclad. Most people's jobs evolve over time. Also, when your
  team, department, or company is in a crunch, be prepared to do
  things that aren't necessarily in your job description.

Control

- **Job hours and location.** Make sure you're clear on the company's expectations. But don't be afraid to ask about working from
  home one day a week, for instance, so you don't have to waste
  time commuting.
- **Vacations.** Negotiate your vacations up front. If you want more
  than is typical, ask, even if it means you'll end up with more
  than others with your title. Fellow employees will likely accept
  it because you'll be seen as a nontraditional hire. And your boss
  will handle it better if you deal with it up front. Tell your employer, "I can start right away, but I've had this vacation planned
  for more than a year now and it's really important to me and my
  family that I be there for it."

The Consulting Relaunch

A consulting relaunch is when you perform project-based work, usually for a larger corporate, nonprofit, or government entity. Short-term
or interim assignments might also be considered consulting. Consultants can work either from home, from an office, from their clients'
offices, or from a combination of the above.

As we noted in chapter 3, consulting has become less of a way
station between jobs and more of a way of life. Yet many relaunchers often end up consulting accidentally. Some women start by looking for a corporate job, but either can't get themselves hired or can't

negotiate the flexibility they feel they need. So they end up taking a consulting project as a sort of consolation prize if it's offered. Others pursue consulting work as a way of easing themselves back in. Still other relaunchers use a consulting assignment as a sort of proving ground to show the client a sample of their work and test their compatibility with the employer. If both parties are happy, then a permanent employment opportunity can be negotiated. In any case, women don't always realize they're consultants until after the fact. But once you get that first assignment, it becomes a more viable and sustainable relaunch option.

Let's look at the steps that will enable you to attract, keep, and profit from clients.

Find a Platform

A platform in this context refers to an established entity, such as a university, volunteer organization, or company, that you can associate yourself with to increase your credibility and exposure to potential clients. In some ways, it's as simple as having an organization to put on a business card, other than Your Name Associates. *You need not be paid by this entity for the platform to be effective.* Rhonda's volunteer position as head of the marketing group of the Chicago Software Association gave her credibility in launching her high-tech marketing consultancy. Maxine's (low-paying) teaching job on the real estate faculty of a major business school helped her secure more-lucrative consulting assignments.

Use Prior Job Contacts, Alliances, Matchmakers, and Employment Ads

With or without a platform, getting that first assignment is probably the toughest aspect of consulting. As when you pursue a corporate job, however, you can use your networks to drum up opportunities.

When former consumer products brand manager Charlene first

sought to relaunch after three years at home full-time, she initially tried to craft a part-time arrangement similar to what she had developed at one of her prior employers. But "with everything I explored, either they didn't want to pay enough, they weren't flexible enough timewise, or they thought I was overqualified. But I found that a lot of people were interested in having me do freelance work. My first client was an ad agency in Philadelphia. They needed a moderator for focus groups. Someone referred me because they couldn't do the job. It was a little scary getting up in front of all those people after having been out for three years. But somehow, the projects are coming in, and I haven't even done that much business development."

If you're shy about selling yourself, try using a matchmaking service such as M Squared (www.msquared.com) or Aquent (www.aquent. com), or bidding on an assignment on one of the freelance Web sites, such as Guru.com. (See the resources section for additional matchmakers and sites.) Even if you don't make much money, you'll be building your portfolio—and your confidence.

As we mentioned at the beginning of this chapter, you can even use want ads to find consulting assignments. If you see a job advertised that requires your expertise, try to get the name of the hiring manager and write to that person directly, offering to work on a consulting basis and enclosing your résumé. Then follow up by phone.

Put It in Writing

Once you have a basic understanding of what a potential client needs, offer to send the client a proposal. This document needn't be more than a page or two that covers the parameters and cost of the assignment. For example, here's a proposal that a consultant might present to a developer of in-store display screen advertising to survey dry cleaners about their willingness to have a digital advertising display monitor mounted in their stores:

Dry Cleaner Survey Proposal
Prepared for XYZ Corporation
Date
Submitted by Jane Real Doe

Purpose: To determine dry cleaner willingness to accept digital display screen advertising in their stores and the terms under which this would be acceptable.

Rationale: XYZ Company believes that dry cleaners may present an excellent location for placement of digital display screen advertising, since they receive heavy foot traffic and consumer wait time is often at least two minutes. Also, users of dry cleaning services represent an excellent target market for XYZ's advertisers, who tend to be local consumer-oriented merchants.

Process: The consultant will develop a questionnaire and target list of survey respondents with XYZ executives. After XYZ has approved the questionnaire and target list, the consultant will conduct in-depth telephone interviews with the owners of 20 dry cleaners from the list.

Required client involvement:
- Assistance in developing the questionnaire.
- Assistance in developing a target list of survey respondents.

Deliverables: In a written report for XYZ management, the consultant will summarize both the numerical results of the survey and key additional findings from survey comments. The consultant will also provide XYZ with copies of the completed survey questionnaire for each dry cleaner surveyed.

Timetable:

- ☐ Development of questionnaire and target list of survey respondents: approximately 4 weeks.
- ☐ Survey time and preparation of report: 4–8 weeks, depending upon ability to reach dry cleaner owners.

Cost and payment terms: See the discussion below on pricing.

I agree to the above proposal:

_____

[Person's name], XYZ Company

_____

The Consultant Relaunch: Price Yourself Right

Don't Forget to Factor in Taxes

Consulting services can be priced a number of different ways. Regardless of the method you choose, however, remember that you're going to have to pay taxes on this money. This includes a self-employment tax of 15.3 percent on the first $94,200 (as of 2006) of income, but you get to deduct 50 percent of it when you are figuring your federal and state income tax. Because this can get complicated and we do not purport to give out tax advice, be sure to consult your tax adviser.

Hourly or Per Diem Pricing

One of the most common pricing methods is to bill, like a lawyer, based on the number of hours you worked. The advantage to this is that you don't have to worry about underestimating how long a project is going to take. Also, if the scope of the project expands as you're in process, you simply keep track of, and bill for, the additional time. Hourly or per diem pricing can also be ideal for interim operating assignments, such as a temporary CFO.

In terms of actual rates, for MBAs, we've heard hourly rates anywhere between $75 and $300. Diane, the Queen of Contract Work, consults for a variety of clients. For the last four years, she's been consulting with about ten students a year who are applying to college or business school and want to improve their odds of admission. "These clients find out about me through word of mouth, and I don't really want higher volume. I'm in touch with them mostly by phone and e-mail so the work can generally be done on my schedule." She's also undertaken marketing consulting projects. "Most of the projects have come from people I worked with at my old employer who then went on to other companies." She charges $150 per hour. "I like this better than charging a flat fee, which can be a crapshoot because it's hard to estimate the amount of time something may take."

Isabelle, a product marketer who also relaunched by doing marketing consulting projects, said a good rule of thumb for estimating your hourly rate is to take your old annual salary and subtract three zeros. For example, if you made $80,000 per year, your consulting rate would be $80 per hour. Isabelle added that if clients thought the price was too high, she would give them references who told them she would take half the time anyone else would to do the project.

For per diems, consultants usually multiply their hourly rate by 8, then round up or down. Rounding down creates a perception of value, but you can round up on the basis that you're going to work more than eight hours a day.

The disadvantage to hourly or per diem consulting is that clients will often try to haggle with you over your hourly rate. Also, many will want you to include an estimate of your hours in your proposal and might only be willing to pay you 10 to 15 percent over that estimate, even if you end up putting in more time than you envisioned. Finally, you may end up leaving significant money on the table by using this method.

Project Pricing

Pricing by the project is another common way to get paid for consulting services. In this method, you estimate how much time you think the project will take you and multiply that by what you consider a reasonable hourly rate. Then gross up the total by at least 15 to 20 percent to give yourself a cushion. The advantage to pricing this way is that you avoid niggling discussions of hourly rates. The disadvantage is that if you underestimate your time, you could end up being underpaid. Isabelle, the marketing consultant we described above, has moved from an hourly to a project-based pricing model because she believes she makes more money that way.

Commission-Based Pricing

Commission-based pricing might also be appropriate in certain situations. For example, before she joined Vivian's executive search business, Heather had thought about trying to raise money for her children's school through telephone solicitation of parents. She figured she could have charged 15 to 20 percent of whatever she raised as her consulting fee.

Value Pricing

A fourth approach is what we call value pricing. It's similar to project pricing in that you price by the project rather than by the hour. The difference is the way you arrive at the price. In value pricing, you focus on what the project is worth to the client, not the time it takes you to accomplish it. To figure out what the project is worth, you research what the client would have to pay someone else—a full-time employee or established consultant—to get the job done, and then discount a bit to create a sense of value. This is a very good way for relaunchers, and most women, to overcome their common tendency to underprice themselves. In the case of the dry cleaner survey described above, for example, the client would probably have to pay an established survey company at least $10,000 for the project. You might propose to do it for s$7,500 or 8,500. If you had priced it on an hourly basis, however, with a rate of $150 and an estimate of thirty hours, you would have made only $4,500. Even a project-based price probably would have netted you only $5,500.

Get Some Dough Up Front

No matter which pricing method you use, always try to get some portion of the payment (or estimated payment) up front, ideally at least one-third. That way you avoid being completely stiffed. After the first payment, bill on a monthly or other periodic basis, so you're not left with a huge balance at the end. And finally, make sure the client agrees to reimburse you for significant expenses, such as travel, document reproduction, outside graphics work, and so forth. Specify all these payment terms in your proposal letter.

Final Thoughts on the Consultant Relaunch

Leverage Each Assignment into Another Assignment

Big-time consultants always joke that the purpose of any consulting assignment is . . . to get another consulting assignment. Imitate their strategies. Propose ways to build on your first assignment, either helping your clients execute your recommendations or doing a similar project in another target market or geographic area for the same clients. If add-ons aren't possible, or to diversify your client base, talk to your clients about whether they might be able to refer you to their vendors or business customers. Finally, propose a similar assignment to a similar entity, ideally not a direct competitor. (You don't want to alienate your early clients by appearing disloyal.) Not only do you get more business this way, but after a couple of projects in a certain field, you can brand yourself an expert in that area.

Invest in Yourself and Your Consulting Practice—but Not Necessarily Up Front

A lot of the how-to books on consulting suggest that you spend a great deal of time up front crafting your mission, your niche, and/or your brand, and creating materials—business cards, brochures, Web site—to support it. We agree that this is valuable for relaunchers as well, but not necessarily at the beginning. Since you'll probably get your first couple of assignments through connections, you don't necessarily need well-developed marketing materials to secure them. And since you've been out of the market, you don't necessarily have enough information to craft an effective brand or message, no matter how much research you do. You'll probably have a better sense of your mission after you've completed a couple of assignments. But once you have a clearer sense of the kind of work you want to do, then you should professionalize yourself—take courses, join associations, attend conferences, and create a logo, Web site, and other materials that reflect your mission.

The Entrepreneurial Relaunch

Consulting is actually just one form of entrepreneurship. In this book, we classify a relaunch as entrepreneurial if it involves the sale of a product or service to a larger public than is typical for a consultant. Still, there's a lot of overlap between consulting and small business, and some of the same critical success factors apply to both.

But how do you actually start a business? Especially if you're trying to mother at the same time? And how do you make sure the business generates dollars, rather than continually consuming them?

Interestingly, as with the consultants, we found many relaunchers are accidental entrepreneurs. They either stumble upon an opportunity or turn to entrepreneurship when spurned or put off by conventional employers. In other cases, however, women deliberately choose to start a business, often a home-based business, so that they can be available to their children when their kids need them.

Home-Based Businesses

For relaunchers, the appeal of a home-based business is obvious: It offers you the chance to make money, engage your brain cells, and still be there for your kids. And today, because of the Internet, the options for a home-based business are virtually limitless. Priscilla Y. Huff's *101 Best Home-Based Businesses for Women* lists everything from the traditional craft-type business such as jewelry and airbrush art to virtual assistant and e-zine publisher.[9] But before you rush to open a pet grooming service or costume shop, make sure you think through the following:

- **Space.** Ideally, you should have a space in your home dedicated solely to your business. That way, you don't have to move your stuff every time you use the dining room table. If you have small children, make sure you can put important papers and supplies under lock and key. The nature of the space will depend on the type of business you're launching. If you're going to be assembling products or storing inventory, raw basement space (without leaks!) will do just fine. But if you're going to entertain clients, you'll need something more presentable. If your conferencing needs are sporadic, you may want to consider renting conference space.

  Besides saving money and allowing you frequent family contact, having a home-based business gives you additional tax deductions. If your work space constitutes 10 percent of your home, for example, then you can deduct 10 percent of your rent or mortgage, utilities, and property taxes (if any) as business expenses. (Consult your tax adviser to avoid audit risk.)

- **Permits.** Depending upon the nature of your business, you may require local permits to operate. You must also be certain you won't be running afoul of local zoning laws, especially if you're going to have customers coming to your home. Check with relevant local government departments to make sure you're in compliance with any applicable laws.

- **Insurance.** Finally, you may need insurance. If you're buying raw materials and/or finished goods and storing them in your home, you'll want to insure them against theft or damage. They won't necessarily be covered by your existing homeowner's policy. If you work in other people's homes, you'll want coverage in case you break something of theirs. And if customers or employees come to your home, you'll want liability coverage in case they trip over the front stoop. Businesses involving cars or trucks may have special insurance requirements. A reputable insurance agent can help you assess your needs.

Although you may start in your home, don't be surprised if you eventually outgrow your domestic digs. A number of the women we interviewed ended up moving from hearth to office park as their businesses grew and their kids grew more independent.

Make Sure You're Self-Disciplined, Organized, and Optimistic

The entrepreneurs we interviewed noted that not everyone is cut out to be an entrepreneur, and those who took regular jobs often admitted that they didn't think they had it in them to go into business for themselves. We posit that the key traits for entrepreneurship include self-discipline, organization, and optimism.

Launch a Business in a Field You Know or Are Passionate About

Almost every entrepreneurial relauncher we encountered or read about built her business based on a developed expertise or interest. Although you'll occasionally read about entrepreneurs spotting an opportunity in some segment of the market with which they're not very familiar and developing a business to take advantage of it, this kind of start-up requires more time and money than most relaunchers have available. Yes, it would be great to come up with the next iPod, but it's hard to do so with three kids in tow. Better to take advantage of your strengths and build from there.

Vicky, a kindergarten teacher who had negotiated a job share after her first child was born, became an accidental entrepreneur after a new principal turned down her job-share request when she tried to return after her second child's birth. Discouraged, she was lamenting the situation on a night out with friends when she came up with the idea of running an after-school enrichment program. The other mothers loved the idea and urged her to make a go of it. Thus her business was born. Initially, she had seven kids in the program, which she ran three days a week in her basement. Four years later, she has forty kids who attend two, three, or five days a week, and she's about to open a second location.

While mulling her work options, Tracy met the father of a fellow alum who had been in the footwear industry. Tracy has large feet and was complaining about the lack of fashionable women's shoes available in large sizes. The footwear veteran said to her, "You've got an MBA. Why don't you do something to revolutionize the footwear industry?" Now she runs a designer shoe business in a posh urban location and a Web site for big and wide feet. "I never thought of myself as an entrepreneur. Now I can't think of myself any other way."

Start Small

As we discussed in chapter 3, don't be embarrassed about starting small. If you seek to remain an involved parent, you don't necessarily want to get yourself in over your head by raising capital and hiring lots of employees right off the bat. You can always expand more rapidly as you get more comfortable with the business and your new routines at home. Also, remember that every new business had a humble start, and that *good execution determines business success, not just a good idea.* Who knows? Your home-based decorating business could turn into a major franchise. But you won't find out unless you give it a shot.

Georgia, who trained as a graphic designer and illustrator, started extremely small. When her children were young, she did graphic design work for friends and family on a very part-time basis. She chose this field specifically so she could work from home and be available to her children. Initially, she didn't advertise, and she used her college's computers, so she essentially had zero costs.

"When my children started school, I invested in some equipment and began advertising to get customers. But it was still just pocket money. In 2000, I went through a divorce and realized I needed to make more income. I also needed the distraction. So I bumped up the advertising and joined my city's chamber of commerce and Business Network International. But probably my biggest source of business is word of mouth and referrals. With business services, your reputation is critical. People are naturally leery about plunking down a deposit for graphics work on someone they don't really know anything about.

"To make sure I had some steady revenue, I approached a local tabloid and offered to do all their ad layout work. We never signed any kind of contract, but basically I run their ad department from my home, and this gives me some regular income.

"In addition to growing my graphics business, I've also started two other related ventures. One is a children's stationery business. This began as a family project with my own children. Together we created some kids' stationery, because they like to collect and trade it. Now I'm selling it at PTO fairs and from a dedicated Web site.

"Every now and then I contemplate taking a real job for the security of a steady income, but after I run the numbers I realize I make more with this business than I'd make as a graphic designer working for someone else. Plus, I can work at night if my kids are home sick or otherwise need me. I've got that all-important flexibility."

Peggy had been a VP at a big ad agency for thirteen years before she quit work. She would have enjoyed going back to advertising, but since she was in a new city, she felt that she didn't have the leverage to negotiate something part-time as she might have had with her old employer. A friend who was running a temple Judaica shop, as a volunteer, was joining a Jewish book distributorship and asked Peggy if she'd like to join as well. (They needed an additional person part-time.) Intrigued by the idea, Peggy signed on. But soon after she joined, the distributorship failed. Peggy and her friend had ideas about how to run the business more efficiently and profitably, however, so they started their own Jewish book distributorship. Although initially they worked without pay, within three years the company became profitable and they were able to draw a salary. Peggy really likes being her own boss. "I'm too old to answer to a corporate person. Also, I like that I don't have to get dressed up every day."

Find a Partner (or Some Other Support)

Sure, you can go it alone. Especially if you're self-disciplined, organized, and optimistic. But most of the women with whom we spoke who had a partner swore by the arrangement. For one thing, working with a partner makes the venture more fun. Entrepreneurship can be very lonely. With a partner, you've got built-in camaraderie. But there are also powerful business reasons for joining forces with a partner, particularly for relaunchers. You can split the work, enabling both of you to spend more time with your kids, and you can serve as backup for each other, allowing you to take vacations with peace of mind. Most importantly, two heads are better than one. With a partner, you'll have twice the network and, potentially, twice the resources. And you can bounce ideas off each other about how to handle problems or take advantage of opportunities.

Selecting the right partner is obviously critical. Look for someone with whom you're compatible, but who's not necessarily your best friend. You need someone whose intelligence, character, and judgment you respect. Also, make sure you have the same level of commitment about the business. Do you intend to spend every waking moment on this venture or are you going to be more low-key? You and your partner should be on the same wavelength in this regard. Ideally, your partner should have skills that complement, rather than duplicate, your own. For example, if you're good at the big-picture stuff, make sure your partner is a stickler for detail. Or if your background is in finance, you might want to pair up with someone from the marketing world.

Whoever you choose, it's a good idea to draw up a simple written agreement outlining the terms of the partnership, particularly how you'll divide investment expenses and profits, how you can exit the partnership if you wish, or how you or your partner can buy each other out. Although a partnership agreement might remind you of a pre-nup—a document you don't want to think about when you're about to embark on your entrepreneurial honeymoon—better to address these issues now than later, when problems have already arisen.

Eileen, a former designer, partnered with a close friend to create a toddler-oriented toy company. But after a few months on the project together, Eileen discovered that their styles and attitudes clashed and felt that the partnership wasn't working. "Tasha was obsessed with the business. She would call me constantly about new ideas and things we had to do. It got to the point where I felt like she was giving me orders. I didn't want to work that way. We didn't have any kind of agreement so I wasn't sure how to handle the situation. I told her I didn't want to work on this with her anymore, but I'm not happy about the fact that she could take our ideas, most of which were *my* ideas, and still develop them with someone else. I don't think she'll do that. But I suppose she could."

If you don't have a partner, at least cultivate a person or two from whom you can seek advice. Your husband may be able to fill this role, although that can create issues of control. Elizabeth, a former CPA who turned her hobby of collecting photographs into a business, relies on her husband for both business and personal support. But that's not always great for the relationship. "Jake wanted me to do the art business his way," Elizabeth confided. "But I realized I had to do it my way, succeed or fail based on my moves. He helps me with ideas about how to make it all work, how to have a holistic life, but I don't listen to everything he says. The most important thing is that he bolsters me by saying, 'It's good for the kids to see you going to work.'"

A trusted employee can even fill the role of sounding board. Or recruit a friend or friends whose business acumen you respect to serve as your board of advisers. As we discussed earlier in this chapter, offer to do something for them in return.

Finally, you might join a local entrepreneurs' group for commiseration and counsel. It might even be a source of additional customers.

Focus Your Resources

There are lots of business maxims with this advice at their core: *You can't be all things to all people. Differentiate yourself. Choose a business where you'll have a competitive advantage. Pick a niche market* . . . and so on, and so forth. They apply all the more to relaunchers who have limited time and, usually, limited resources. So no matter what your business, focus, focus, focus.

Instead of becoming just another shoe retailer, Tracy bored in on the underserved "big-foot" market. This allows her to charge premium prices and sidestep (no pun intended) most footwear competition.

Peggy and her partner didn't open a book distribution business, but a *Jewish* book distribution business. This allows them to focus their time and money on marketing to a reasonably sized but relatively narrow and well-defined set of customers.

Although Georgia's graphics business produces everything from brochures to Web sites, she has a tight geographic focus for her marketing efforts. As a result, she chooses local media to advertise her business. She also doesn't try to create in every conceivable style. If a client wants a caricature on a business card, for example, she'll subcontract the artwork to a cartoonist. "I've lost some business, but that's okay. I can't be all things to all people."

Give Out Free or Discounted Samples

Take a cue from the big consumer products companies and dispense free or discounted samples to high-profile or high-potential customers. You can do this with a service as well as with a product. That's in essence what Vivian did when she prepared and gave a mini seminar for free to a company that offers writing seminars for executives. Lawyers do this all the time when they meet with prospective clients; they give these prospects a little free advice, hoping they'll later engage their services. Offering your product or service at a discount for school or community fund-raisers can also help put your business on the map. Just make sure you're strategic about how you offer these freebies and discounts.

———

And now, whether you relaunch by taking a job with an employer or working for yourself, let's look at how to rejigger arrangements at home to ensure that your relaunch is a success.

CHAPTER 6

Channel Family Support

"Mom," my children would tell me when I came home at night, "you're so much less stressed now that you're working." In the evening, I was energetic and thrilled to spend time with them, talking, playing, reading, or helping with homework. They liked the new me. I began to wonder if it wasn't better for them to have an enthusiastic mom in a great mood on evenings and weekends, instead of a stressed-out, not-so-happy mom full-time. My husband had similar thoughts.

—Carol

Husbands

Without getting into a marital counseling role, we must talk frankly about husbands and their response to their wives relaunching. Key to this discussion is the impact the second income has on the family finances. If your income truly lightens the financial burden on your husband and takes some pressure off him as the sole provider, he may be thrilled that you're thinking about relaunching your career. However, if your income will be a drop in the bucket compared with your husband's, he may be far less supportive. Also, if your husband can see that your return to work is critical to your mental well-being, he may be more supportive than otherwise. Finally, if your mother-in-law had a career, your husband may actually expect you to return to work.

Loving the Status Quo: What If Your Husband *Doesn't* Want You to Go Back to Work?

Although some husbands can't wait for their wives to return to work, others have the opposite reaction. A wife's relaunch threatens the turn-key operation of the household as he has come to know it, and this poses a problem for him. Larry, a potential relauncher's husband, commented, "I like my life the way it is with my wife running everything at home. I'm concerned when I hear her talking about wanting to go back to work. I don't want to take on home-related tasks." Many of the things that happen in the house that he takes for granted will no longer happen, or will happen more sporadically. The house will be messier, there won't be a dinner prepared regularly in the evening, the house will run out of staples—milk, toilet paper, and so on. And some husbands have become accustomed to high levels of pampering. According to Virginia, "I used to replace my husband's shaving cream before he even realized it was getting empty. Now it just runs out and he has to replace it himself when he gets around to it."

Some husbands display mixed emotions. "I think my husband felt relieved the financial burden was being shared," Connie told us, "but also a feeling of abandonment, that all the things he was used to having me do for him and the kids were suddenly not happening anymore."

Taking Your Husband from Relaunch-Resistant to Relaunch-Friendly

- **Share your feelings.** You must have an honest talk with him about the long-term effects of your staying home. Let him know that you honestly feel your mental and emotional well-being may be threatened by the status quo. Tell him you are not sure you can continue to be the sole household manager. There are over-whelming numbers of mundane tasks involved for someone who used to deal with interesting and complex issues. Also, it's hard to imagine responding to the endless demands from the kids and from him indefinitely—always being in "give" mode.

- **A vacation is not the solution.** If he offers a weekend away for you alone or for both of you, let him know that having alone time or time just with him is wonderful, but it's not fulfilling some of the broader dimensions of who you feel you are intellectually and creatively. If he suggests pursuing a hobby or a particular interest, you must explain that you've done this already and it just isn't cutting it anymore, either because you're not sufficiently engaged by it or because you're still uncomfortable with the dependency issue, having held your own financially in the past.

- **There's a storm beneath the calm.** Tell him that everything may seem fine on the surface, but things are not really fine deep down inside you. Let him know that you're afraid of who you will become if those emotions of resentment and desperation are left to fester and make their way to the surface.

- **Remind your husband why he married you.** When you first met, your husband was probably attracted to your brains and energy, maybe even specifically to your ambition. Remind him that if you had only been interested in taking care of his needs, he probably wouldn't have married you. Tell him that you deeply miss the work part of your life. Explain that you were willing to put your career on hold when the children were young and needed hands-on care, but now that they're more independent you want a chance to develop your own potential.

- **Let's work together.** Let him know that you both can work together to figure out which household tasks neither of you wants to do. With your additional income, you may be able to devote a portion of it to hiring a person or a service to handle some of the mundane tasks (grocery shopping, cleaners, post office—you know what they are), or even someone to cook dinner a few times a week or a tutor to help your children with homework.

- **More daddy time can be beneficial for the kids.** You know your husband and whether mentioning this would be helpful or not. For details, see "The Go-To Guy (or Gal)" later in this chapter.

- **Timing is everything.** Initiate these conversations at the best possible time and place. And plan to revisit the issue several times. Your husband's attitude toward relaunching may improve if you give him a chance to get used to the idea. Don't despair if your husband reacts in horror the first time you bring up the topic. By the third go-round, he may be far more open-minded. The same goes for any particular chores you try to assign to him.

Working Around Your Spouse

Let's be realistic. If you flunked part 2 of the Relaunch Readiness Quiz and the above tips fail to help, then you may need to rethink your relaunch strategy. Lucy knew her domestic role would not change if she began working, so she took a part-time job. "At home the division of labor is the same as when I wasn't working. Now I'm working twenty hours a week as a speech therapist. But I'm okay with that. My husband doesn't cook meals, do dishes, or do laundry. My day is divided into pieces. After work, I have to grocery shop or do other errands and housework, but I also have a small window that's for me. My husband never devalued me based on my work status. He never pressured me to go back to work. What is really important to him is that I give him attention. If I don't, this is the only time he'll react. He wants to remain a priority in my life."

Children

Don't expect your children to be thrilled with the idea of your going back to work. Any change in their routine may throw them. They're not going to relish coming home to a babysitter in the afternoon rather than to you. The daughter of Linda, a teacher's assistant, complained that her mother had no time to take her shopping for clothes anymore. "Also, my son was unhappy at first. He said Mom is supposed to be first and foremost *his* mother! This changed after we were able to share school stories. This was positive!" Like your husband, your children are used to a certain level of service, and now you're cutting back on the amenities.

Terry, the software programmer, put it in a nutshell: "I think one of the hardest things about going back is the feeling that my kids would rather have me home all the time. They had me home for six years and then suddenly I'm not home as much. I wonder sometimes if it was fair to do that to them. Initially, my son would ask me what train I would be getting in the morning and he would wake up early just to see me and tell me I should go in later! That was hard. The good part was that my husband started going in a little later in the morning and had some time alone with the kids that he had not experienced before. That was very good for all."

As we noted in chapter 3, *presenting yourself consistently as a working parent is the key to making the transition easier.* For example, if a mom switched to a four-day workweek when her first child was born and kept that schedule through the births of subsequent children, then that four-day-a-week work schedule is all her kids have ever known. It's a given. The *consistency* of it is what makes it work. Change it, and an adjustment is required. This is also true for moms who have continued to work full-time while their families have grown. For relaunching moms, a transition is required, either sudden or gradual. This is why we say a gradual relaunch will make you appear more consistent to your kids. Even leaving your children for volunteer work or social events can help accustom them to your absence.

First and foremost, you need to explain to your children, early and often, that *your desire for a job is not a rejection of your current life with them, but rather a chance for you to develop a part of yourself that's been dormant for a while.* If that seems too hard to grasp for your younger children, tell them that you used to work and now that they are older you want to work again because you enjoy it. Don't bribe the kids by saying you'll be able to buy them more goodies with your income, or take better vacations. You want them to understand that work can have value in and of itself. Once you've determined your schedule, then the details of the relaunch need to be discussed frequently and repeatedly, so that each family member can understand how it will affect him or her.

Donna's decision to go back to school and then to take a position as an ESL teacher caused drastic changes in the routines of her son and daughter. She worked only four hours a day, Monday through Friday, but she had to leave for work right after her son's wake-up time. (Her fourteen-year-old daughter left for the school bus before her son woke up.) Her eleven-year-old son had to make his breakfast, set the house alarm, lock the house, and get himself to the bus all on his own. He was only in fifth grade. Her friends couldn't believe she would let him do this, but Donna felt he was mature enough to handle it.

Sharon believes her relaunch was a reality check for her children. "I think it's good for kids to see life isn't perfect. They should experience getting their needs met *most* of the time, but not all the time."

Frequent communication with your children is key to making the transition smoother. Laura, a mother of three boys who relaunched by entering a full-time, no-summers-off rabbinical school program, took stock with her family after her first year in the program: "My youngest [age five] kept reminiscing about the time we used to have after school together: 'Remember you used to pick me up from nursery school and we would play together in the afternoon?' I reminded him he was in school all day now and he wasn't home in the early afternoons to play anymore, either. But I also realized that I always wanted to talk to him when we both got home and find out how his day went and he just wanted to go outside and bat a ball around. *So I decided to spend time with him on his terms instead of mine when we were both home from school.* I don't engage him in conversation right away; instead we do whatever he wants to do. Of course that means

I'm ignoring my other children for that time, but they are doing their own thing anyway.

"My thirteen-year-old son said he didn't like that he had to get things done so I could start my homework. He just didn't like me talking about my studying. So I decided to stop mentioning that. He also said he wished he had a traditional mom who was home and baked cookies, et cetera. I told him that was not going to happen. We've all made some concessions in order for me to take this big step in my life."

Making the Relaunch Transition Easier for Your Kids

- **Ideally, try to make any changes in their routines or responsibilities well before you begin working.** Carol stopped cooking dinner one night a week months before she went back, to get the family used to fending for themselves. "It basically became fruit and yogurt night." If you're hiring a sitter, bring her on board before your start date, so that you can train her adequately and allow the children a transition period to get used to her. If you'll be enrolling your children in an afternoon program, sign them up a semester early so that they can adjust to their new routine and don't necessarily equate the change with your return to work.

- **Get your children involved in the running of the house as much as possible.** If you've assigned chores, enforce the rules. You're not going to have the time or the energy to load the dishwasher because "Billy didn't feel like it tonight." Don't feel guilty about this. It's character building. And kids like to feel needed.

- **Hire the best-quality child care you can afford.** This will differ based on your children's ages and activities. According to Terry, "Finding quality child care is absolutely the toughest piece in all of this, partly because the children are older. They don't want a housekeeper type; they want someone young who will go out and kick a soccer ball or play Monopoly. I've been back to work for just sixteen months and I'm already on my third person. This one is the best, but she has to leave in August. Frankly, if I end up leaving my job, one reason will be so I won't have to begin the child care search again."

- **Periodically, take stock with your kids.** Like Laura, listen to them carefully, make the changes they request that are realistic for you and your family, and stand firm on those that won't work in your post-relaunch life.

- **Make sure you spend some time with your kids on their terms, not on yours.** This takes some discipline, a high level of sensitivity and patience. Observe how you interact with each of your children. Hold back and listen to them first before directing the conversation or activity. You may get some clues as to how they want to spend their time with you or what they want to discuss with you, especially your teenagers. One mother confided: "With my fifteen-year-old son, I literally have to bite my tongue sometimes to keep from chiming in when he has moments of silence in his conversations with me. If I sit there long enough and say nothing, he eventually comes out with his next thought or concern. I'm often floored by how much he is willing to confide in me, if only I'm patient enough to keep my mouth shut and stifle my tendency to drive the conversation and focus on what has to get done."

The Investment Period

If you seek to relaunch in a full-time capacity, you're going to have to build in a contingency plan for spending extra time at work during your first year, while you're ramping up and learning the ropes. We call this the Investment Period. It doesn't have to be a whole year, but rather *a designated period you estimate you need to set aside to completely focus on getting up to speed on the job.* Killing yourself to succeed at work is not going to be sustainable for an indefinite period, but it should be realistic to make this investment at the beginning of your relaunch.

In order to pull this off, you need the complete support and cooperation of your husband (or other close friend or relative) and children. Your return to work will require continuing the family conversations you began when you were just contemplating returning. The more and the earlier the family knows, the better. Uncertainty, and the idle speculation it causes, disturbs kids more than contemplating the reality that Mom is going to be away at work some or all weekdays. If you anticipate an intense ramp-up period, your family will feel more comfortable knowing that it has a beginning and an end.

The Go-To Guy (or Gal)

Whether your husband can be the point person to pick up the slack in your absence during your Investment Period depends on many factors related to his job, his personality, and how he views his role. If he is unavailable, you may need to enlist the services of a grandparent, sibling, or close friend to step in while you are investing in your future success on the job. This person should be available even if you end up hiring a babysitter or utilizing an after-school program for the afternoon-into-early-evening hours. Your kids will need a go-to person if you are not available, for real or perceived crises, advice, homework help, or just someone close to hang out with for a while.

When Tammy relaunched in the mid-1980s, she and her husband worked out a sharing schedule that was quite progressive for the time. "My husband could put in his eight-hour day at any time working for the IRS. So he worked 7 AM to 3:30 PM and then picked the kids up from school. I worked nine to five and did the morning drop-off. We also split the household chores. Then we moved and my husband took a more conventional corporate job. He was working nine to seven. I began with a part-time job for a small company that couldn't afford full-time help initially. Less than a year later, they asked me to switch to full-time. When this happened, I needed coverage from four forty-five to six every day, which was the gap between when the kids got home and when I got home. I found two thirteen-and-a-half-year-old girls in my neighborhood who were best friends to provide this coverage. They guaranteed that one of them would be available to cover this time slot every day. They were there, without fail, every afternoon for two years. I could never have done this without them." (We like the idea of two kids handling one babysitting job and working it out between them to provide 100 percent coverage.)

Tolerate Disorganization (and Enjoy Your Children's Growing Independence and Pride in You)

"Since I went back the household stuff is definitely more out of control," Linda admitted. "Now we all rush out of the house at the same time, and there is no one to clean up the dishes and food left on the table. Beds are unmade. There's no one to go around and straighten up and clean. This is especially hard when my mother-in-law is visiting. She tends to judge me a little by how I keep or do not keep up the house."

Expect that, at least at the beginning, children's lives might become a little more haphazard as lunch preparation, mitten finding, and backpack organization are less carefully supervised. Ultimately, this may engender more independent kids (and husbands, for that matter), but the transition will be bumpy as everyone adjusts to their new roles. Minimizing the bumpiness will depend on communication, preparation, and a positive attitude among all involved, led by . . . who else? Mom. Humor and the ability to laugh at situations gone awry will also help a lot.

The Household

"I do a lot of Crock-Pot cooking." Donna explained: "One night a week, we have sandwiches for dinner. One night a week, we have what we call 'Sonoma night': a cold meal with cheese, fruit, bread, boiled eggs, cold veggies, leftovers. We barbecue a lot. Sometimes the kids make dinner on their own with canned soup, frozen dinners, and/or fresh fruit."

Although Donna was able to get dinner on the table, she confessed, "I find it hard to relax. I have to consciously give myself permission to not do anything sometimes because there is always something that needs to be done at home. I have less time to do the same number of household tasks."

In her landmark book *The Second Shift*, Arlie Hochschild studied the division of home responsibilities among dual working couples. She found that there is a fundamental difference in the amount and type of home responsibilities husbands and wives tend to take on. "Women do more childcare than men, and men repair more household appliances. A child needs to be tended daily while the repair of household appliances can often wait 'until I have time.' Men thus have more *control* [our emphasis] over *when* they make their contributions than women do."[1]

Relaunching poses unique challenges in handling the division of home responsibilities. *The relaunch forces a fundamental shift in how these responsibilities are shared between husband and wife*—and sometimes kids. Suddenly, your husband will need to carry some of the load that has a low "control factor," as Hochschild referred to above. Alternatively, if you are in a position to devote a portion of your new income to some paid household help, it is possible to transfer some of this housework to a third nonfamily person.

Steps to a Streamlined Household

- **In the words of one relauncher, "You've got to let go of domestic perfection."** No matter how hard you try, your household is likely to be a little messier and a little more disorganized once you go back to work. "The housework has gone downhill and I don't care," confided Michon. "The house is not as clean and we don't entertain as much as we used to. When we do entertain, I cook a very simple menu." Elaine explained, "I like that if I am working, things that are undone at home don't really bother me as much. Like those pictures that have been leaning against the wall for the last two years that need to be hung."

- **Contract out as many routine jobs as you can afford.** Hire as much help as you can in order to free up time you can devote to your children, your spouse, and yourself. Use grocery delivery and dry cleaning delivery services whenever possible. For transporting your children to extracurricular activities, join car pools (if you haven't already) or consider paying a responsible adult (another mother?) to take and retrieve your child. If you can afford to hire someone to do the heavy housecleaning, and/or the laundry and light housekeeping, this gives you the maximum free time to devote to your family and yourself.

- **Shop by catalog or online whenever possible.** Purchase clothing staples and school supplies by catalog or online. Even with mailing costs, the time saved is often worth it. Stock an inventory of age-appropriate birthday presents and wrapping paper at home. That way, when a child has a party to attend, he or she just picks a gift from the at-home store to wrap and give. For grocery delivery, have a set time of the week to place your online order. Even better, save a set list of weekly household staples you can use for your order if you don't have time to look through all the online grocery aisles. Then you can order whenever you happen to be thinking about it. You might try delegating this to one of your middle school or high school kids as a weekly chore, or to a babysitter if you have young children.

- **Put your routine under a microscope to cut out inefficiencies.** Many at-home women say, "I'm so busy now, how could I possibly think about working?" If they examined how they were spending their time, however, they probably could free up huge chunks with a little more planning and organization. For example, how many of us end up driving to the supermarket two and even three times a week? If you don't want to shop online, at least create a standard shopping list and take a thorough inventory so that you can reduce your food shopping runs to one weekly visit. Ditto with shopping for other basics, such as children's underwear, socks, and the like. In addition to reducing the frequency of shopping trips, think about shopping when working women do—at night or on weekends. Yes, the stores are more crowded, but you then have more time during the week for job hunting or work-related projects. Taking your kids along may slow you down, but it also provides good face time.

- **Remember that a simple or take-out dinner a couple of times a week never killed anyone.** Don't feel you have to prepare a banquet every night. Pilar believes she actually cooks more than a lot of her stay-at-home friends, who often eat at fast-food places while they're driving their kids to and from extracurricular activities. But she keeps the meals simple. "We have a lot of pasta for dinner now, or eggs, or even cereal and fruit when I can't get around to making anything." Kim, a gourmet, resorts to takeout when she can't get home early enough to cook a decent meal. Her husband doesn't care, as long as there's something hot and nutritious on the table.

- **Make friends with your neighbors.** If you're not already acquainted, try to forge a cordial relationship with your neighbors before you return to work, especially if they're at home during the day. There may be times when a little favor from them could be a lifesaver for you. For example, if you're expecting a delivery, perhaps your neighbor could accept the package or open your house for a drop-off.

- **Do favors for your friends** (so you won't feel guilty when you have to ask them to do a favor for you). To ensure that you're not always the one asking for favors, offer to do something for your friends whenever it's easy for you. For example, if you're heading to the grocery store, call a nearby stay-at-home mother and ask her if she needs anything. If you have a light week, offer to take over someone else's carpool duty and ask them to drive for you when you're busy in return. This builds on that same principle of the "emotional bank account" that we describe in chapter 5.

You

No matter how difficult the transition is on your husband, your children, or your house, the transition will be hardest on you. You're the one taking on a whole new set of responsibilities and completely changing your routines while still, most likely, retaining the lion's share of the responsibility for your children and your home. This is, again, why the gradual approach may work best, as you give yourself time to develop and implement new systems.

We see the transition from stay-at-home mother to relauncher as a continuum—a process of reclaiming. It begins the day after your youngest child was born as you reclaim your body after giving birth and, later, after nursing. It then moves toward reclaiming your professional interests and ambition after devoting yourself to family issues full-time. As part of this effort, you might reclaim a work space in your house, a place from which you can plan your relaunch (or even execute it if you pursue the consulting or entrepreneurial route). Finally, and sometimes coinciding with these last two events, you must reclaim your professional reputation outside your home as you seek an actual return to paid work.

Snapshot of a Transitioning Family

We caught Shelly right at the moment she had accepted her job as a clinic physician, about a month before her start date: "I'm feeling tremendous uncertainty, a tremendous urgency to get everything in place before I start work again. Now I'm realizing all the roles I really had."

Shelly methodically reorganized her household. She didn't want to be frazzled and have a hard time with the kids. The transition, which she referred to as "the letting-go moment," involved listing all the household tasks and dividing them up; presenting to the kids the concept that they owe the family thirty minutes of helping-out time every day; making a responsibility chart that assigns duties to each family member; and reclaiming a room of her own—a home office where she can review medical paperwork. This final step involved a lot of moving things around and was disruptive to her husband. Essentially, she displaced him. But together they realized that having a home office was an important part of her resuming her role as a working parent.

Lack of Time

Everyone we interviewed claimed that they had less time for themselves but that they weren't too bothered by it. They were so energized by their work, they were willing to forgo that alone time. Celeste, a social worker, noted, "What I sacrifice is personal time. My out-of-work peer relationships are gone. I never see my women friends anymore. Exercise is really reduced or gone. That's an okay trade-off for me right now. Some of my social needs are met at the office."

But the time pressure can be daunting. More than simply feeling pressed, relaunchers reported occasionally feeling completely overwhelmed, especially when a holiday or special event throws a wrench in the system.

Compounding the problem, you won't get much sympathy from your family. According to Susan, a former management consultant who relaunched full-time revamping the public school system of a major city, "I can't complain about my schedule because I *chose* to do this."

Making the Transition Easier on *You*

- **Take care of yourself (or at least try).** At the risk of sounding like your mother, don't completely ignore your own needs. You've got to recharge to keep operating at peak performance. Sure, it would be ideal if you ate well, got enough rest, exercised, and monitored your health. However, we are both guilty of violating all of the above advice and we know how hard it is to follow this kind of healthy regimen consistently. So just try to stick to it whenever you can.

- **Drop time-consuming volunteer commitments.** Give yourself permission to let go of volunteer commitments that consumed your life while you were at home full-time. You're taking a break from them. It doesn't mean you're leaving them forever. It also doesn't mean you're a bad person because you're now saying no. Remember, you logged five, ten, or even thirty hours of volunteer work per week during the time you were at home with your children. So you've paid your dues. The next few years are yours to focus exclusively on *you and your career* within the constraints of your particular family obligations.

- **Ditto for "obligatory" but unfulfilling social engagements.** "It takes a monumentally important event for me to be out on a weeknight," explained Sharon. "I now say no to almost every evening request for my time, whether it be a fund-raising event, dinner with friends, or a college alumni get-together. I will admit I made an exception for the Paul McCartney concert!"

- **Step back after intense bouts of work.** After completing an arduous project, try to take a break to spend a little extra time with your family to gain some perspective.

Peer Reactions

When you make a huge change in your life, like relaunching, it may prompt the women in your peer group to consider whether they should be making a similar transition. *All of a sudden, the doing rather than the talking about it forces the issue.* Your friends are now asking themselves, "Hey, Ellie stopped talking about it and she actually went back! Does that mean I should be going back, too? What do I really want to do about this? Just talk about it some more or take some action?" Ellie, meantime, is sensing her friends watching her progress almost as a proxy for their own possible back-to-work scenarios.

Just as your relaunch may cause friends to question their at-home status, leaving a relaunch job that doesn't work out can spark the opposite reaction. Christine left her first relaunch job because she tired of the long commute. "Upon finding out I'd left, my friends said things like, 'Oh, so it didn't work out? It was too hard?' *I think they almost wanted it to not work out so they wouldn't feel compelled to think about actually returning themselves.*" As we discuss in chapter 1, many women who have the choice are conflicted about the idea of returning. They do and they don't want to go back.

"Socially, my world changed," Carol noted. "Instead of standing in the 'wife circle' at parties talking about school and kids, I was in the 'guy circle.' Suddenly, my friends' husbands wanted to hear my views on the bond market, companies, current events affecting business, you name it, and I was happy to oblige. Later, some of my closest women friends confessed to being a little uncomfortable with me, because their lives seemed insignificant compared with mine, now that I was working. At some level, this was astonishing. Could I really have transformed myself from ordinary housewife to intimidating executive in just a few weeks? I was the same person who, a few weeks earlier, had been a stay-at-home mom just like they were. Yet by returning to the workforce, I had somehow entered a new realm that made me slightly unapproachable.

"I think this speaks to the core insecurity many women feel if they are not working for pay. It just doesn't count as a career without the office and the money. True, my volunteer work had been complicated, political, and involved managing the behavior of large, unwieldy groups of people—including many men. Yet I wasn't being paid for it, so that still placed me in a less intimidating category. Now that I was working, everything was different for my at-home friends, too."

Ongoing Conversations

Once you've started your job, new challenges will occur that you need to discuss with your husband. Try to set aside some time when you can talk about these issues, even if it is date night. You don't want to spend your entire romantic evening on work or home management topics, but you can probably, from time to time, use this occasion to have a heart-to-heart about concerns you may have in your new roles (we're sure he will have some, too). For example, on one of their Saturday-night dates, Vivian asked her husband if he could hold down the fort from four to six-thirty on Tuesdays, when he tends to have a shorter workday. Although he didn't agree to the exact proposal, he did start stepping in with dinner and homework supervision on Tuesday nights, giving her some much-needed evening work time. The restaurant setting and the bottle of wine made it much easier to discuss than when on a cell phone or while tending to the kids.

We caution you, however, not to make your relaunch the only topic of conversation with your husband. Vicky, the teacher who ran the kindergarten after-school enrichment program out of her home, not only was a solo entrepreneur, but also worked with kids all the time, not adults! So it was a double whammy in terms of lack of peer interaction. She felt isolated and had only her husband to talk to about the business. So that's all she talked about with him. The blurry home–work line and her lack of a professional peer group became an issue for her personally and in their relationship. Eventually she made some changes, which we discuss in detail in chapter 7.

———

When you relaunch your career, it requires a major, long-term family lifestyle adjustment. In terms of the work itself, gearing up and getting the job are just the beginning. Once back on the career track, you may face all sorts of new challenges, from managing your twenty-seven-year-old boss to learning new technology. In the next chapter, we take a close look at exactly what you're likely to encounter on the job, and what to do if your first relaunch isn't working out.

CHAPTER 7

Handle the Job
(or Find Another One)

Up: The day finally came. In my new work clothes, looking sharp, and heading off to work, I was relishing every minute of it. There was the sheer excitement of having made the leap into such an outstanding job. The office, the interesting co-workers, the intellectual freedom, the business cards, I reveled in all of it! I was in the best mood. Weeks later, still basking in the glow, I told my husband, "This is so great, sometimes I even forget I'm being paid!"

Down: I remember thinking I gave up a lot to be here at this job. I gave up everything at home. I'd leave in the morning and my son would still be sleeping. I also felt this incredible need to prove myself to myself and the world that I could do this. I didn't want to let down the woman who took the risk to hire me.

—Two relaunchers

No matter where you work, and no matter how long you've been out, you're likely to face major changes from your last experience on the job. For one thing, you may feel a little different from your colleagues, especially in a conventional work environment.

Don't Call Me Mom or Grandma

Depending upon your age and those of your colleagues, you may well be the oldest in your group, potentially even older than your boss. While you shouldn't feel compelled to hide your age, younger colleagues will probably warm up to you more easily if you don't constantly date yourself by referring to cultural icons of the 1960s, '70s, and '80s. You should be especially careful not to lord it over your teammates by saying things like, "When I was first in banking we had to do all the calculations by hand."

If your boss is younger than you, she may be just as uncomfortable about this as you are. Don't dwell on this potentially awkward differential. Be honest and open about what you do and don't know. People will take their cue on the age issue from you. If you don't make a big deal about it, neither will they. Just as confidence and a positive attitude got you through the job search process, so they should help you adjust to your new work environment.

At age forty-two, Carol began as an associate, along with others just a few years removed from business school. Her bosses were in their midthirties. Working side by side with her were the analysts, bright and eager college grads more likely to share musical tastes with her kids than with her. She loved working with all of them, but was torn between thinking of herself as their peer and as their surrogate mother. One young analyst in particular, who was far from home, eventually started coming to her family's holiday dinners.

These young people, all so technologically savvy and bright, were ready and eager to soak up and use the unique brand of consulting and financial analysis demanded by Carol's new employer. They could work night and day—just as she could at their age. They were simultaneously refreshing, exciting, and threatening to her. "But I didn't have any hang-ups about being older or out of it, and would readily admit when I didn't understand something. I think my colleagues appreciated the genuine and enthusiastic approach 'Grandma' took to her new job, and it helped me ramp up."

The Technology Challenge

"Without a doubt it was the huge changes in technology that made going back most difficult," recounted Bonnie, who initially relaunched with project work from temporary-staffing company Robert Half, then segued into a full-time position with a large oil company. "*Being technologically backward and hiding it became something of an art.* It took me a couple of years to really feel comfortable with the technology tools. But I didn't actually feel as though I had truly caught up to the rest of the world until I began working for my current company. The pace is so fast here and the changes come so quickly, there's always some new process or technology to implement."

Carol also struggled with technology. "I was pleased to find that my financial modeling skills came back fairly easily. But I felt behind in every other aspect of technology. Compared with the new analysts fresh out of college, I was slow in importing contents of annual reports and other documents into my own files and positively hopeless with graphics. Mastering these skills, which were second nature even to my children, was a struggle. It was just not easy for me to turn data into charts and graphs with the help of technology, and the PowerPoint tutorial I took before relaunching was nowhere near enough. In the past, if I didn't understand something I would spend the extra hours at work until I nailed it. This strategy proved a lot tougher with a husband and four kids waiting at home."

Occasionally, a relauncher will have the opportunity to learn a new technology right along with her colleagues. Kerry, who chose the field of library science as her original career because she knew it would give her flexibility through various life phases, was the first employee at her suburban library to get pregnant.

While home with her children, Kerry offered a toddler storytelling presentation she created, Baby Book Talks, on a sporadic basis, and reviewed books for the *School Library Journal.* When her husband changed careers, they decided she should go back to full-time work. Fortunately, a local library called with an offer to run the children's room. "While I was out of the field, libraries became computerized. But they kept changing the circulation systems they were using, and librarians were constantly having to learn new systems. So even though I missed the change to computerization, I could learn a new circulation system with everyone else when they changed to it."

The Gender Gap

In addition to adapting to youth culture and getting with the technological program, you may find yourself—or more precisely, your husband may find himself—discomfited by all the new men in your life. According to Nora, "A more amusing aspect of working was the newly discovered tension my husband felt from my being in a mostly male environment. Instead of being 'safe' at home with my women friends, I was surrounded by men every day and going on the occasional business trip with a male colleague. I think this equalization in perception of each other's work environment is healthy. While I never worried about my husband and all those female associates, partners, clients, and support staff, I was aware of them. On some level, I enjoyed the fact that he now could share this 'awareness.'"

Between Two Worlds

Even though you've officially joined the working-mothers club, you're likely to feel divided loyalties in the mommy wars. In an office environment, you might get upset when people malign stay-at-home moms; not so long ago, you were one of them. If you have your own business or work from home, you may feel even more like you're between two worlds. It may be hard for you, your family, and your friends to accept that you can't necessarily go to the park anytime you want; that you've got patients or clients or customers who count on you to get a job done. You've got to come to grips with the fact that you can no longer completely control your time. However, there are things you can do that will allow you to have some level of control over the time you spend working.

Tricks of the Trade: Working as an Employee

Do for Colleagues so They'll Do for You

Just as you should bank favors with your neighbors at home, so you should build goodwill with your colleagues at work so they'll cover for you when you're in a jam. Don't wait until you need them. Volunteer to proofread a report or check someone's numbers. Even though you're pressed for time, try to establish yourself as a giver and colleagues will want to give back to you. You don't want to be known as the one who can never help out "because of the kids."

Don't Necessarily Label Every Absence as Due to the Kids

Speaking of the "because of the kids" excuse, one of the interviewees in Deborah Swiss and Judith Walker's *Women and the Work/Family Dilemma* noted, "I don't talk about family issues at work unless it's critical to do so. Their [her kids'] doctor's appointments become my appointments. If I need to go to a teacher's conference in the morning, I simply call in to say I'll be an hour late."[1] Remember that all employees, including men and childless women, take personal days or duck out for an hour here and there.

On the other hand, there may be times when you want to invoke family to make your priorities clear. Early in her career, Ann Fudge, now CEO of Young & Rubicam after a stellar career at General Foods, followed by a highly publicized two-year break, famously told her boss on her first day of work that she had to leave because her son was injured on the playground. When her boss asked if this was going to be a regular occurrence, she said her family would always come first, but she didn't expect it to affect her job performance. She told him she only wanted to hear from him if it did.[2]

Don't Agree to Unrealistic Deadlines or Goals

In your zeal to impress your new boss you may be tempted to say you can get an assignment done quickly, a lot more quickly than is realistic. Or you may sign on to a "stretch" sales target or other goal to demonstrate your ambition. Don't make these mistakes. Even if you think a task is a piece of cake, remember that it's likely to take you longer because you're rusty. Also, with external factors (that is, children), you never know what might happen to derail your plans. Come up with any argument you can to buy yourself more time at the beginning. (*I need to get information from other departments; I want to make sure I produce quality;* whatever you can think of.) Companies dealing with Wall Street analysts try to underpromise and overdeliver; you should do the same.

Tricks of the Trade: Working from Home

Whether you're a consultant, home-based entrepreneur, or telecommuter, the following ideas will enable you to stay productive without turning into the sorcerer's apprentice.

Take Breaks During the Day

Far from lacking discipline, relaunchers report powering through hours of work at one sitting. But they often find they're more productive if they pry themselves away from their desks for a brisk walk, a little stretch, or—dare we say it?—lunch. If you were in an office, you'd almost never sit that long without stirring. So don't do it at home, either. Charlene, the former brand manager who relaunched herself as a marketing consultant, feels compelled to work "every second my kids are in school." But she realized this wasn't optimal, and eventually carved out a little time for herself.

Take a Break for a Day (or at Least a Night!)

Home-based relaunchers all revel in the convenience of having an office close to the kitchen. But they also recognize that, in addition to loneliness, working from home carries another major potential liability: the inability to leave the job behind.

Vicky, the former teacher who started a home-based afternoon enrichment program, had trouble with the home–work boundary. She had spent twenty thousand dollars to finish the basement—adding a bathroom, storage space, and a lively, child-friendly decor—so she felt enormous pressure to make the money back. Her husband was supportive to a point, but then felt she went too far. Concerned about whether her venture would be successful, she started immersing herself in the business, retreating to the basement to work on it all the time.

After a confrontation with her spouse, she realized she had to make some changes in order to be able to run the business, mother her growing family, and not go crazy. She lessened her expectations of herself. She now feels she does a pretty good job 80 percent of the time, and that's good enough. She scaled back by telling people her classes were full and she couldn't take any more kids. She hired a Saturday-night babysitter (who also folded laundry) so she could have a regular date night with her husband, and she made sure to take a ladies' night out as well. She also retained the services of an accountant and an assistant, despite the impact on her profits.

We recommend taking a full day off from work each week. In *Free Agent Nation,* Daniel H. Pink proposed that home-based workers—or "soloists," as he called them, "take a Sabbath. Choose one day during the week when you don't work. Don't go into your office, don't check your phone messages, don't answer your email."[3] Vivian observes the Jewish Sabbath—doing no work from sundown Friday until sundown

Saturday. "I can push myself all week, because I know I'll have that day to recharge. And I always return to my assignments with renewed energy and insight."

Check and Respond to E-Mail and Voice Mail Frequently

This way, colleagues and clients will think you're there even when you're not. Diane, the Queen of Contract Work, swears by this strategy for making clients feel like they're your top priority. If you're home-based but frequently on the go, consider a BlackBerry, even if you have to pay for it yourself. But—in keeping with our advice above—don't check messages obsessively on your day off.

Tricks of the Trade: Consulting

Work from Home and Rent Conference Space as Needed

Organizational strategists Marcie Schorr Hirsch and Lisa Berman Hills are both moms. They've made some decisions about the way they run their consulting business, Hirsch/Hills Associates, to accommodate the dual role of Hills, whose kids are still relatively young. For example, they decided not to have an external office. Instead they have a home office in each of their homes. Since most of Hirsch/Hills's *visible* work is done at their clients' offices, they access conference and meeting space only on an as-needed basis. This not only saves money, but also enables Hills to be accessible to her children when they're home from school.[4]

Control Project Selection with an Eye Toward Providing Excellence

Don't be afraid to turn down a project if the parameters are outside the scope of your expertise, or if the client's expectations are unrealistic. According to Hirsch and Hills, "If we don't think we can deliver a superior product to the client, we turn the client down. Our reputation is based on providing the highest-style quality work, and we won't compromise that if we feel the project is not the right match for our services."[5] Vivian made a pitch to a prospective client that she thought would make a great addition to her mix of business. But when she reflected on her meeting, she realized the company's expectations were unrealistic and would be extremely difficult to meet. So she decided not to pursue the assignment further.

Have an Assistant or Information Source Inside Your Client Company

Diane, the Queen of Contract Work, asks her client companies to assign an internal assistant to work with her. She gives this assistant her cell phone number so she can always be reached. If a client calls, the assistant takes the message, but calls Diane on her cell phone to let her know the call came in. That way Diane can be instantly available to her client, if she chooses to be, without completely sacrificing her privacy. She also asks her clients to pay for a dedicated phone line and connect her home computer to their e-mail system.

If you don't think you have the leverage to obtain these freebies from your clients, you should at least try to cultivate a low- to midlevel contact at your client company who can help you access resources you may need. And if you're going to bill the client more than once, try to develop a relationship with someone in accounting so that you can track the status of your payments without having to continually follow up with your consulting contact.

Take the Lead in Scheduling Meetings

No company expects consultants to be available 100 percent of the time. So if a client proposes a meeting that conflicts with something important on the family calendar, just say that time isn't good for you and suggest another. Better yet, try to be the meeting initiator so you can suggest dates and times that work for you.

Tricks of the Trade: Entrepreneurship

Slow Business Growth While the Children Are Young

Unlike many male entrepreneurs who are looking to make a killing ASAP, "mompreneurs" often eschew fast growth initially in order to have more time for their children.

Nancy Connolly (whom we profile in chapter 8), founder of printer cartridge recycler Lasertone, made her daughter her priority throughout the development of her company. "I wasn't looking for a big payoff early on." Although the company grew quickly, that wasn't necessarily her goal. "I focused on the growth of my child before I focused on the growth of the company. Even though we had a meteoric rise, I never put her schedule off."[6]

Leverage Core Strengths to Grow Revenues with Little Additional Investment

When you're ready for growth, don't think you'll have to invest double the effort to make double the money. If you identify and build off your core strengths, you can add revenue without racking up substantial additional hours. Once she opened her store for large-size footwear, Tracy easily increased her revenues by putting up a shingle on the Web as well. Georgia, the graphic designer, was already producing children's stationery and selling it at PTOs when she decided to take the product online. Vicky already has curricula, a customer base, and accounting support for her after-school program. In opening a second location, she'll be leveraging these existing assets. Her only major additional task will be recruiting and supervising teachers.

Hire, Outsource, Collaborate

Although we made Vicky's new task sound easy, learning to delegate or let go of some aspect of the business is probably one of the toughest challenges for relaunchers. As a mother, you may be so used to doing everything yourself that it's hard for you to trust someone else to take care of your "baby." Home-based businesses also face the privacy issue. "I've considered hiring an employee to handle the phones and do some routine work," Georgia said, "but my office is my private space. I often work in my pajamas. I just don't feel comfortable letting someone in here."

Elizabeth recently hired an employee for her art business and found it "hugely liberating." By taking on a second recruiter, Vivian has been able to more than double her revenues with very little additional time invested.

Don't worry if you can't offer someone a full-time job or high pay. There are probably a lot of women who would be willing to work with you on reasonable terms in return for a little flexibility.

In the absence of additional employees, consider outsourcing parts of your business. Peggy and her partner hire help during their busy season to assist them in packing and shipping book orders. Vicky farms out billing to a bookkeeper. Georgia subcontracts design work that isn't up her alley, as well as all printing. Don't feel you have to do everything yourself.

Continually Reevaluate Strategy and Tactics

Your business is up and running. You glide from kid to customer with the greatest of ease. You think you've got it made. Our advice? Don't hit the cruise control button. In today's fast-paced, competitive environment, you have to constantly scan the market for new developments—both positive and negative—that could have an impact on you and your business. Nancy Connolly's company Lasertone lost a huge customer that represented 30 percent of her firm's revenue. In response, she's diversified into other related areas and vowed not to chase big contracts again. She also started a new company that leases office equipment to business customers.

Moving On: When the First Relaunch Isn't Working Anymore

Like anyone else who works, at some point after your initial relaunch you may want to make a change in your professional situation. Unlike others, however, relaunchers may change jobs as a result of changes in their personal lives, not just in response to new professional opportunities. Relaunchers may also make a change if their true career objectives do not become clear until after they are well into their first relaunch.

Ratcheting Up

As your children become more independent, you may find yourself willing and able to commit more time and energy to your work. After a few years as a marketing consultant, Charlene, whom we described in chapter 5, was offered a great full-time job as head of marketing for a new venture in consumer health care. "It's making the home juggling act tougher, but my kids are older, and it was too good an opportunity to turn down."

Ratcheting Down, if You Find You've Overstepped

If you've taken a demanding full-time job, you may find yourself regretting it. Don't assume you have to quit in order to get your life back in balance. Just because you didn't ask for flexibility up front doesn't mean you can't request it later. Remember, now that you've proved yourself, your bosses should, theoretically, be even more willing to make adjustments to keep you happy. But also remember that requests for flexibility or other adjustments in your employment situation should be a win–win for employer and employee. Think through how you can maximize the company's benefit in return for willingness to comply with your requests.

Marcia, an MBA-nurse, found her first relaunch job as a residency program administrator in a hospital to be much more intense than she'd anticipated. Because of the commute, she was gone from 7 AM to 7 PM. On top of that, she faced a huge learning curve and a churlish staff: "I hate this job and I'm looking around," one of them greeted her on her first day.

Eventually, Marcia asked her boss if she could create a job share with the person who had held the job before her and now was a consultant to the hospital. "I was able to convince my boss to give this a try. She wanted to set an example of corporate opportunity for part-time or job-share employees, so this was another motivation for her to approve it. She knew there were limited opportunities for women to work in substantial part-time jobs."

Now Marcia works Monday through Wednesday, while her job-sharing partner (the person she "splits" her full-time job responsibilities with) works Wednesday through Friday. The hospital pays the extra day so they can work together for a smooth transition. Marcia loves her two days at home. She has picked up yoga again. She's home when her two kids get home on those days, and she can cook dinner for the family two additional nights per week. Marcia is really satisfied because she was able to relaunch at a good level and a decent salary. But she's not sure she could have sustained it long-term without the job share. Her company benefited, because although they have to pay for the one extra day a week, when both partners work on Wednesdays, they did not lose any continuity, or have to go through the long and expensive effort of recruiting and training someone else.

Coming to Terms with the Prospect of Quitting

Sometimes quitting appears to be the only solution to an all-consuming relaunch. Even the quitters we encountered, however, intend to relaunch again. *Indeed, not one of our interviewees expressed a desire to return to full-time stay-at-home motherhood on a permanent basis.*

Carol's pent-up desire to work after eleven years at home made her an enthusiastic interviewee who came across as willing and able to sell her soul to the company that hired her. "I had this idea, which I suppose was tied to my wanting to regain my former image of myself as the high-powered businesswoman, that the job I took had to be a killer job with a prestigious company. My desire to be in there with the big boys overshadowed the reality of my personal situation, which was that I wanted to remain an involved mother *and* have an intellectually challenging, high-paying job. The prestige of the firm and the compensation potential, in addition to an environment filled with motivated, highly intelligent people and interesting work, were too hard to turn down." In retrospect, Carol believes she oversold herself, although that was difficult for her to face.

"It was very hard for me to quit my investment management job one year after I went back to work. It was difficult on two levels. On a personal level, it felt like a failure. Could I just not cut it, or was it too hard for me to be successful in this particular type of job because it was so all-consuming, I was still learning the business, and I had four kids at home whom I was trying to be there for as much as I could? I was not used to failure in connection with my career—I had only experienced significant career achievement in the past."

Also, Carol discovered, in the middle of her first relaunch, that her professional interests had changed. "It wasn't until I was well into that job that I realized I had been forcing myself to do quantitative work my whole professional life and I didn't want to do it anymore. I had always loved business writing, which was certainly helpful when preparing investment recommendations and client presentations. I also loved interacting with and motivating people. I had done a lot of it in my volunteer work and I was a natural at it. But the point is, I *had* to return to the finance job before I realized my true interests had changed.

"I had to separate my personal situation from the situations of other women returning to work. We all have our own personal constraints and our own personal experience relative to the job we are taking, which will determine our success or failure when we resume our career. Maybe if I had fewer kids, or if I was going back to a job I already knew how to do from past experience, I could have been successful.

"I left in order to reevaluate my career goals. I was not ready to be at home again by any means, but I needed to find something that was engaging and that would allow me to work around my kids' schedules and still have a little time left over to take a deep breath periodically and regroup."

Marcia's and Carol's experiences argue in favor of a more gradual approach to relaunching if at all possible, especially if you have two or more young children. We don't want to discourage those of you who need or want to accept full-time positions immediately. Rather, we want to alert you to the potential pitfalls of a sudden switch from being at home full-time to working full-time. Make sure you focus your search on relaunch-friendly roles and organizations and negotiate key variables that may make the transition easier.

Also, if you're faced with an untenable situation and end up quitting, don't brood over your "failure." Use the knowledge you've gained about yourself and the market to zero in on an opportunity that's a better fit for your strengths and life situation. And don't berate yourself over the idea of having let your employer down. Men quit, too. And when they leave a job, they often join the competition, wreaking havoc on their old employer. So who's betrayed a firm's confidence more? You, who have decided to recoup and regroup? Or the guy down the hall who bolted to your firm's biggest competitor?

PART II

→

THE RELAUNCH MOVEMENT AND BEYOND

←

In part 1 of this book, we examined the issue of women returning to work from *your* perspective, and we outlined a 7-step process to help you relaunch your career. In part 2, we take a look at the big picture. Why are so many well-trained women currently at home? How many are there, actually, and how many want to go back to work? How do employers view stay-at-home moms? Are they doing anything to try to recruit and reintegrate them into the workforce? What *should* they be doing? What about colleges and universities? Have they developed any programs for their female graduates who are now at home?

We begin part 2 with a look at relauncher role models. These are women we all can learn from in thinking about women transitioning from home to work.

CHAPTER 8

Inspirational Relaunchers

Retired Supreme Court Justice Sandra Day O'Connor. Former politician Geraldine Ferraro. Academy Award–nominated actress Annette Bening. What do these women have in common? They're all relaunchers whose careers reached stellar heights after time at home raising children. A few of these women were real pioneers, who overcame great obstacles. Not only were they among the first women to *reenter* their fields after years at home, they were among the first women to even *enter* those fields, with none of the support systems that working mothers take for granted today. We had the privilege of interviewing a few of these inspiring relaunchers and share their stories in this chapter. We also highlight the careers of other prominent women we have identified as relaunchers.

Retired Supreme Court Justice Sandra Day O'Connor

The story of Sandra Day O'Connor's rise from a cattle ranch in Arizona to the first female on the US Supreme Court is legendary. By now many people know that although she graduated number three in the Stanford Law School class of 1952, no law firm in San Francisco would hire her because she was a woman. "I couldn't even get an interview," she related, "without pulling strings to get someone's father to talk to me." Few official profiles reveal, however, that she took five years off to stay home with her three sons early in her career.

Spurned by the private sector, O'Connor took a job as a deputy county attorney of the Northern California county of San Mateo. She stayed there only a year, since her husband, who was in the class behind her at Stanford Law, was drafted immediately upon graduation and posted to Frankfurt, Germany. Sandra followed him and worked there as a civilian lawyer until 1957, when they returned to the States to settle in Phoenix, Arizona. Again facing no interest from any private law firm, O'Connor opened her own law office with a partner, doing landlord–tenant work, family disputes, and other walk-in client business. "Not exactly Supreme Court material," she said, laughing. She had her first son the following year. Two years later in 1960, when her second son was born, she decided to leave her practice to stay home full-time. "I had a wonderful babysitter, but she left after my second child was born. It was a disaster for me because there were no day care centers in those days and I tried, but I could not find another competent sitter. So I had to leave my job." Four years later, O'Connor's third son was born. In 1965, she returned to work.

"With all the trouble I had had before, I was really worried that I would be unemployable, but I had to take care of those children. To keep my foot in the door, I realized I had to do something in the field even if it didn't pay. I wrote and graded bar exams for the state of Arizona, which kept me current in the law. I set up a lawyer referral plan for the local bar association, which was a good way to get acquainted with other lawyers. I took a position on the county planning and zoning board and agreed to be a juvenile court referee. I also accepted some small bankruptcy appointments." In addition, she dabbled in politics, becoming the precinct committee person for the Republican Party.

By the end of 1964, "I became busier than I wanted to be. I was putting in more hours than if I had a full-time paid job. Of course, no part-time jobs existed back then." Through her volunteer activities,

O'Connor had become well known in Arizona political circles, and in 1965 she got a job in the Arizona Attorney General's office. O'Connor reminisced: "I loved the job. It was the most fun I had in my career." But she wanted to work part-time, not full-time, so O'Connor made a bold move. "*First I tried to make myself indispensable.* Then I proposed working two-thirds time. I told them I would make them a great deal, because they'd only have to pay me for half time and I'd work two-thirds time." Thus one of the original less-than-full-time legal paths was created. O'Connor continued at the Arizona Attorney General's office until 1969, when she was appointed by the Court of Supervisors to fill a vacant state senate seat. She was reelected twice.

"I have a high energy level. I like to work, and I'm efficient in my work ethic. You give up friends or time for yourself. You make choices." O'Connor's choices certainly paid off. She moved to the state judicial branch when she ran for and was elected judge of the Maricopa County Superior Court of Phoenix, where she served from 1975 through 1979. Then Governor Bruce Babbitt appointed her to the Arizona Court of Appeals in 1979. From this post, she was nominated and confirmed as the first woman to serve on the US Supreme Court. "I'm the only Supreme Court justice with experience in all three branches of government," remarked O'Connor. She's also the only Supreme Court justice who relaunched her career.[1]

Relaunch Lessons from Sandra Day O'Connor
- **Take volunteer positions that keep you current in your field.** Justice O'Connor's law-related volunteer work as a juvenile court referee and as a bar exam writer and grader, although unpaid, kept her legal skills sharp.
- **You can make valuable contacts from your volunteer positions that will be critical in your relaunch.** O'Connor's extensive volunteer work for the Republican Party gave her invaluable contacts that helped her get hired by the state's Republican attorney general.

- **Make yourself indispensable** if you have relaunched full-time and are eyeing a future shift to less than full-time. Justice O'Connor made herself indispensable in the Arizona Attorney General's office as a full-time employee before proposing the then unheard-of two-thirds-time arrangement.

Margaret Rayman, PhD, one of the world's leading experts on the mineral selenium in human health and in cancer prevention

"Tell the National Institutes of Health they're wrong!" exclaimed British scientist Dr. Margaret Rayman, referring to their career reentry grant program that deems ineligible women with degrees more than eight years old. She is living proof that women with degrees older than eight years can have high-impact scientific careers.

Dr. Rayman had been away from scientific research for fifteen years, and her doctorate was almost twenty-three years old, when she relaunched as a volunteer researcher in a chemistry lab while applying for a Daphne Jackson Fellowship for restarters. Dr. Rayman believes she may be the fellowship recipient with the most years away from the lab bench, but it certainly didn't stop her from obliterating any stereotypical assumptions about degree obsolescence. She is now a reader, the British equivalent of associate professor, in nutritional medicine at the University of Surrey School of Biomedical and Molecular Sciences, and is one of the world's leading experts on the presence and effects of the mineral selenium on human health, and especially in cancer prevention.

Rayman graduated with her D Phil (PhD) in inorganic biochemistry from Oxford University in 1969. After two postdoctoral research fellowships, she took a part-time university lecturer (assistant professor) position upon the birth of her first child in 1973. In 1977, her second child was born, and three weeks later she moved to Paris due to her husband's job transfer. There she focused on her children and learning the French language. After seven years in Paris, her husband was transferred back to England. After running her own kitchen design business, she decided she wanted to resume her scientific research career. However, her job search came up with nothing—until she learned to use her own contacts rather than answering classified ads.

One contact was a member of the University of Surrey faculty with whom Dr. Rayman had worked many years before at Oxford. She called him up, and he remembered her right away. They had lunch, and he told her about the Daphne Jackson Fellowship program. *Through this professor, Rayman found a researcher she wanted to work with at Surrey and started as a volunteer while she went through the fellowship application process.* Her husband's income had increased by this point, so she didn't have pressing financial need.

When asked how she managed to get the researcher to agree to sponsor her for the fellowship, Rayman felt her dated but stellar credentials (an Oxford PhD and her first honors undergraduate status) were the key. "A person's intellectual capability is what is most important, regardless of the years they have been away from the field," she commented. "You never lose your sense of approach and how to study. It is much more about approach and intellect than obsolescence."

Interestingly, during her fifteen years away, Dr. Rayman had not done more than read "layman's diet and health books." Yet she didn't have a problem jumping back into scientific lab work or literature. *This was partly because she entered a new research field when she relaunched: She had to start over in building her research base anyway.* Her chemistry background did give her a greater understanding of structures when studying nutrition topics. She worked eighteen hours a week in the lab, but spent an additional eighteen hours a week reading. Her youngest child was fifteen at the time she began the part-time lab work, so her kids were pretty independent by then and the schedule worked for all of them. The only area in which she felt she was really behind was technology. She was tutored for five days in word processing and Excel. Then "I was shot into complex electronic and computer-controlled instrumentation. This was my weakness. But the science itself was no problem at all."

After her two-year Daphne Jackson Fellowship ended, Rayman had a setback. She thought she was going to get funding for a dyslexia and nutrition project, but it never materialized. After some false starts, she finally received a fellowship, and later a full-time position. Dr. Rayman quickly established herself as an assistant professor at Surrey, and built her reputation over the next ten years as a selenium expert. She also created and now administers the UK's first master's program in nutritional medicine at the University of Surrey Medical School.

On Margaret Rayman's résumé, in addition to the endless papers, presentations, awards, and accomplishments, she proudly includes "1977–1994: Career break."[2]

Relaunch Lessons from Margaret Rayman

- **Your intellectual approach is often more important than having up-to-date knowledge.** Rayman's study habits and approach enabled her to master new material quickly, even though she had been away from her field for more than fifteen years.
- **Learning a new area in your old field helps you make an obsolescence leap.** In Dr. Rayman's case, she did not have a problem jumping back into scientific lab work or literature. Her old knowledge base in chemistry gave her an advantage in studying her new field of nutrition.
- **Persevere through downtimes.** Twice Dr. Rayman had setbacks—when she first decided to return to her original field and was rejected, and when a grant didn't come through after her fellowship was over and she hadn't figured out her next career move. Both times, she hunkered down and worked her way out of these low points to great achievement.

Ruth Reardon O'Brien, retired partner, Ropes & Gray law firm

Like O'Connor, Ruth Reardon O'Brien was a pioneer. She won a full scholarship to Vassar College, and was one of four women who entered the Yale Law School class of 1956. Following her graduation from Yale, where she also received a scholarship, O'Brien landed a prestigious clerkship on the Massachusetts Supreme Judicial Court and then secured a coveted spot at the old-line Boston law firm of Ropes & Gray. After leaving the firm to accompany her husband during his military service, she returned to Ropes and worked there until 1960, when she became pregnant with their first child. "I loved my time at home. I liked to cook, and I know this sounds funny, but I even liked doing the cleaning. I liked having babies and taking care of them. I was always very content." Then, after eleven years at home raising five children, O'Brien relaunched in a part-time role at Ropes & Gray. Her sixth child was born after her relaunch. Six years later, she switched to full-time work, and in 1978 Ruth Reardon O'Brien became the second woman to make partner at the firm.

When O'Brien had been at home approximately ten years, she thought about going back to school. She talked to people at Harvard Law School about pursuing an advanced degree, but was essentially "casting about. I had not defined any details about what I was interested in, about household organization, or how it would all work." She was in this mode when she ran into a partner from her old firm one day while shopping. Their conversation was casual, but he called her two weeks later, said he had spoken to some other partners in the firm, and they wanted her to come back to work there. "He told me I could go back to Harvard Law School, but then I'd still have to spend time learning how to practice again, so why didn't I just come back to Ropes & Gray directly and learn there?" We asked her how she felt when this happened. "I was flattered. It was unexpected. I would never have dreamed of asking for it because I was too rusty."

Two weeks after her phone call with the partner, she walked into

Ropes to talk about the possibility of her returning. She told them straight out, "I couldn't come back unless it could be less than full-time. I said I couldn't be out of town and away overnight. I was thirty-nine when they asked me back. My husband traveled, and it was important to me to be home by dinnertime with the children. After I said all this, I told them, 'I don't know if you will want me under these circumstances.' I would have understood if they didn't.

"They asked me how often I wanted to work. I answered maybe four days [a week], but I would start at three and a half days a week. What I didn't tell them was I would spend all my extra evening and weekend time reading [to get up to speed again] and generally greasing the wheels.

"When I did go back, I brought my oldest child [who was eleven] in with me for a visit because he was the most concerned with my new role. I showed him around and told him, 'This is where I'll be and here's my office and my number where you can always reach me.' I made a promise to my children they would always be able to reach me when they called, wherever I was, and I kept that promise."

We asked O'Brien whether she had any confidence issues at the time she was relaunching. "My confidence level was okay going in because I was straightforward with the firm about my limitations. I told them I had been out eleven years, and I had not read anything to do with the law during that period. Plus, I told them, I had spent most of my time with people who did not use more than two-syllable words and who pointed a lot! I told them not to tolerate me if they didn't think I could do the work. I needed them to agree to tell me if I wasn't doing the work well—and I promised to tell them if I didn't think I could do it. But neither of us said anything to the other all the time I was working there, so I guess we all thought I could do the work!" She also advised, "If you don't tell anyone you are scared, they won't know. There's no law out there that says you have to talk about being frightened."

After her return, the firm started O'Brien in the real estate department, because the partners believed she'd have more control over her schedule there. However, when she began, the partner in charge of the department was ill and in the hospital. There was only one other attorney in the department, a woman, who mentored her. O'Brien had to take calls for the absent partner right away. Since she usually didn't know the answers to some of the client questions, she told people on the phone she was in a meeting and would get back to them shortly. Then she would familiarize herself with the client's file and skim the answers in law books. "I wanted everyone to think I was reliable and did good work, but I had forgotten everything. So I was playing above my head for a couple of years."[3]

In the meantime, daily life at home was well organized, but hectic. Approximately one and a half years after her relaunch, O'Brien's sixth child was born. She had planned to take some time off to recover from this pregnancy, but while she was on maternity leave, the attorney who had mentored her left to become a judge and the firm wanted O'Brien to come in as soon as possible to deal with 141 Appellate Tax Board cases that were pending. Her immediate response was that she wasn't qualified. The firm persisted and O'Brien went back, although she was scared about the possibility that she would not succeed in this daunting task. Of course she succeeded, and this field became an important part of her legal practice for the rest of her career.

O'Brien was firm about setting limits for her involvement in matters outside work and family. Her ability to say no was key to her success in managing her career and making her family her priority. "Tom and I decided together to cut out a lot of socializing when I went back to work. We wanted to spend all of our extra time with the children." O'Brien's husband was extremely supportive of her return to work, and he was involved in daily duties of child care as well. "We were in lots of car pools, and with six kids, both of us drove them. Our deal with the other parents was, O'Briens would do the morning car pools, and other families would do the afternoon. Sometimes I'd be at a corner dropping off three of the kids, and I'd see Tom whizzing by with his car pool!

"[My sense was] this is either going to be enormously successful or a huge failure. I told the firm the kids came first, and they did. I took good care of my family and my work, but one thing I didn't do was get involved in firm or bar committees or outside roles in the community. I said no to these things because I didn't have time to do them.

"The times of illness were the hardest. We had a couple of devastating accidents in the family. One of my daughters broke her back on the schoolyard [when she was ten]. I got this phone call from the school telling me my daughter can't move and they are taking her to Children's [Hospital]."

In the days following the accident, "The men I worked with at the firm were fantastic about covering for me. [One of the managing partners] came in and said, 'I'm not going to ask you how your daughter's doing because everyone told me if I do you'll start crying, but I can help you work on this deed or that file or do some other paperwork for you, can't I? Can you give me a few jobs to do?' When I think about the most thoughtful things someone else has ever done for me, the gesture by this partner is very high on the list.

"My daughter was ten and very athletic—she was the most athletic of all the kids, who were generally athletically inclined. Tom went out and bought her the fanciest fielder's mitt he could find. She couldn't even hold a pencil yet when he bought this for her—it was only a short time after the accident. She saw it and said, 'Dad, I'm never going to be able to use that.' Tom said 'It's all up to you. I'm going to fold it up [to soften it] and put it under your mattress.' Well, years later she ended up on the all-star softball team when she was at Brookline High. I still remember them announcing her name over the loudspeaker and feeling so proud—proud of her, proud of Tom, and proud of the firm for supporting me during that difficult period.

"The men I worked with were terrific about covering for me when I needed them to. I would say to them, 'If you can do this for me, I'll pay you back.' And I did. They never complained to me that they were shortchanged, and I hope they never felt that way!"

In 1977, six years after her part-time relaunch, O'Brien switched to full-time. "I used to come into the office a lot on Saturdays. But I'd always ask the kids who would want to come with me, and a couple of them always did. We'd bring a picnic lunch, and whoever came in got to have a conference room all to themselves where they could spread out all of their homework. The biggest draw was that each child who came got coins for the vending machines, which were a big deal back then. This worked for everyone. I felt it was important the kids not feel isolated from me if I was working on the weekend."[4]

Relaunch Lessons from Ruth Reardon O'Brien

- **Manage employer expectations carefully,** especially if you are returning to your old employer, where you previously might have worked a heavy schedule and traveled a lot. Understand your time and travel limitations now that you are also a mother, and make sure you are explicit about them up front.

- **"Always be totally reliable and dependable.** Do not ever disappoint your clients, co-workers, or anybody with whom you have a working relationship," advises Ruth Reardon O'Brien. This credo was central to O'Brien's successful reintegration into law practice, and then as she rose up the ranks to become a partner.

- **Exchange favors.** O'Brien relied on a system of give-and-take in her work life and home life to keep both parts under control. At home, she and her husband both drove car pools in the morning so other families could help them by driving in the afternoon. At work, Ruth knew she had credibility asking other lawyers to pitch in for her when she needed it, because she always returned the favor.

Katharine Wolf, MD, pediatric cardiologist turned psychiatrist after her relaunch

Dr. Wolf, another pioneer, graduated from Harvard Medical School in 1963. Following med school, she continued her training with internship, residency, and then two fellowships in pediatrics and cardiology. By the time she had completed all this training, it was 1969, and her first son was born. Dr. Wolf left medicine completely for almost five years and returned when her second son was two and a half. "My first son was independent at two so I thought I'd give my second son an extra six months and go back when he was two and a half. But the truth was, he was a different kid and really could have used some more time with me at home.

"When I was in med school, the women were not counseled about which specialties were amenable to attending kids' recitals, sick kids, et cetera. I wasn't really thinking about this and became a pediatric cardiologist. Also, my mother and grandmother were both physicians. Both had worked full-time, and finding competent child care was never an issue for them.

"But when I had my own kids, I realized I could not work full-time in this specialty—and it didn't lend itself well to part-time, either. My husband is a cardiologist, and when either one of us would have an emergency it was a life-or-death situation. I could not pick between saving the life of someone else and being with my own sick child [her older son was sick as an infant]. So I had to quit."

At one point during her hiatus, a male physician friend opened a pediatric HMO practice. The new medical school graduates he hoped to hire to staff the office couldn't start until they graduated. So he asked Wolf if she could work part-time until the new graduates arrived. She agreed, and worked there two mornings a week. Wolf felt her skill recovery was like riding a bike. "I reupped quickly. I was board-certified in pediatrics and in cardiology, so I had lots of extra training." Also, she was not alone—there were other doctors around to answer her questions if she was stumped. But she found most of the pediatric issues to be fairly straightforward.

Following that brief back-to-work experience, Dr. Wolf thought long and hard about what kind of medical career she could have that would be compatible with working part-time. "At first I thought child psychiatry might be the right thing, especially because I already had the pediatric background. But then I realized that geriatric psychiatry was a better field because older people actually liked having their appointments between 10 AM and 3 PM, which is when I wanted to work!"

When Wolf finally made the decision to return, she explored a number of psychiatry training programs but couldn't find one that would let her attend part-time. A friend and college classmate was able to arrange the first part-time residency in Boston (hers was in pediatrics). Although her friend experienced hostility from other residents—they resented that she was taking someone else's full-time place and assumed she was goofing off by attending half-time—Wolf was inspired by her friend's experience, and attempted a similar arrangement. When accepted to the full-time psychiatry residency at Beth Israel Hospital, she inquired whether it would be possible to go part-time at some point. The hospital considered it and allowed her to switch to part-time after the first year. The hours were 9 AM to 3 PM plus night call. By this time, her husband was a junior faculty member and had more clout at work; he could get the time needed to cover at home when she had night call. Also, occasionally she'd have to go in at 7 AM, and he was able to cover her for this, too.

The metamorphosis of the attitude toward the half-time residency program was striking. After Betty Friedan's *The Feminine Mystique* had its second printing in 1974, "the ferment was happening. Nurses started coming to work in white slacks instead of skirts!" commented Wolf. Her shift to half-time status in her residency program began in 1974 in the midst of the second wave of the Friedan reaction. "People began, just barely, to think that maybe a half-time program would be okay."

But there's more. In the first half of the first part-time year of her residency, Dr. Wolf had been farmed out by Beth Israel to Cambridge Hospital. When she applied for board certification in psychiatry a few years later in 1980, both hospitals denied she had been there! They did not want to acknowledge they had allowed a part-time residency arrangement, which might be viewed as some sort of insult to the prestige of the program. Then, in 1992, when Dr. Wolf applied for board certification in the subspecialty of geriatric psychiatry, both hospitals claimed she had attended. This was because by the early 1990s, it was considered a feather in your cap to have a half-time program.

Dr. Wolf has given talks at Harvard Medical School about how to stay married, have kids, and pursue a medical career. But the school doesn't always want her to speak. She thinks this is because the med school administrators are afraid she'll scare the students.

"Once I attended a medical lecture where a male physician said terrible things were happening because women were attending medical school and then not working full-time. I marched up to the front and he said, 'Yes, Mrs. Wolf.' I said, 'That's Dr. Wolf to you!' I then went on to cite the study of Dr. Carol Johns, at Johns Hopkins. It was a survey of women medical school graduates. It indicated that the women who were working part-time had more clinical intensity to their careers and were actually taking care of people and in medical teaching positions as opposed to the many male doctors who ended up working for drug companies or taking administrative posts like deans of medical schools. Dr. Johns also said women physicians practice longer in part because they live longer, and in part because they often are part-time at some point in their careers, they feel compelled to retire at much older ages than their male counterparts."

The Johns Hopkins survey nicely complements the anecdotal evidence represented by Dr. Wolf's career that women physicians can have long, productive careers after time at home.[5]

Relaunch Lessons from Dr. Katharine Wolf

- **Design your career around your children's schedule.** As you consider relaunch options, if working school hours is a priority for you, think about which customers or clients are likely to want to do business specifically during those hours, and tailor your career in response. Dr. Wolf switched specialties to geriatric psychiatry because seniors preferred office hours during the school day, and only minimal on-call time was required.

- **Be resilient in the face of criticism.** Dr. Wolf and the friend who preceded her in the part-time residency program endured ridicule for being lazy by taking the part-time track and for taking up a space someone else could have had for a full-time slot. Even today, female doctors who are working part-time schedules are subject to comments by others, usually male doctors, that they "wasted" a spot in medical school.

- **Your ramp-up may be quicker than you anticipate.** Indeed, Dr. Wolf's relaunch ramp-up time was short— "just like riding a bike." Likewise, she did not experience any professional ramp-up issues when she was back in her residency program. The adjustments were primarily logistical.

Dinny Stearns Taylor, Chief Technology Officer, Williams College

Dinny Stearns Taylor started her postcollege life traditionally enough after her graduation in 1968. "I was married two weeks after graduation. There were a lot of weddings that summer." Taylor admitted to having lower career expectations at that time. "The really radical feminist movement was just coming in," she said, but hadn't quite taken hold; traditional views prevailed. She began teaching elementary school near Boston while her husband pursued his PhD at Harvard. She loved it. She also received her master's degree in education during this time.

Her son was nine months old when they moved to Williamstown,

Massachusetts, where her husband started teaching at Williams College. At Williams, the brand-new women faculty who were pursuing their academic careers and putting off their personal lives in the process "looked at me with contempt that I had made the choice to have a baby." Taylor gravitated toward women in the community with children, and these were the women who became her friends. They had a rotating child care arrangement, trading one morning a week taking care of four children in exchange for three free mornings a week while the others did the child care. Taylor, who had an undergraduate psychology degree from Connecticut College, used this time to work six hours a week at a three-dollar-an-hour part-time job during the academic year in the Williams College Psychology Department.

"Somewhere along the way, someone talked me into learning how to teach LSAT [Law School Admissions Test] workshops. So one to two times a year, I led seminars I put together to prep students to take the LSAT." Taylor characterized these minimally part-time and sporadic work experiences as "ways to get out of the house a few hours a week at most." Aside from these occasional work opportunities, Taylor was out of the workforce for ten years, from 1973 to 1983.

Her daughter was born in 1976. "I had no overall plan for what life was going to look like, work or no work." Taylor had loved teaching when she could come home to a childless house, but somehow couldn't fathom returning to teaching knowing she would now come home to more kids, even though they were her own. She had always been interested in math and science; in high school, she'd attended a National Science Foundation institute in biology for high-ability students. In college, she had signed up for a course in the programming language Fortran, but couldn't keep up with it in addition to the academic demands of her major, so she dropped it. But even that brief encounter with computer programming made her realize she had possibly found her work passion.

So she enrolled in computer programming courses and talked to local companies, asking, "When you are hiring, what are you looking for?" *It was a top priority for her to work within Williamstown, so she wanted to find out specifically the kinds of skills the college and the local businesses were seeking.* This helped her decide not to get her PhD, but instead continue to train in systems analysis.

After a stint in North Carolina (due to her husband's sabbatical), where she got her first programming job, she returned to Williamstown and started looking for work right away. "When I returned to Williams, I started talking to people about programming jobs because people knew me there. There was an intro programming analyst job opening at Williams, and I applied for it and got the position.

"This was a full-time job, but the proximity and environment of the college campus were helpful. My husband worked from home a lot, and he was usually there when my daughter came home from school." Her seventh-grade son was involved in activities after school, so it was less relevant to him that she wasn't home then. Since her husband was home in the afternoons and since she was still cooking, managing schedules, and running the household, she thinks the transition was pretty smooth for her kids. It helped that she was in a small town with available babysitters, and it was easy to take the kids to appointments, go to school plays, or have the kids walk over and hang out on campus.

Meanwhile, Taylor was thrilled with her new job. "Four of us were working on this big project together and no one was stepping up to the plate to lead the project, so I stepped up. *Motherhood is one of the best preparations for project management. You need skills in communication, organization, time management, and managing different personalities.* Ten years at home gave me the project management skills I needed to take the lead on this project." This experience led her to move to more senior positions. "As openings came along, my administrative skills made me a clear candidate. Williams conducted searches for all these positions, but I was able to come out on top and get the job."

Taylor commented that she didn't really see her programming jobs as a career until later. "I've been at Williams twenty-two years in technology, but I've had a different job every year." She found that her combination of technical and administrative management skills made her unusual. So many of the technical people she worked with did not have management strength. This quality gave her an enormous advantage as more senior management positions popped up. As Chief Technology Officer, she manages a forty-two-person staff. "Now I joke I'm writing more memos than programs."

We asked her what role confidence played as she moved up in seniority. "*My initial success increased my confidence as I was going along, and that enabled me to do more things.* Once I was working, I realized I had these leadership skills as well as technical skills. Other people told me I was good at what I was doing. When I began leading projects, I discovered a skill set I didn't even know I had."

Looking back, Taylor was glad she had her children young and was able to manage her career path the way she did. She noted that when she started, there were no day care centers. She was twenty-six years old when her son was born and thirty when she had her daughter. Now her daughter is a twenty-nine-year-old lawyer in New York, and her daughter-in-law, who has a new baby, will soon face the back-to-work decision. Taylor thinks it's a lot harder to make these decisions today than it was when she was making them. She didn't even appreciate the magnitude of the work-related decisions she was making at the time! Only in hindsight did she realize how her choices melded to produce the successful career path that led to where she is today.[6]

Relaunch Lessons from Dinny Stearns Taylor

- **If proximity is a value, look around to see what skill sets are needed locally.** Taylor believes that working in close proximity to your home and kids gives you the opportunity to do it all. We also think the somewhat less traditional setting of a university campus helps give employees the freedom to work atypical schedules.
- **Mothering is key preparation for project management.** Taylor

feels her skills in communication, organization, time management, and managing different personalities were developed while she was a mother at home.

- **Pursuing your work passion can lead to a satisfying career.** Taylor took a low-key but methodical approach to her career. She didn't even know she was building a career when she first started. She was just doing what she loved.

Nancy Connolly, Founder and CEO, Lasertone

Nancy Connolly got married after two years of college and spent her young adulthood driving around in a van with her new husband doing odd jobs and having fun. She fell into a start-up in office technology that was funded by Exxon and discovered her penchant for business. The firm, called Vydec, grew to a hundred million dollars a year in sales, and she stayed there eleven years. She then worked for Exxon in New York acquiring and integrating office systems companies. The one thing she couldn't seem to do was have a child: "I had six miscarriages in seven years." When she finally gave birth to her daughter, "I made the choice early on that she was my priority. I told myself that if I can't work around her schedule, I won't work. I wasn't a stay-at-home type, but I knew I didn't want to go back to the kind of job I had at Exxon."

Because her daughter was born ten weeks early and had some health problems, Nancy elected to stay home. One day after she'd been home for three years, the husband of a friend called and asked her to help him start a company recycling and remarketing toner cartridges. Although she didn't know the cartridge business, her background in start-ups had trained her to recognize good potential business opportunities. And she thought this was one. But she made it very clear that her daughter came first. "I knew I'd never have another shot at being a mother. So I set reasonable growth expectations. When we started the company, my daughter was in preschool but not in extended-day.

When she was five, I initially signed her up for all-day kindergarten but she came home one day and said, 'I want to have lunch some days with my best friend,' so I cut her back to only three full days.

"Initially my partner and I worked out of our houses. We each invested five thousand dollars. We kept overhead low. I knew from my experience at Exxon that overhead can kill you. But it was still an adjustment. I was used to all the perks at Exxon. When I went to the big Boston law firms to try to sell them on our recycled cartridges, they'd say, 'Lasertone? Who are you?' We'd get the door shut in our faces. So we decided to focus on small companies in Cambridge and up Route 128 that were bootstrapping the way we were and more willing to take a chance on us. They had all left big companies, too, so they knew how it felt.

"We got additional start-up cash from friends and family, and eventually were able to get a bank loan. Fortunately, we didn't need to look for outside investors. We were profitable pretty much from the get-go. But I always took seriously any offers we received to buy the company. It's not your child. Everything's for sale at a price."

As the business grew, her partner grew increasingly uncomfortable. "He wanted to keep the company small and homebound. Eventually, I bought him out." Nancy relished the management challenge. "I either hired people who didn't have constraints on their time—or if they did, I set the expectations up front and let them figure out how to get the job done. I found that when I gave people flexibility, it reduced turnover."

Although the partnership broke up, she had a board member from day one who's still with her. "I do suggest an advisory council for small non-venture-backed companies initially, with a more formal board of directors later on if required. Sometimes the formality of votes gets in the way when the board is not easily accessible, and with governance issues an important consideration, some candidates are opting out of board positions."

The only hiccup in her company's growth was the loss of a major client that temporarily cut revenues by 30 percent. The original toner cartridge recycling business has become less profitable due to competition, so she's taken Lasertone into other areas, such as laser printer servicing and computer hardware servicing. She's also avoiding big contracts that make the company too dependent on one customer, and she's started a new company, called Smart Page Technologies, which leases office equipment, such as copiers, laser printers, and fax machines.

Nancy is justifiably proud that, within fifteen years, she built Lasertone into a company with revenues of over thirteen million dollars and sixty-three employees. In fact, it's the largest woman-owned business in its industry. But she's even prouder of her daughter, now also a budding entrepreneur, and happy that she put the time in to raise her.[7]

Relaunch Lessons from Nancy Connolly

- **If you have your own business, grow it around your children, not the other way around.** Connolly couldn't have said it better: "You only get one [or two or three, maybe] shot at motherhood. If you don't make your kid your priority, you may regret it."
- **A business partnership doesn't necessarily last forever.** If you and your partner knock heads frequently, consider exit strategies for one of you.
- **Learn to let go.** Connolly's ability to hire, train, and delegate enabled her to build her company without sacrificing time with her daughter. This is critical to executives working for others as well as for entrepreneurs.

Look at These Inspiring Prominent and Celebrity Relaunchers!

- **Kirstie Alley.** The former *Cheers* and *Veronica's Closet* star took four years off to stay at home with her children. She relaunched at age fifty-three in the high-profile but short-lived sitcom *Fat Actress,* and has since become the best-known spokesperson in weight loss program Jenny Craig's history.

- **Brenda Barnes.** The woman who became famous in 1998 for leaving her powerful position as president and CEO of PepsiCo North America to be home with her family made the headlines again when she relaunched her professional career six years later as president and chief operating officer at Sara Lee Corporation. Within nine months of her return, she was promoted to chief executive officer of Sara Lee, making her one of the few female executives in the country running a major corporation. In November 2005, *Fortune* magazine listed her as number three in its annual ranking of the 50 Most Powerful Women in Business.

- **Annette Bening.** The Academy Award–nominated actress took three years off in 2000 shortly before her fourth child was born. At the time her three older children were ages eight, five, and three. In 2003, she resumed her on-screen career in a role opposite Kevin Costner in *Open Range.* Then, in late 2004, she starred in *Being Julia,* for which she received her third Oscar nomination.

- **Geraldine Ferraro.** Although best known as the only female major-party candidate for vice president, Geraldine Ferraro began her career as a second-grade teacher while she pursued a law degree at night. Following a thirteen-year career break to raise her three children, Ferraro worked at the Queens County District Attorney's office before her election to the U.S. House of Representatives in 1978. After serving three terms, she was selected as Walter Mondale's running mate on the 1984 Democratic ticket.

- **Teri Hatcher.** The *Desperate Housewives* star took six years off after her daughter was born in late 1997. From 1993 through 1997, she'd starred in the television series *Lois and Clark: The New Adventures of Superman.* Her last major cinematic role before her career break was in the James Bond movie *Tomorrow Never Dies.* Hatcher's relaunch on *Desperate Housewives* at age

forty in 2004 earned her two Screen Actors Guild awards and a
Golden Globe for best actress in a comedy. A media favorite, she
has achieved formidable celebrity status. Her best-selling book,
Burnt Toast, was published in May 2006.

CHAPTER 9

The Relaunch Movement

As we noted in the introduction, when we each tried to relaunch our careers in 2000 we felt very much alone. But since we started working on this book, we've run into a veritable army of relaunchers. And we don't think it's just because we were looking for them. We think the whole concept of relaunching, and the growing corps of relaunchers, is reaching a tipping point.[1] The question is: Why? Why are there so many relaunchers all of a sudden? How many are there, *actually*? And what efforts are under way to cater to or court this new category of worker?

Obviously, to be classified as a "relauncher," you have to have had a career in the first place. Although women have been in the US workforce for decades, prior to 1970, according to Katharine Bradbury and Jane Katz of the Federal Reserve Bank of Boston, "Almost half of all college educated women did not work, and those who did tended to be concentrated in nursing, elementary and secondary school teaching, and other traditional female occupations."[2] As you can see from the following chart, less than 12 percent of first-year students at professional schools in 1970 were female.

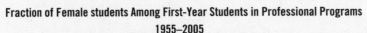

Fraction of Female students Among First-Year Students in Professional Programs 1955–2005

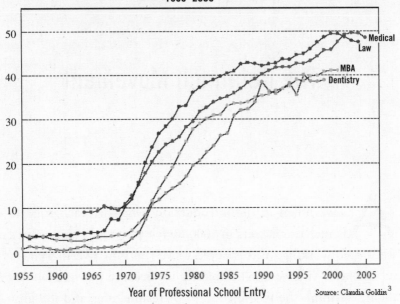

Year of Professional School Entry   Source: Claudia Goldin[3]

Our point is that prior to the mid-1970s, career women were few and far between. In her book *Getting It Right,* based on a survey of Stanford Business School alumnae, psychologist Laraine Zappert calls women who graduated from Stanford Business School prior to 1976 "the Pioneers."[4] In the pioneer era, those who made it professionally weren't likely to give it all up for children. According to a longitudinal study of female Harvard Business School graduates published in *Fortune,* the 1973 graduates ". . . have stayed in the work force full-time much longer than women from the class of 1983. That probably reflects both a lack of part-time options in the 1970's for the Pioneers and a determination to have the careers they struggled so hard for."[5] Inspired by the feminist movement, and having overcome quips and quotas to climb the corporate ladder, most early career women weren't about to relinquish professional ground—baby or no baby.

Even if some of the career pioneers did quit in order to raise their children, those who left may never have sought to return, channeling their energies instead into volunteer work or hobbies. How many of the pioneers opted out and then relaunched their careers? Who knows? No one tracked these women. Prior to the new millennium, the number of relaunchers was so small, they escaped notice. And the few pioneers who did manage to relaunch their careers, such as Sandra Day O'Connor, became better known for their accomplishments during round two than for their years at home.

Sequencing

Although relaunching was not widely discussed prior to 2000, Arlene Rossen Cardozo identified the phenomenon more than twenty years ago. In her groundbreaking 1986 book *Sequencing,* she told the stories of women who established careers, took time out to raise their children, then returned to work once their children started school. "Sequencing is the solution more and more women choose of having it all—career and family—by not trying to do it all at once, at all times in their lives," she wrote in her introduction.[6] "The purpose of this book is to provide mothers who have begun sequencing their lives . . . a guide for making the most of their full-time mothering years, and an exploration of career reemphasis options specifically tailored to the woman who wants to reincorporate professional activities into her life without compromising her mothering priorities."[7] Trouble is, when *you* started your career, you might not have heard of the concept of sequencing. Moreover, even if someone had tried to tell you about it, would you have paid any attention?

If you began your career in the late 1970s, the 1980s, or later, your experience probably differed considerably from that of the pioneers. As a result of the passage of the Equal Employment Opportunity Act of 1972 and affirmative action, as well as women's increased access to higher education, many women launched careers almost as easily as their male peers. You didn't have to fight to get those coveted jobs at big professional service firms. If you had the right stuff, you simply sailed in. Moreover, for ambitious young women of the late 1970s and '80s, life was all about careers. You probably didn't worry (or even think about) how you would balance work and family. When you started your first job, you were probably still single, or at least childless, and you figured you'd manage somehow. *Being superwoman still seemed possible.*

Opting Out

But after you married and started to have babies, reality began to set in. Managing work and family wasn't as easy as you'd thought. *Unlike the pioneers, however, you probably didn't feel the need to prove yourself by sticking with your career at any cost.* Although ambitious and successful, you felt comfortable and confident enough to step back from your career to be at home for a while. And unlike the pioneers, you probably didn't feel guilty that you were letting the movement down when you opted out. Mothering is at least as important as working, if not more so, many women reasoned. And with young children, it's difficult to do both well at the same time. So women started to leave, first in a trickle and then in larger numbers. Indeed, according to Bradbury and Katz, "the labor force participation rate of prime-age (25–54) women with at least four years of college rose in the 1980s and early 1990s, leveled out in the mid-1990s, and then declined. Between 1994–95 and 2003–04, the rate declined from 84.7 percent to 81.8 percent." Furthermore, "the decline was most pronounced for married women with children under the age of three, whose participation [in the labor force] dropped 8 percentage points."[8]

This trend has been well chronicled. The subject even made the cover of *The New York Times Magazine.* In October 2003, the *New York Times* work and family columnist Lisa Belkin penned "The Opt-Out Revolution," which described a group of Princeton women, including lawyers, a teacher, a television reporter, and a marketing manager, among others, who had "opted out."[9]

In March 2005, the Center for Work–Life Policy released the first large-scale study of the opt-out phenomenon. Titled "Off-Ramps and On-Ramps," the study was based on a survey of 2,443 "highly qualified" women aged twenty-eight through fifty-five, as well as a smaller group (653) of "highly qualified" men in the same age bracket. *Highly qualified* was defined as having a graduate degree, a professional degree, or a high-honors undergraduate degree. According to their survey, 43 percent of highly qualified women with children "left work voluntarily at some point in their careers," as did 37 percent of all highly qualified women (with or without children)."[10]

How Many?

The Belkin piece, and indeed the whole trend of women staying home to raise their children, has actually generated quite a bit of anger. Some argue that only a sliver of wealthy women enjoy the privilege of staying home with their children. So, of course, we wanted to find out how many women are home raising children and figure out a way to estimate how many of those women are contemplating a return to the workforce.

Data from the Bureau of Labor Statistics Current Population Survey indicate that in 2005 there were an average of more than 9.1 million women between twenty-five and fifty-four years of age with children under eighteen who were *not* in the labor force. This represents 28 percent of women in this demographic.[11] In other words, *more than a quarter of women with children under eighteen are not working for pay.* One could certainly argue that not all these stay-at-home moms *chose* to be home with their children. Other factors could be contributing to their decision to stay at home; maybe they gave up looking for work because they couldn't find anything that paid more than the cost of child care. But even if some of these women are not home by choice, the number and percentage are high enough to suggest that the "opt-out" revolution runs much deeper than the Ivy League.

But let's get back to the issue of how many *career-oriented* women have opted out and may want to opt back in. Focusing on women with a BA degree or higher, the numbers are also impressive. In 2005, more than 2.3 million college-educated women between the ages of twenty-five and fifty-four with children under eighteen were *not* in the labor force. This represents 24 percent of women in this demographic.[12] In other words, *almost one quarter of college-educated women with children under eighteen are not working for pay.*

And how many of these women are interested in relaunching? The "Off-Ramps" study notes that 93 percent of the "highly qualified" women surveyed who have taken time out indicated that they want to return to their careers. Applying this percentage to the more than 2.3 million college graduates among the stay-at-home-mom population, we estimate that there are over 2.1 million former career women currently at home who are interested in relaunching. (Note that this is a dynamic number, as mothers are constantly opting out of and returning to the workforce.) *Thus, there is a large cohort—more than 2 million—of educated and, in many cases, experienced women not currently in the workforce, but interested in returning.* This number is important because it indicates to potential relaunchers on a career break that they are far from alone, and it tells employers that this cohort of women is a force to be reckoned with from a hiring perspective.

The Conversation Shifts

By mid-2004, we detected a shift in the media conversation from the topic of opting out to the topic of opting in. Why did it take so long? Why weren't we talking about women reentering careers ten or fifteen years ago? Again, pure demographics are behind the trend. Enough years had to pass for women who launched their careers in the late seventies, eighties, and beyond, to invest at least five years in their fields and have a couple of children, then quit when their second child was born (let's say after seven years at work), maybe have another child, and then wait until the youngest child was in kindergarten. Quick, there go fourteen years. The 1993 grad, for example, is now, in the year 2007, home seven years with three school-age children. What happens? She's ready to go back to work (possibly dying to go back) and she has the time to make a go of it. We graduated in the mid-eighties and began thinking about relaunching in 2000; again, an approximately fifteen-year cycle from graduation to relaunch. That's why we believe the issue of career reentry is only now gaining prominence, as the women who began leaving the workforce to raise their children in the eighties (and beyond) now seek to relaunch their careers in larger numbers.

The Relaunch Movement

Just as the women's movement of the 1960s and '70s opened professions to women, so the Relaunch Movement of the twenty-first century is opening the workplace to stay-at-home mothers. Like the earlier movement, it will require women's initiative, corporate America's openness, and legislative action to make it complete. Although some of the most critical laws are already in place—such as nondiscrimination laws, equal work for equal pay, and the obligation of large employers to provide unpaid maternity leave—there is still work to be done on the legislative front. Laws mandating paid parental leave, fair part-time pay practices, prorated insurance coverage for freelancers and part-timers, and access to higher-quality child care would obviously make relaunching easier. In fact, Workplace Flexibility 2010, a policy and research organization run out of Georgetown Law School, is working on developing such legislation. But gaining government support for this sort of change takes time. And frankly, you may not want to wait for legislation to be put in place.

Corporate Concerns

The corporate picture is more complicated. US corporate culture places a premium on uninterrupted work experience. This makes it difficult for women to relaunch themselves into conventional corporations. When women leave the workforce, they may be perceived as sending a "negative signal," tainting their employment prospects from that point on.[13] Author Susan Lewis agrees. She wrote in 1999 in *Reinventing Ourselves After Motherhood,* "There has been and still is a common notion that women who choose to stay at home with their children are less ambitious, serious and even reliable as professionals."[14] They are no longer viewed as loyal employees, because they have turned away from their companies for a higher personal priority. Employers may also fret that these women's skills are not up to date.

Lack of Flexibility

Possibly the greatest obstacle to women seeking to relaunch their careers in a corporate setting is the lack of flexibility in most workplaces. Despite the Internet and the rise of telecommuting, many jobs still require most employees to be on-site from nine to five (or even eight to six, or longer). And then, as Arlie Hochschild argued in *The Second Shift,* after putting in overtime at the office, women face another almost full-time job at home.[15] This has clearly discouraged a lot of highly skilled stay-at-home moms from even *trying* to get back to the paid workforce. And those who do show up at interviews often face managers expressing skepticism about their ability to put in the hours "required."

What's in It for the Companies? The Business Case for Flexibility

Many firms have discovered, however, that offering their employees flexibility, both within the workweek and over the course of their career, can improve their bottom line. According to Ellen Galinsky, president and co-founder of the Families and Work Institute, "There has been a generational shift in values, possibly as a result of 9/11, years of downsizing, the movement to an ownership business culture, and the aging of the workforce. Older and younger workers want more flexibility over their careers. This results in defining flexibility more broadly than just flex time and includes career flexibility with times in and out of the workforce."[16]

The green eyeshades in the accounting industry, of all places, were among the first to offer career flexibility—and not out of charitable or feminist impulses. Hard-nosed economics have dictated their moves. After crunching the numbers, management at Ernst & Young, among other firms, realized that the consistent exodus of midlevel female employees, the so-called brain drain, is more than a nuisance; it drags profits down. According to the "Off-Ramps" study, "Turnover in client-serving roles meant lost continuity on work assignments. And on top of losing talent that the firm had invested in training, Ernst and Young was incurring costs averaging 150% of a departing employee's annual salary just to fill the vacant position."[17]

So the need for consistent client teams, the high cost of replacing a lost employee, and the write-off of the financial investment made in training employees who leave, all purely economic concerns, forced E&Y (and the accounting industry generally) to focus on retention of their female employees. And as soon as firms start to formulate solutions to the problem of female retention, flexible work schedules almost always figure in the mix. According to Sue Shellenbarger, *The Wall Street Journal*'s work and family columnist, "Flexible scheduling invariably ranks Number 1 in surveys of workers' most-wanted supports."[18]

In addition to accounting firms, many other employers have also begun to grasp the business case for offering employees flexibility. Corporate Voices for Working Families, a Washington, DC, nonprofit, released a study in November 2005 titled "Business Impacts of Flexibility: An Imperative for Expansion." This study draws on internal research performed by twenty-nine large US firms from a variety of industries and "provides evidence that employers can gain tremendous benefit from providing flexibility in when and how work gets done. . . ."[19] For example, "In its 2003 global employee survey, Discovery Communications learned that 95% of employees in the US say that availability of flexible work arrangements is a critical factor in taking a job."[20]

The study also includes numerous examples illustrating that firms that allow workers flexibility, even occasional flexibility, enjoy increased employee satisfaction, increased employee engagement and commitment, and reduced employee stress. Lest you think this veers into the realm of the touchy-feely, the consulting firm Watson Wyatt has found that "firms with high employee satisfaction scores have decidedly higher market value—and that a flexible work place is associated with a 9% change in market value."[21] Additionally, the study notes that employee stress costs US business about three hundred billion dollars a year in lost productivity, health care costs, and replacement costs.[22] Reducing stress, by providing flexibility, decreases these costs.

Most importantly, the report describes a number of studies that quantified the positive impact of offering employees flexibility on a company's bottom line. The bottom line for you is that the Corporate Voices report successfully argues that employers should move from viewing flexibility as a perk or accommodation that benefits only the recipient to a management strategy that can drive profit.

The Business Case for Part-Time, Contract, or Consulting Work

In particular, allowing employees to work on projects primarily from home and/or on a part-time or flexible basis can also be a boon to companies' profits. It potentially lowers companies' real estate and benefit costs, in addition to reducing turnover, recruiting costs, and training costs. Those women who prefer to work part-time and who already have medical benefits through their husbands' companies don't have to receive benefits. This can be a huge potential savings to employers. If more employees job-share, telecommute, or work on a contract basis, firms may be able to make do with less office space, again a potential savings.

Finally, contract employees (those who are hired as independent consultants) can have special appeal to companies because they represent a variable cost, as opposed to the fixed cost of a full-time employee, and can be brought in on an as-needed basis.

Pulling It All Together—Overlooking Résumé Gaps and Offering Flexibility

To date, the goal of most employers' flexible and part-time programs has been to retain valuable employees and, to a lesser extent, to reattach former employees. But corporations would also enjoy cost savings if they allowed *relaunchers* to work in flexible arrangements, *not just current or former employees.* Perhaps more importantly, offering flexibility to relaunchers would allow employers to tap into a pool of high-caliber talent that might not be willing to work on a conventional full-time basis, but that could give their employers a significant competitive advantage.

The Relaunch Pool Is High Quality

If you think we're just dreaming this up to make you feel good, we're not. At a Merrill Lynch–sponsored 2005 job fair we attended in New York, designed specifically for at-home moms seeking to return to work, name-brand firms in finance, strategy consulting, law, and accounting were represented. We interviewed nearly all of the recruiters, and they consistently commented on how unusual it was to find such highly qualified applicants at a job fair. With almost 50 percent of the job seekers sporting graduate degrees, it was no wonder the recruiters were impressed.

Job fairs targeting stay-at-home moms suggest that cutting-edge employers have become more open to candidates lacking current experience. Indeed, Anne Erni, chief diversity officer of Lehman Brothers, commented that Lehman "is trying to impress upon every employee that the [relaunch] pool is a viable hiring pool just like the college and graduate school pools."[23] This is a pivotal development in the Relaunch Movement. But for the movement to really take off, employers have to not only open their doors to women with résumé gaps, but also give them the flexibility that will enable them to thrive in their new roles. With data now available documenting the positive impact of flexibility on profitability, convincing more employers to take both these steps seems possible.

Macroeconomic Factors

In getting employers to be more creative about whom they hire and where and how they put them to work, we're talking about major structural change. As evidenced by the relauncher success stories in this book, as well as the more family-friendly employer policies we describe here and in chapter 10, structural change has already begun. More people work in unconventional ways than ever before. Envisioning additional adjustments in the workplace, however, is more realistic in a full-employment economy. Fortunately, in terms of employer demand, long-term demographics are on relaunchers' side. "One reason businesses are getting serious about the brain drain is demographics. With boomers nearing retirement, a shortfall of perhaps 10 million workers appears likely by 2010," *Time* magazine reported.[24]

And these workers will not easily be replaced. According to the "Off-Ramps" study, "The baby bust generation is about to hit 'prime time,' with the number of workers in the 35 to 45 year old age group shrinking. Productivity improvements are flattening out [and] immigration levels are stable."[25] Finally, more than half of all college graduates today are women. Consultants Hirsch and Hills argue that there must be a sense of "organizational urgency" on the part of employers in order for them to hire new types of employees. We believe that the anticipated labor shortage and other factors noted above are creating "organizational urgency"; this will prompt employers to open their doors to relaunchers and to offer them the flexible work alternatives that will make their return more feasible.[26]

Your Role in the Relaunch Movement

Just as the early Stanford Business School graduates Zappert profiled were Pioneers, you are the pioneers of the Relaunch Movement, and you can help determine its course. By relaunching yourself, you'll be demonstrating to employers, still-at-home friends, and young women just starting their careers that returning to work after taking time out *is* possible. One of our goals for the Relaunch Movement is to trumpet so many examples of relauncher success that a résumé with an employment gap is immediately recognized as a relauncher's, with no stigma attached. When the number of relaunchers reaches critical mass, the word *relaunch* itself will become part of the vernacular. *Instead of asking how long a maternity leave a prospective mother is taking, people may inquire whether she is planning to take maternity leave or if she is going to take a few years out and then relaunch.*

Ideally, as a result of the supply-side push (from the increasing quantity and quality of the relauncher population) and the demand-side pull (from employers experiencing a labor shortage), a seismic shift in the labor market will occur. As more relaunched women successfully participate in the workforce, corporations will devote more resources to recruiting, accommodating, and integrating women from the stay-at-home pool. Professional schools will offer career relaunch educational programs. Women's organizations and work–life balance institutes will put career relaunching on the agenda. Indeed, a whole new industry will spring up to focus on relaunchers' personal and professional needs. Even the government may jump on the bandwagon with relaunch-oriented legislation. In fact, all of this has already started to happen. As you'll see in the next chapter, the Relaunch Movement is well on its way.

What Employers, Universities, and Others Are Doing for Relaunchers

Elsewhere in this book, we focused on how *you* can relaunch your career—the specific detailed steps you can take to identify and secure an opportunity that meets your personal and professional needs. In this chapter, we focus on the other side of the equation: what employers, universities, and others are doing for you, as a relauncher. As we indicated in the last chapter, many institutions have finally realized that the world does not divide easily into "women who work" and "women who don't." Employers have started to acknowledge that many of the women currently working full-time will leave if not given some flexibility, and that many of the women currently at home would gladly work if given a chance and/or, in some cases, a flexible schedule. More importantly, employers have begun to perceive the financial benefits of recruiting from the relauncher pool and of offering employees workplace flexibility.

Employer Initiatives

In fact, we think there's been a sea change in employer attitudes toward relaunchers. For example, in 2005, at least two job fairs were held in New York City where professional services and other primarily white-collar employers sought candidates from the stay-at-home pool. At the first fair, sponsored by career expert Tory Johnson's Women for Hire in June 2005, recruiting companies included Morgan Stanley, ADT Security Services, and Wachovia. The second fair, organized by Mothers Can Do It in October 2005, included Deloitte & Touche, IBM, Merrill Lynch, the Federal Reserve Bank of New York, and McKinsey, among others.

At the Mothers Can Do It job fair, we talked to a Federal Reserve Bank of New York representative who explained that *since there have been so many layoffs in the financial services industry, they are used to seeing people with gaps in their résumés.* A two-year gap, she said, they "could skip over" without much problem. Even women with longer résumé gaps, as many relaunchers have, were still considered viable candidates. "We would put these women through the same training programs as any new employee."

A different take on ignoring a résumé gap came from the representative for the strategy consulting firm McKinsey & Company. The very pregnant rep was about to begin her first maternity leave, after working there only eighteen months. She noted that the firm sometimes hires people (who are not relaunchers) who are older and making a midcareer change into consulting. She said these lateral hires start as associates, but their career trajectory may differ from that of a starting MBA because of their previous work experience. A woman who had not worked for McKinsey earlier in her career, and who was hired by McKinsey after a number of years at home, would have a status similar to that of these lateral hires. The rep also explained that a relauncher joining McKinsey wouldn't necessarily have to spend consulting's infamous weeks on the road. Travel requirements vary from office to office, depending upon the density of the local client base.

As further evidence that employers are looking more favorably upon relaunchers, a survey by CPRI (now Aquent), a Chicago company that places marketing professionals as temporary workers with Fortune 500 companies, "found that 94 percent of Fortune 500 companies were likely or somewhat likely to hire back a sequencing mother, but the biggest concern was familiarity with technology."[1]

On the flexibility front, we discovered a variety of corporate efforts, including the institution of flexible work arrangements, job shares, and mentoring programs, all aimed at preventing talented women from leaving their jobs in the first place. More importantly, companies are rolling out programs to encourage and enable women who want to take time out to stay connected to their firms and eventually return. Employers' increased openness to relaunchers and growing acceptance of flexible work arrangements signal huge paradigm shifts that should continue to benefit relaunchers.

The following is by no means an exhaustive list of relaunch-related initiatives, but merely a sampling to give you a sense of what's out there. Our goal in highlighting these model corporate practices is to inspire more companies to do the same. *We also want to give you the ammunition with which to approach employers and say, "Here's a successful model of how companies are making this work. Maybe we can try the same thing."*

The Lehman Brothers Encore Program

On November 1, 2005, Lehman Brothers kicked off the Encore Program in New York City, as an initiative designed to facilitate networking and professional development opportunities for women who have left the field of finance and are interested in reigniting their careers. As one of the sponsors of the Center for Work–Life Policy's "Off-Ramps and On-Ramps" study, Lehman Brothers made it a priority to respond to the study's findings, especially the idea that more than 90 percent of off-ramped women want to return to work, but only 74 percent have been able to do so. "The percentage of these women who have been able to return is probably even lower for women who were in the financial services industry," noted Anne Erni, who spearheaded the program.[2]

Erni herself is passionate about the issue. After eighteen years in corporate finance and sales and trading, Erni was one of the first women in the trading division to negotiate a flexible work schedule. For Erni, this came at a time when several of her female friends had already left Wall Street to start their own families. In 2001, Joe Gregory, Lehman Brothers' president and COO, asked Erni to found the firm's women's initiative and, ultimately, to make a move off the trading floor to become the firm's chief diversity officer.

Subsequent to the release of the 2005 "Off-Ramps and On-Ramps" study, Erni and other senior managers from Lehman Brothers launched the Encore initiative to recognize stay-at-home moms—or others who take time off—as a viable alternative talent source. "We recruit at undergraduate schools, grad schools, and competitors, but in terms of achieving diversity goals, there's just not enough talent there. If you want more women applying, you have to look at the at-home pool."

Lehman Brothers' inaugural Encore event included a panel discussion called Since You've Been Gone: A Look at the Trends and Developments in Investment Banking Over the Past Three Years. This panel was followed by a storytelling workshop, which helped the women practice articulating their own personal stories in anticipation of sharing them with potential employers and recruiters. Erni said, "Many women are either very insecure about their time at home or don't know how to talk about it without apologizing. By showing them how fables are constructed, we tried to give them those storytelling skills."

The Encore event concluded with a networking luncheon and an invitation to attendees to submit their résumés to the firm's lateral recruiters for employment opportunities. Within twenty-four hours, several of the seventy-one attendees followed up, and the firm has already hired some of the Encore participants.

Jodi Garner began her career as a bond trader at Lehman Brothers, later worked as a teacher overseas, and then switched into training and development at JP Morgan when she returned to the States. After taking two years off to spend time with her preschool-aged twins, she contacted former colleagues who encouraged her to attend the Encore event. Within six months Lehman Brothers offered her a job doing leadership development and sales training, working under her former boss from JP Morgan, who had joined Lehman Brothers. Jodi returned full-time, but works from home on Fridays.

Lehman Brothers held a similar Encore event in London in February 2006 and is developing plans for an event in Tokyo and a second New York event in the fall of 2006.

Ultimately, the firm's goal is not only to solve the brain-drain problem, but to brand Lehman Brothers as the best place on Wall Street for women.

Goldman Sachs' New Directions Program

Not surprisingly, another Wall Street bank, Goldman Sachs, also a sponsor of the "Off- Ramps" study, launched a similar program with approximately seventy women in New York in May 2006. New Directions: The Next Step in Your Career included an update on trends in finance, a workshop by Women@Work Network on how to brand yourself as you go through the recruitment process, and a panel discussion with female Goldman Sachs professionals who had taken career breaks and returned to the firm in high-powered yet family-friendly roles.

One of the panel participants, Analisa Allen, had worked for ten years in Goldman's fixed income technology department in New York before leaving to try to start a family with her boyfriend in Africa. Five years later, she returned to the States, with a husband and two little ones in tow. "In terms of the job market, I had three strikes against me. My tech knowledge was five years old, I was a returning mother, and people thought I was weird because I'd been living in the bush. I didn't get many offers, and the few I did get I didn't like." After four months of searching on the West Coast, she sent a letter to some of her former colleagues at Goldman in New York. She recieved an offer for a job that was challenging, but not overwhelming, and she has since become a managing director, as well as co-chair of the firm's women's initiative.

Elaine Phillips initially returned to Goldman to replace a woman in her old department who was on maternity leave. But when the new mother's leave ended, she decided she didn't want to come back full-time. So the two women requested and received permission to structure a job share. They're in the fifth year of their successful arrangement.

The six-hour New Directions event also included a networking lunch with current Goldman Sachs executives. Most important, the firm made it very clear that it's interested in recruiting from the at-home talent pool.

Other Initiatives, Financial Services

Merrill Lynch, Citigroup, and UBS are also involved in relauncher-oriented initiatives. Merrill Lynch sponsored the Mothers Can Do It job fair. Citigroup is sponsoring Dartmouth's Back in Business program (see below), and UBS, taking a grassroots approach, is also reaching out to former finance professionals now at home. These financial services industry titans obviously believe that recruiting relaunchers offers them a competitive advantage. Clearly, structural barriers to career reentry in the professional services are crumbling.

Extended Leave Programs

Extended leave programs have been around longer than the programs we described above. They enable companies to keep talented employees who have opted out from disappearing forever. They tend to be offered by large corporations with sizable inventories of job openings at any given time. Although they'll be of little use to you if you didn't work for one of the companies that offer them, you can use this information to goad your old employer into looking more favorably upon you and other former employees now at home. Here are two examples of successful extended leave programs.

Deloitte & Touche's Personal Pursuits™ Five-Year Leave Program

Personal Pursuits™ debuted in June 2004. When we interviewed W. Stanton Smith, Deloitte's national director of next-generation initiatives, in May 2005 about the details of the program, there were twenty-eight participants. Personal Pursuits gives employees the opportunity to take up to five years of unpaid personal leave and keep current through classes and mentoring during the leave period. The participants are guaranteed a job at the end of their time out, although not necessarily the same job they left.

The impetus for the program was the realization that "the really good people are hard to replicate in the market. What happens is we lose people at the higher levels and hire at the lower levels." *So while Deloitte's average employee count is stable, it does not reflect the net decrease in experience level.* Personal Pursuits is "a way of replacing employees who leave with experienced employees at very little cost to Deloitte," explained Smith.

Deloitte's program is offered to "high-performing"employees with a minimum of two years at the firm. The initial group was formed when Deloitte identified promising women who had already left the firm and asked if they wanted to participate. In the future, people will either self-nominate to the program, or nominate someone else they think would be a good candidate.

"The whole idea is to keep the participants connected with the firm. They are matched with a mentor who checks in with them and answers questions about access to the firm's resources. The Deloitte Learning Center offers courses to the Pursuits participants so they can keep current," explained Smith. Additionally, Deloitte pays professional association fees for women while they are on leave. The program keeps networks strong by scheduling professional and social events during the leave period.

At the time of our spring 2005 interview, Personal Pursuits was running as a pilot program. But when we checked in again a year later, the pilot had proved so successful that Deloitte was rolling it out firmwide. By June 2006, there were fifty participants, and although the program is open to both men and women, all but one were female.[3]

Eli Lilly and Company's Three-Year Leave Program

In 1991, one of Indianapolis-based pharmaceutical giant Eli Lilly's high-potential female employees had her first child and wanted to stay home, but was also committed to Lilly and wanted to leave the door open to return at some point. After she delivered her resignation speech, her boss, the executive vice president of compensation and benefits, instead of offering the usual *Good-bye and good luck,* responded, "Why do we want to lose such talent?" and conceived the idea of a three-year leave program right then and there.

The program, which is open to all Lilly employees, has become a signature benefit of the firm. One of the reasons it works so well is the company's size. There are approximately twenty thousand Lilly employees in the United States and forty-two thousand worldwide; at any given time, there are hundreds of opportunities in the Lilly internal job posting database for people returning from leaves to consider.

In March 2005, when we interviewed Candice Lange, then head of long-term leave programs at Lilly, about the program, she explained that 50 percent of participants return after their three-year leave, a much higher percentage than had returned from standard maternity leaves in the past. Most relaunch at the same level they left. Some find part-time work or job shares, both viable options at Lilly.

Not only has the leave program helped solve Lilly's talent retention problem, but it's also a powerful recruiting tool. Indeed, it's one of the reasons the firm has been named one of *Working Mother* magazine's "Top 10 Companies for Working Mothers" seven times, and a "100 Best Companies for Working Mothers" winner for eleven consecutive years.[4]

Flexibility Programs

According to a 2000–2001 survey of a thousand major US employers, Hewitt Associates found that 73 percent offered flexible work arrangements, up from 67 percent five years earlier.[5] We don't have the space here to detail all the new flexible arrangements that exist somewhere in the US employer universe. But we do want to throw out a few to stimulate your thinking. Pharmaceutical giant AstraZeneca has promoted job sharing and part-time sales jobs in its field sales force, yet the productivity of those involved in these programs, as measured by various metrics, has equaled that of their full-time peers. Marriott piloted a process in which hotel property managers were encouraged to "do whatever it takes to get your job done, but be flexible in how you do it." After six months, managers reported working, on average, five hours less per week than they had prior to the pilot with no negative impact on customer service scores. In various pilots testing a compressed workweek at PNC Bank, operational and financial metrics improved.[6]

Indeed, according to *The Wall Street Journal*'s Sue Shellenbarger, in addition to expanding their flexibility programs to cover a wider group of employees, employers are insisting that employees take more responsibility for the success of these programs and, in some cases, justify their requests for flexibility in terms of their impact on the bottom line. "To make flexible scheduling more fair, some employers are: allowing all employees to apply for flexible schedules; requiring proposals that outline how the plan will work; evaluating flexible setups regularly; making scheduling a team responsibility; training people to back up co-workers."[7]

With an overwhelmingly female workforce (80 percent), Children's Memorial Hospital in Chicago has married flexibility with an effort to pull new mothers back to work after maternity leave. They allow nurses to work three twelve-hour shifts or office staff members to work four ten-hour shifts. Another important change has been dropping the number of hours needed to qualify for benefits from eighty hours in a two-week period to seventy-two hours. This made it much easier for new mothers to return to Children's Memorial on a full-time basis. Additionally, the hospital lifted the cap on the number of part-time positions it could offer. According to Barbara Bowman, chief human resource officer at Children's, "A lot of hospitals budget for only a certain number of part-time positions," so a worker who wanted part-time hours would have to wait for a part-time position to come along. We realized that was counterproductive." On a combined basis, these initiatives have cut the hospital's turnover from 28 to 13 percent.[8]

High-Caliber Part-Time Positions

Medicine

And while we're on the subject of hospitals, as a result of an almost insatiable demand for health care professionals in certain regions of the United States, this industry has transitioned from being one of the most traditional (Marcus Welby, MD, treating patients 24/7) to one of the most progressive. Kaiser Permanente, the nation's largest HMO, hires per diem and part-time doctors, including relaunchers, in its Southern California region, where physician demand is acute. A major perk is that Kaiser's malpractice insurance policy covers doctors with part-time or per diem status. Private practices around the country have also reached out to relaunching physicians in an effort to round out their specialty offerings and provide female physicians to patients who might prefer them.

Leah, the thirty-five-year-old internist who had not practiced for three years whom we described in chapter 1, was invited to join a private practice run by two male friends from her residency. Some of their patients had repeatedly asked to see a woman physician. She worked two mornings per week, took no calls, and had her malpractice insurance payments picked up by the practice. "It makes me feel so good to hear about women entering medicine who plan to take off completely for a while to raise children. In the medical world, I feel very alone and odd to be so 'traditional' and 'nondriven' in my profession." In our view, the Leahs of the medical world are becoming much more common.

Management and Marketing Consulting

Change is also afoot in the competitive world of management consulting. To help combat consultant burnout, Marakon Associates, a large international strategy consulting firm, recently developed a benefit that could be a real boon to relaunchers: the "10&2" program. Under this program, any employee who has worked at Marakon for at least a year can take off up to two months on an unpaid basis every year. Surprisingly, according to Chief Operating Officer Lori Massad, "both men and women have taken advantage of this benefit."[9]

In general however, the all-consuming lifestyle of management consulting has prompted scores of women at the big firms to jump ship. For the most part, smaller firms have been the beneficiary of this exodus. We spoke to a couple of boutique consultancies that rely on big-firm alums to staff their client engagements. They have no problem hiring women with a résumé gap, as long as their prior experience was on-point. Indeed, the head of one such firm considers the relauncher pool a gold mine. "Hiring at-home moms with big-firm consulting experience on a part-time, project basis is a win–win for everyone: It helps me manage the ups and downs of demand, provides intellectually challenging, well-paid, but flexibly timed work for the consultants, and great-quality work for clients."

Mavens & Moguls, another boutique consultancy, also contracts with independent consultants on an as-needed basis. It promotes its revolving staff as one of its chief selling points. According to CEO Paige Arnof-Fenn, the source for these consultants is wide-ranging, but one important group is high-level former marketing consultants or corporate executives who are parents, including many moms. Consultants are called upon as particular assignments come in that fit with their background and geographic location.[10]

Booz Allen Hamilton's Adjustable Programs

Although smaller firms have been in the vanguard in tapping at-home talent, megasize management consulting firm Booz Allen Hamilton has created three programs for strategy consultants with varying restrictions on work hours and travel, usually due to child care considerations: the Internal Rotation Program, the Ramping Up, Ramping Down Program, and the Adjunct Program.

Borrowing its name from academia, the Adjunct Program is the most relevant for relaunchers. Under this pilot program, Booz Allen "unbundles" consulting assignments and farms out discrete components as contract work to high-potential consultants who have decided to take a career break to be home with children. Not only are there fifty-five Booz Allen alums in the program, but forty-five more women and men from competing consulting firms and industry also participate. Projects include client proposal writing, background work for responding to a client request for proposal, customer or competitor interviewing for due diligence (much of which is done by phone), regression analysis, and financial modeling.

According to DeAnne Aguirre, senior vice president, "This program is targeted at alums who leave voluntarily for work–life balance issues, but whom Booz Allen wanted to retain because they had partnership potential. These are people we didn't want to lose in the first place and who are valuable to meet our continuing growth trajectory."[11]

Maria Corina Perez worked full-time in Booz Allen's Venezuela office for two years before her daughter was born. Wanting to remain at Booz Allen, but no longer willing to travel, Maria Corina signed onto the Adjunct Program to ensure local assignments. Now she may work full-time for three months and then have a month off, and most of her projects are in Caracas, the city where she lives. Her occasional travel is limited to nearby cities, requiring at most one or two nights on the road, a major improvement over her former travel schedule. Her second child was born a month ago. "I'm not worried about adjusting to work and two children because I proved to myself I could maintain this work arrangement after having my first child. The Adjunct Program has allowed me to continue working at Booz Allen. I know I would have left if this option was not available, and I feel fortunate to have been able to take advantage of it."

Using Booz Allen's "Unbundling" Process to Carve Out a Perfect Job

We believe this unbundling process is transferable to other workplaces. Hidden within many organizations, discrete components of work can be identified and outsourced to relaunchers, whether former employees or not. We're not talking about scut work here. We're talking about meaty, résumé-worthy assignments. The onus to find such projects isn't on the employer alone; relaunchers themselves can identify and suggest a potential contract consulting assignment in order to test the waters with a company.

We see two ways to use unbundling: vertically, which means that instead of taking a full-time job managing an entire group of products or programs, you contract to *manage everything about just one of them;* or horizontally, which means *taking a single function across a group of products or programs.* Let's look at examples of each type of unbundling.

In chapter 3, we recount Carol's experience considering a full-time job with a nonprofit, where she would have been responsible for overseeing the launch of an umbrella of health care initiatives for low-income families. If Carol had only wanted to return part-time, or on a project basis, she might have proposed that the nonprofit hire her as a consultant to take on the launch of *just one* of the initiatives, reporting to a person in charge of the larger campaign. This is an illustration of vertical unbundling.

A university lecturer position is an example of horizontal unbundling. Tenured university professors usually focus on research and advising and teaching graduate students, while lecturers teach introductory courses to undergraduates. The lecturer may teach only one particular course, or she may string together lecturer assignments at the same or different educational institutions. Lectureships are becoming increasingly common because they bolster an academic department already heavily laden with tenured professors, at minimal additional expense. But the same principle of horizontal unbundling of assignments could be used in other, nonacademic environments.

Tapping Corporate Alumni

In an article addressed to women trying to reenter the workforce, Rhona Kisch, organizer of the 2005 Mothers Can Do It relauncher job fair, said, "Corporate America wants you. But they can't find you."[12] Increasingly, firms ranging from McKinsey, accounting firm Grant Thornton, law firm WilmerHale, to credit card company Capital One have taken steps to ensure that they don't lose track of their retiring talent by setting up corporate alumni Web sites. Modeled on the alumni Web sites of colleges and graduate schools, these online communities enable former employees to keep in touch with their former bosses and co-workers as well as with one another. From the firms' perspective, "An alumni network is a gold mine of skilled, experienced rehire candidates, referral resources, new business opportunities, and marketplace intelligence."[13] Although none of these alumni programs targets relaunchers per se, the growing popularity of these efforts suggests that employers increasingly realize the value of their *former* employees as potential *future* employees. This change in corporate attitude from out of sight out of mind to valuable potential recruitment pool will clearly benefit relaunchers.

University Initiatives

Professional schools have also started to realize that they have a role to play in preparing their alumnae (and others) to reenter the world of work after a long absence. We venture that more institutions will develop and promote course offerings to this constituency as they begin to understand the value generated by efforts such as those we describe below.

Harvard Business School

In May 2001, Harvard Business School (HBS) Professor Myra Hart led a new seminar for female HBS alums titled Charting Your Course: Alumnae Career Choices & Transitions. (This is the seminar that Vivian mentioned in the introduction.) The impetus for the program was the school's dawning realization that many of its female graduates were not currently in the full-time workforce but may, at some point, wish to reenter, and that HBS could *and should* help them negotiate this transition.

Then, in April 2006, HBS launched The New Path: Setting New Professional Directions, a five-and-a-half-day residential reentry program. The New Path offered participants "an opportunity to brush up on the latest business news, knowledge and skills plus build an effective job plan for the career that will bring personal and professional fulfillment."[14]

Tuck School of Business at Dartmouth

The Tuck School of Business at Dartmouth announced its relauncher reentry program, Back in Business: Invest in Your Return, in early 2006. Held over four weekends in New York City and Hanover, New Hampshire, in the fall of 2006, the residential program featured review and refresh components and a critical extra element: recruiters. Led by Citigroup Corporate and Investment Banking, corporate sponsors were on board to recruit program graduates. Women with

MBAs from leading schools and/or significant prior business experience participated.

Tuck sees this program as complementary to its existing summer "Bridge" program for liberal arts undergraduates who are about to begin business careers. The Bridge program has been so successful that many companies actually pay for their fresh-out-of-college recruits to attend it in preparation for their upcoming jobs. A similar model might appeal to companies for the Back in Business program. Companies might foot the bill for relauncher recruits to attend the Tuck program, or similar programs, because they believe it will significantly decrease the relauncher recruits' ramp-up time once on the job.[15]

Other University Initiatives

As of spring 2006, we had heard of three other business schools that were in the process of developing, or had developed, reentry seminars. The University of Virginia's Darden Graduate School of Business Administration held a two-day Re-Entering the Workforce workshop for its alumni and other business school graduates in the DC area in the fall of 2005. It will be partnering with other universities and companies to offer the program in various cities around the country in late 2006 and 2007. Baruch College's Zicklin School of Business in New York City distributed a detailed proposal for a reentry program still in development tentatively called Back to the Future: Re-entry Program for Women Returning to Work at a conference for MBAs thinking about resuming careers. And in May 2006, Babson College's Center for Women's Leadership in Massachusetts launched ACT II: Women Stepping Back into the Workforce. The five-hour introductory session, open to all comers, enabled participants to preview a more in-depth program to be held during the fall.[16]

Check our Web site (www.backonthecareertrack.com) for updates on additional reentry programs, and please contact us via this site if you hear of any new university programs for relaunchers.

Reentry Fellowships

In addition to the specific reentry programs described above, we uncovered several fellowships to fund relaunching women who need or want to update their academic credentials. Most of these grant programs are offered either by nonprofits, such as the Society of Women Engineers, or governmental institutions like the National Institutes of Health (NIH). As we mention in chapter 4, searching for "reentry scholarships" on the Web should pop out the latest possibilities. Following are two cutting-edge European reentry grant programs, as well as a similar program at the NIH. We hope the European programs will inspire more US institutions to develop similar reentry grants and fellowships for relaunchers.

The British Daphne Jackson Fellowships for Reentering Scientific Careers

The Web site headline for the Daphne Jackson Fellowships says it all: "The Daphne Jackson Trust enables scientists, engineers and IT specialists to return to work after career breaks."[17] Scientists who have taken *at least* a two-year career break to tend to family matters are eligible to submit a research proposal, *no matter how long they have been away from the field*. The grant is for a two-year half-time position with a corporate- or university-based sponsor. In an example of "what goes around, comes around," Dr. Margaret Rayman, a former Daphne Jackson fellow whom we profile in chapter 8, sponsors Daphne Jackson fellows in her lab.

European Molecular Biology Organization Restart Fellowships

This two-year fellowship targets research scientists who are returning to the laboratory after taking a career break of at least one year to care for children. Eligible candidates are researchers, female or male, who hold a PhD degree in the life sciences, and who have published at least one first-author paper in an international peer-reviewed journal.[18]

The National Institutes of Health Reentry Grants for
Scientific Research

Established in 1992, this program targets women who have been away from research for at least two years, but no more than eight years. Seventeen NIH institutes and centers support the grant program. Reentry supplements are viewed as a "bridge to independence" for a researcher. Candidates can be either out of the workforce or working in a non-research field when they apply. Grant applications are accepted year-round and usually fund two years of research but can sometimes cover three. According to Joyce Rudick, Director of Programs and Management for the NIH Office of Research on Women's Health, candidates must have a sponsor who is a "principal investigator of an existing NIH research grant with at least two years left on the grant. The supplement to the grant would be used to expand his or her grant to include your extra related research."[19]

In addition to the eligibility cap, NIH reentry grant candidates need to present evidence that they have kept up with the literature in their field. However, if your knowledge is already years stale, don't worry. Dr. Margaret Rayman hadn't eyeballed a scientific article in more than fifteen years. She caught up by spending concentrated time reading up on her field. *She feels strongly that you don't have to be reading all the way through your time away.* If you anticipate applying for one of these grants, designate a study period of several months to update yourself on new developments since you left your field.

Organizations and Businesses Serving Relaunchers

In addition to corporations and universities developing relauncher initiatives, other organizations now offer a variety of services that target women seeking to reenter, corporations seeking to recruit and/or retain women, including stay-at-home moms, or matchmaking between the two. Services for women include one-on-one career consulting, reentry seminars, newsletters, and advice regarding entrepreneurship and home-based businesses. Services targeting employers include recruiting and programs to aid parents at work. Matchmaking services include online job postings, career fairs, and seminars.

We highlight two of these below so you can get a sense of the types of services these organizations offer. For a more complete list of these organizations and businesses, please see the resources section.

The Women@Work Network Reentry Seminars

Women@Work Network, a Ridgefield, Connecticut, firm dedicated to helping moms who have taken time out to raise children get back into the workforce, offers reentry seminars and relauncher networking events. In April 2006, the group hosted a program titled MBA or MIA? How to Maximize Your Degree at All of Life's Ages and Stages, to discuss the realities of resuming work after a hiatus, from the perspectives of both employers and potential employees.

The Minerva Helping Women Work Reentry Program

The Minerva Foundation of Vancouver, British Columbia, has a longer-term relaunch program that begins with a two-day orientation retreat, then meets for five hours twice a week for three months, and concludes with a two-month job search period. The program helps women identify their long-term career goals as well as short-term steps they need to take to get going in the right direction. The participants, called protégées, also receive assistance overcoming mental blocks and emotional obstacles that may have prevented them from returning in the past. Each participant develops her own career reentry plan with support from a mentor group of top Vancouver professionals. Armed with the strategy and skills developed in the program, the protégée then embarks on her job search with Minerva staff available to counsel her during the process.

As we noted at the beginning of this chapter, the employer, university, and other initiatives we have described are only a sampling of the developments in the relaunch arena. Furthermore, we think the number of employers, universities, and others offering programs to recruit, train, and successfully integrate relaunchers will increase exponentially over the next ten years. In our epilogue, we peer into the future, both short-term and long-term, to see what's in store for those of you trying to relaunch now and for those who are just beginning their careers—the relaunchers of tomorrow.

The Future

People in the baby boom generation realize what they gave up to get ahead in the workplace, and a lot of times it's their families. They realize that it doesn't have to be that way.

—Executive at Best Buy, a company that is moving toward a completely flexible workforce

I'm petrified for my daughters about all this stuff. The two older ones are young lawyers. They're going to have to make some very hard decisions. They both look at their work as a job; they're less ambitious than [they] might appear. They want to raise their children the way they were raised [with Mom at home]. It's exhausting to have little children, and they want to do it well. They want a husband to be the primary breadwinner.

—Kim

The idea that these students think they will be able to drop out for ten years and then suddenly just reappear as if they never left is really offensive to those of us who stuck it out at work through our childbearing years. It is also incredibly unrealistic.

—A working mother's reaction to current undergraduates contemplating future relaunching

I s it realistic to think a relaunch-friendly world could ever exist? If so, what would it look like? As we describe in chapter 9, we believe a number of macroeconomic trends will drive change that benefits you, as well as future relaunchers. As the need for skilled labor intensifies, more and more workplaces will do everything in their power to protect their investment in their workforce. Companies will adopt and/or expand flexibility programs to keep highly trained workers from leaving. They will institute extended leave programs to maintain contact with and cheaply re-recruit and reintegrate employees who have, despite employers' best efforts, decided to take a break. Over time, an "extended leave track" will develop alongside other flexible career models. To assist these efforts, universities and other educational institutes will market reentry programs both to relaunchers and to employers.

In a parallel but nonetheless important development, independent consulting and entrepreneurship will continue to lure women away from traditional jobs, whether after a break for child rearing or not. However, the entrepreneurial sphere and the employer sphere are interdependent; if you become a consultant or entrepreneur, you'll buy from, sell to, and partner with conventional employers. We therefore expect more people to move into and out of consulting, entrepreneurship, and employee status at various phases of their lives. In short, just as you had dramatically more career options than your mother, we believe your daughters will have dramatically more *family-friendly* career options than you did, including more *relaunch* options.

For example, a unit of Wal-Mart in the UK has started offering older employees winters off so they can migrate to a warm climate during the cold season. The snowbirds then return to work for the summer. Similar approaches could and, we believe, will be applied to attract and retain relaunchers, who would probably appreciate reduced workloads during the summer months. Perhaps innovative employers might pair a snowbird with a relauncher for a year-round job share.

In addition to the impending workforce shortage due to retiring boomers and the paucity of workers in the succeeding generation, *the very nature of this next generation* is prompting employers to change. Surveys suggest that "Gen-X employees view work as secondary to their lives outside the office."[1] As a result, employers will continue to roll out flexibility programs to keep this talent from hopping to a more lifestyle-friendly workplace. Gen Yers or Millennials also demand special treatment: "Millennials aren't interested in the financial success that drove the boomers or the independence that has marked the Gen-Xers, but in careers that are personalized."[2] They want totally tailored, customized jobs that help them learn and grow as individuals. Thus, although Gens X and Y subtly differ in their attitudes toward work, they're both forcing employers to cater to their needs as human beings, and that's good for relaunchers of any age.

Change that benefits you and future relaunchers is inexorable. And it's getting bolder. Best Buy has been experimenting with Results-Oriented Work Environment, or ROWE, since 2002. Under this program, employees can work when and where they like, as long as they get the job done. Entire departments join the program together, so that no one is made to feel like a lightweight. Technology, such as "software that turns voice mail into e-mail files accessible from anywhere," gives employees the option to leave the office and work from home. By July 2006, twenty-three hundred employees at Best Buy's Minneapolis headquarters were participating, representing nearly 60 percent of the corporate employee population. The company is working on a version of the program for its hundred thousand US retail employees.[3]

Leaping from the Mommy Track to the Extended Leave Track

Gen X, Gen Y, and boomers aside, an additional underlying motivation for many of these moves is the recognition that women constitute a significant part of the workforce, and that "women have babies and men don't."[4] Indeed, Felice Schwartz, founder of the working women's advocacy group Catalyst, and coiner of that pithy phrase, was one of the first women to explore the ramifications of this obvious fact on employers, as well as on female employees. In her widely misunderstood 1989 article in *Harvard Business Review* titled "Management Women and the New Facts of Life," Schwartz asserted that "the cost of employing women in management is greater than the cost of employing men,"[5] as a result of career interrupting, plateauing, and turnover by women. To address this problem and enable employers to recoup their investment in women without losing valuable talent, Schwartz proposed that employers offer women who want to maintain their careers through their early mothering years an opportunity to work in part-time, flexible, or job-share arrangements. Unfortunately, within weeks of the article's publication she was assailed both for calling attention to a truth that no one wanted to acknowledge—that employing women was more expensive than employing men—and for advocating a subpar mommy track for women, whether they wanted it or not.

We think that Schwartz was not only wrongly maligned, but positively prescient. She never suggested that mothers be *pushed* onto her so-called mommy track, just that the option should be made available to them. *In fact, all the accommodations and backroom deals for flexibility that mothers have negotiated over the last twenty years are, in essence, mommy tracks.* Accounting firms' and others' recent flexibility and retention programs are also mommy tracks, although you'll never hear any of their proponents call them that.

But the fact remains that we need an extended leave track, one enabling women who have opted out to rejoin their company after a career break. From employers' perspective, women who opt out tend to leave their companies after five to ten years, just when they are on the brink of their highest productivity and profitability levels. By hiring these women back after a period of years away, employers can recoup their initial investment in them.

We purposely do not call the extended leave track the relaunch track, because not all relaunchers will return to their former employer. Yet the benefits of an extended leave track will trickle down to other relaunchers. *The presence of an extended leave track at prestigious firms destigmatizes the résumé gap.* More importantly, other employers will start to realize that there's talent worth considering in the relauncher pool, beyond just their own alumnae. Employers will start to view relaunchers from competing companies in the same way they view potential lateral hires who did not take career breaks. Your résumé will no longer be rejected simply because you haven't worked for five years.

Relauncher Recertification Programs Benefit Employers, Universities, and Relaunchers

The relaunch-friendly world of the future will most certainly include generic as well as customized relauncher ramp-up or recertification programs. A company could contract with a business school or other graduate school to enroll groups of relaunchers in an off-site but customized recertification program prior to their returning to work. Companies would then have a completely outsourced alternative for ramping up their relaunching employees, and a comfort level that these employees would hit the ground running. Universities would be able to leverage their generic recertification programs across a number of client companies, thereby turning them into profit centers. And relaunchers would get a concentrated review-and-refresh boot camp underwritten by their employer. Just as MBA programs proliferated, so will relauncher recertification programs. And as with the MBA programs, this expansion will also lead to increased specialization: distance learning, and programs with a special functional or employer emphasis, such as marketing or nonprofits, will develop. A win–win for all involved.

The Next Generation

In September 2005, *The New York Times* ran a story titled "Many Women at Elite Colleges Set Career Path to Motherhood."[6] According to the article, 60 percent of 138 Yale freshman and senior women indicated in an e-mail survey that when they had children, they planned to cut back on work or stop working entirely. The article then quoted various professors and students at Yale and other elite universities who corroborated these findings.

Although critics argued that the Yale e-mail survey was based on way too small a sample to be valid, our sense is that the survey accurately identified a shift in women's attitudes toward careers. Young women coming out of college and graduate programs today have a heightened awareness of work–family trade-offs in stark contrast to the near-tunnel vision that many women in prior generations displayed.

Part of the reason, cited by the *Times,* is that today's graduates observed their mothers struggling with work–family balance and concluded that "having it all" is too difficult. But part of the reason may also be the new Gen-X and Gen-Y attitude toward work. As we noted above, *balance* has become the watchword not just for the women of Gens X and Y, but for the men as well.

Are Family-Friendly Careers the Way to Go?

The multimillion-dollar question for the women of the Yale survey, and others just starting out, is whether they should choose their career based on work–life balance considerations.

We're conflicted on the answer to this question, and obviously influenced by our own experiences. Because we were both highly ambitious, we pursued killer jobs out of business school with no thought as to how we'd manage our careers once we became pregnant. We thought we were as talented as the guys sitting next to us, and we believed women could and should compete neck and neck with male peers for the highest-paying jobs. And to a large extent, we still hold that belief. On the other hand, we know that many women who chose less demanding careers (with lower starting salaries) were able to integrate motherhood more easily into their lives, without opting out. Their lives, overall, have been more balanced. And their lifetime earnings will probably exceed those who opted out, unless the latter relaunch.

Maybe if women vote with their feet and avoid the killer jobs, not only will their own lives be easier, but they'll eventually force the killer employers to become more family-friendly. If women choose to work at companies precisely because they offer relauncher-friendly programs and policies, then growing numbers of employers will view having these programs and policies as a competitive advantage.

From the perspective of women's advancement, however, we wouldn't want to see women give up hard-won ground; we'd hate to see the former men's clubs of finance and physics become men's clubs once again, because women decide to pursue careers in more family-friendly fields from the get-go. This will reinforce the old stereotype that women can't hack it in these arenas. Moreover, if women coming out of college and graduate school primarily take lower-paying "lifestyle" jobs while men continue to grab the highest-paying positions, then over time an imbalance will develop between average starting salaries of men and women graduates. Most business and law schools focus on the starting salaries of their graduates as a way to establish a peer ranking. Some institutions might conclude that one way to raise the averages would be to reduce the number of women admitted to each class. While we think this consequence is unlikely, the salary imbalance itself is disturbing.

Bottom line: We don't think we can give one-size-fits-all advice about whether young women today should choose their careers based on their family friendliness. There are strong personal and societal arguments to be made on both sides. Probably the best advice we can give is to pursue your passion, whether you're just starting out or re-launching. If you're fired up about finance, for example, go for it. Don't restrict yourself to more family-friendly options if you're compelled by something else. And don't assume a certain field is family-unfriendly without a thorough exploration. Medicine, for example, has become a surprisingly flexible career, as we've noted throughout this book. On the other hand, if you're drawn to family-friendly fields, pursue them. Their family-friendly nature will be an added bonus.

Taking Turns

Some women opt out with the thought that when they relaunch, their husbands might be able to downshift as they themselves begin bring-ing in money. Carol and her husband, Steve, had the idea that over a five-to-ten-year period, Carol would ramp up her career and Steve would ramp down his. Essentially they would trade places during this transition period. She realized after a year into her very demanding relaunch job that, if she and her husband were serious about this goal, she would have to spend longer days at the office. She would essen-tially have to pay her dues all over again. Carol had worked long days the first time around, but in a different company and in a related but different field. Plus, she didn't have any kids back then! Paying dues with four children at home wasn't practical. And although her hus-band could downshift a bit, *her income would not become large enough, quickly enough, to enable him to drop down to a part-time situation.* So unless you're on an extended leave track with your old employer (and can therefore eliminate the dues paying), and your retirement and kids' college accounts are fully funded, taking turns with your spouse will be difficult, if not impossible, to achieve.

Advice About Opting Out and Relaunching for Women Just Starting Their Careers

Despite our reluctance to push one type of career over another, we are willing to take a position on opting out. We believe that keeping a toe in the water, through consulting or some sort of part-time position, makes a future relaunch much easier. Although some of the women we interviewed either desired a complete break or involuntarily found themselves at home as a result of a spousal relocation, employer bankruptcy, or downsizing, most would have preferred to stay involved in the work world on a part-time or flexible basis. A few of our interviewees confessed, however, that although they might have preferred to work part-time rather than quit, their years home full-time gave them the freedom and distance to reevaulate their career goals and pursue different, more satisfying directions when they relaunched. Nevertheless, we believe that the compromise of maintaining some professional activity while at home allows you time for family and self-reflection but still keeps you professionally connected.

For the benefit of women just beginning their careers, we present below the collective wisdom of our interviewees, career experts, and the two of us on the subject of opting out and relaunching. If the advice seems conflicting, that's because it is. We're trying to address the range of situations in which women may find themselves over the course of their career.

Establish a Strong Professional Reputation

No matter how difficult, try to invest at least five or so years in your career up front. This gives you time to make a mark at your employer, as well as get a start on building a professional network. Having done this puts you in a better position to negotiate either flexibility or extended leave time during your early childbearing years, or to relaunch based on old relationships. The ideal goal would be to maintain a long-term working relationship with one employer, and resume full-time work when the time is right for you. However, the references and connections you gain from having established a strong reputation early in your career will serve you even if you end up relaunching in a different direction.

Acquire Transferable Skills

Susan, the former management consultant who relaunched into the public school system, weighed in with some savvy advice. "If I were to do it over again, I don't think it's so much a question of whether I'd take the killer job or the lifestyle job; I'd focus on getting certain portable skills, like learning how to sell and negotiate. That's what I'd tell women just starting out to focus on."

Know When to Quit

Charlotte, a managing director at a Wall Street firm who relaunched at a major executive search firm, left the workforce twice over her long career. Her first leave was to be home full-time with her kids; her second, to care for her aging parents. Her number one piece of career advice was given to her by her mother—ironically, a stay-at-home mom: "Leave the party when you are having the best time." In other words, if you do your very best work and leave on good terms, your professional reputation will remain intact for when you want to return later. This is why Charlotte left a second time. "I didn't see how I could do a good job at work and be involved in caring for my mother. I didn't want to hurt my professional reputation. So you need to know when to quit. Don't wait too long to leave until you have too many conflicts and are not doing your best work. Quit when you are at the top of your game."

Pay Your Dues Early On so You Don't Have to Quit

Women who have paid their dues by working hard for five or more years with the same company build up enormous credibility and have the best chance of successfully negotiating special requests to accommodate changes in their personal lives. You need to be fortunate enough to be in a company that (a) is around for that long, (b) you enjoy working for enough to stay around for that long, and (c) finds you valuable enough to keep you that long.

If you manage to gain flexibility, you may never feel the need to opt out. This is probably the optimal situation for you and your family. If you work while your children are young, your children will take it for granted that "that's what mommies do." The problem with certain fields, such as news reporting and producing, big-firm strategy consulting, big-firm law, 24/7 high tech, investment banking, and tenure-track academia, is that the dues paying typically spans at least ten years. In addition to seeming interminable, these years also happen to coincide with women's peak fertility period. Thus, many professional women, particularly those who attend graduate school as single women in their late twenties, face incredible pressure to establish a fabulous career, marry, and get pregnant, all within a five-year time frame. This practically impossible scenario was the central theme of Lia Macko and Kerry Rubin's 2004 book *Midlife Crisis at 30.*[7] The interview subjects of Sylvia Ann Hewlett's 2002 book *Creating a Life* failed to pull it all off; demanding careers combined with their dates' distaste for high-powered women kept them from marrying and/or having children.[8] A sobering thought for those just starting out.

Don't Wait Too Long to Have Children
Which brings us to our next point. If you want a family, don't put it off for too long. We all have far too many friends who fell for the media propaganda that they could have babies whenever they wanted, and put off getting pregnant until their late thirties or forties, only to encounter infertility and complicated pregnancies. And these problems not only thwart families, but also can wreck careers.

If You Do Leave, Stay Connected

Although you may be tempted to wallow in motherhood, cut ties to the office, and plunge headlong into your maternal world, don't. If you ever hope to return to work again, the more you keep in touch with colleagues and trends in your field, the easier it will be. Even if you think you'll want to make a career change, maintaining your professional connections will boost your confidence, and that will serve you in any profession.

The Dream Job of the Future . . . Today

Before we close (and let you get on with relaunching), we want to tell you about Robyn Davis and Mary McNamara, two close friends who have job-shared the managing directorship of Angel Healthcare Investors LLC since January 2000. Both had downshifted from intense careers, yet together managed to compete for, win, and successfully sustain a high-level job share in the demanding field of early-stage venture capital investing. Following a high-powered career at Fidelity Investments, Mary "stepped off the MBA track" to spend more time with her family, and started consulting projects after being home for one year. Robyn held full-time positions in management consulting and merchant banking until 1996, when she had her second child, and eventually took on consulting assignments.

Mary and Robyn talked on the phone often, swapping stories about their children and their work. One day, Robyn had an epiphany. "I distinctly remember it. I had just spent the whole Thanksgiving weekend in New York on a big consulting project for a major financial institution, with a five-year-old and a three-year-old back in Boston. I was exhausted and frustrated. I was talking to Mary and I remember telling her, 'I want a job I can do from home, that is Internet-dependent, that is part-time, where I can work with an incredibly stimulating group of people in a growth industry, and I want equity!'" They both laughed and promptly forgot about it.

Two days later, Mary received a call from a business school classmate who said he had been offered an interesting job, but that it didn't
have the career path he was looking for. "However, he told the folks
who offered him the job that he knew an MBA who was looking for
part-time work—that would be me—and thought she would be a perfect fit. It sounded like a great opportunity, but the time was not right
for me. My father had died just six weeks before and my mother died
six weeks prior to my father. It would not have been prudent to take on
something so unknown in terms of 'share of mind' given my state of
mind. But it was an opportunity too good to let slip away.

"So I called Robyn and told her I found a great job that was what
she had described to me literally days earlier." Robyn said, "Only if you
do it with me. We can job-share the part-time job." Mary responded,
"That's nuts. There's no way they will go for that." Robyn replied:
"Then we won't get the job."

On that basis they went in and applied together. To their surprise, they
found that two of the founders were co-CEOs who job-shared (though
they didn't call it by that name), and they were open to the idea.

When Robyn and Mary began their managing director job share
at Angel Healthcare LLC, there were thirteen angel investors and only
one investment. Now, six years later, they have an investor group of
forty-seven people and twenty-five completed deals, representing seventeen million dollars of equity in over a billion dollars of transaction
value. "I thought we would be working ten to fifteen hours a week each
the first year," Robyn related, "but the reality was we were each working
twenty or sometimes even thirty hours a week that year. The market
became challenging, yet our growth trajectory continued. We realized
we needed some help and hired a twenty-dollar-per-hour MBA student intern to work ten to fifteen hours a week. When he graduated, we
offered him a competitive package for a full-time job. We have trained,
mentored, and promoted him. Now, although we are much bigger, we
each work ten to fifteen hours a week because we have our MBA director full-time and the business is well oiled and efficient."

They also credit technology as the major component that allowed them to pull this off. "We are Web-based, and we use many of the new virtual tools. We share a work e-mail, voice mail, and an assistant, so we don't spend a lot of time updating each other in person. We laughingly call ourselves 'seamless and redundant.'"

Mary added: "Our founder's single stipulation of seamless communication laid the foundation for our success. We each stood behind any and all work that the other did. While one of us would occasionally handle a situation differently than the other, never did Robyn or I ever blame or fault the other. On numerous occasions and to this day, we each will take the brunt of the other's decisions simply because we are on the receiving end when a client has a question, challenge, or issue. Our trust in each other is implicit and is reaffirmed over time. United we stand—hokey but true—that is why our partnership thrives." By harnessing technology, maintaining steadfast loyalty to each other, and leveraging their professional relationships, Robyn and Mary crafted a dream job share in a demanding, competitive field with work that is meaty, fairly compensated, *and flexible.*[9]

You, Too, Can Get Back on the Career Track!

Like Robyn and Mary, relaunchers everywhere are tearing at the traditional fabric of the job—challenging their own and employers' assumptions about when, where, and how work gets done. This ultimately will help make the workplace more flexible for everyone—from new mothers seeking to spend more time with their children to men and women with other caregiving responsibilities or extensive nonwork interests. As the pool of qualified relaunchers swells and labor markets tighten, employers will increasingly welcome nontraditional candidates and approaches. The most forward-thinking US institutions—both large and small—have already taken steps toward creating a more relaunch-friendly world.

Don't get us wrong; we're not Pollyannas. Relaunching your career still isn't easy. But *it is doable*. Like the relaunchers we interviewed for this book, you, too, can find or create work that works for you. As you begin your relaunch, we'd love to hear your story and keep you updated about developments in the Relaunch Movement. Log on to www.backonthecareertrack.com to stay informed and let us know how it's going.

Resources

The following is not a comprehensive list of resources, but rather a sampling of what is offered in each category. Check our Web site, www.backonthecareertrack.com, for updates.

Chapter 2. Learn Confidence
Confidence Building

Michele Phillips: Confidence/self-esteem seminars, consulting. www.keyseminars.org.

Chapter 3. Assess Your Career Options
Compensation Rates for Specific Positions and Industries

America's Career InfoNet Wages and Trends: Detailed wage directory by occupation and location. www.acinet.org/acinet/occ_rep.asp.

Monster.com: Has a "Salary Wizard" that calculates your market worth, but you have to supply your e-mail address to receive the results. http://promotions.monster.com/salary/?WT_srch=1.

Salary.com: A quick read on salary information. www.salary.com.

The Wall Street Journal: Web site has career section with a feature allowing you to pull up salary information on various jobs and functions. www.careerjournal.com/salaryhiring.

Diagnostic Tests (such as Strong-Campbell) to Assess Career Interests and Skills

Career Leader: Career diagnostic site designed specifically for people interested in business. Alumni from dozens of universities are eligible for a discount. www.careerdiscovery.com.

Quintessential Careers: Career information site includes a table that rates a number of online career assessment tools in terms of price, ease of use, and efficacy with direct links to those tools. www.quintcareers.com/online_assessment_review.html.

Books

See Bolles, Burton/Wedemeyer, Ibarra, Jansen, Lassiter, and Ryan in "Recommended Books."

Assessing Career Options

The Entrepreneurial Parent: Business and personal advice and information for parents looking to balance work and family on their own terms. www.en-parent.com.

Flex-Time Lawyers LLC: "A networking and support organization for lawyers who work a flexible and/or reduced schedule." Flex job board. Members meet monthly for lunch. www.flextimelawyers.com.

Franchise Solutions for Women: Directory of franchise opportunities that can be accessed by size of investment required and other criteria. www.franchisesolutionsforwomen.com.

Home-Based Working Moms: "A professional association and online community of parents who work at home and those who would like to." www.hbwm.com.

Jobs and Moms Career Center: Focuses on all career options for women, including contract work. Job board, newsletter, advice column, and more. www.jobsandmoms.com.

Jobs for Moms: Focuses on working from home and directory of home-based businesses. www.jobsformoms.com.

Mom Inventors—Moms Helping Moms: Advice, news, "Mom of the Month," and a retail eBay site for inventions. www.mominventors.com.

Mom M.D.—Connecting Women in Medicine: Online community for women physicians. Job board for women physicians including flexible and part-time options. Also articles, forums, and resources for doctors in all life stages. www.mommd.com.

New England Mothers Organization: Job board, advocacy, and scholarships. www.nemothers.org.

Women for Hire: High-caliber career expos for women (not just relaunchers), speeches, seminars, career-focused magazine, and online job board. www.womenforhire.com.

Chapter 4. Update Your Professional and Job Search Skills, and Prepare for the Interview

Relaunch Scholarships and Grants (also see chapter 10 resources below)

The Educational Foundation for Women in Accounting: Women in Transition Scholarship for women returning to school to earn a bachelor's degree in accounting. www.efwa.org/scholarships.htm.

Institute of Physics, UK: British organization awarding grants to attend physics conferences to stay in touch with the field while on career break. http://careers.iop.org/Resources/Awards.html.

National League of American Pen Women: Scholarships for "mature women," female undergraduates thirty-five or older, majoring in art, writing, or music. www.americanpenwomen.org/membership.

New England Mothers Organization: Funding for classes that help a relauncher realize her career goals. www.nemothers.org.

Society of Women Engineers: Engineering reentry scholarships for moms who have been out at least two years. www.swe.org (look under "Scholarships" and then "Reentry").

University of California–Riverside: Reentry Scholarship Program: For UC Riverside alums who are "reentry student[s]—over age 25, pursuing a bachelor's degree after an interruption in their education of at least two years." *Check your own alma mater to see if a similar scholarship exists.* www.alumni.ucr.edu/about/reentry.html.

Women's Enterprise Development Center, Inc.: Small Business

Administration–funded microenterprise development program providing training on how to start your own business, microloans and grants for
starting small businesses, and life skills workshops to get over hurdles to
starting businesses. www.wedc-westchester.org.

University Relaunch Programs

Babson College, Waltham, MA: Act II: Stepping Back into the Workforce
is a two-day program open to all, but Babson alums get a discount. www.
babson.edu/CWL/events/Act-II-Stepping-Back-Into-the-Workforce.

Baruch College, Zicklin School of Business, New York, NY: Back to
the Future: Re-entry Program for Women Returning to Work, in development; certificate program, one day a week on alternating Fridays and
Saturdays, for twelve weeks. Bachelor's degree in any subject required. Contact Cynthia Thompson, PhD, at (646) 312-3644 or cynthia_thompson@
baruch.cuny.edu for updates and more information.

Harvard Business School, Boston, MA: A New Path: Setting New
Professional Directions, a five-day residential reentry program for HBS
graduates only; and Charting Your Course: Discovering Working Options,
a two-day nonresidential career transition assessment seminar for graduates of leading business schools. www.alumni.hbs.edu/lifelong_learning/
alumni_programs.html.

Hastings College of the Law Center for WorkLife Law, San Francisco,
CA: Opting Back In and Forging Ahead: Helping Women Return to the
Law, a four-session program focusing on job searching and updating legal
skills. Check www.worklifelaw.org. Also, see the center description below
under chapter 9 resources.

Tuck School of Business at Dartmouth, Hanover, NH: Back in
Business: Invest in Your Return includes eleven (residential) days over
four alternating weekends in Hanover and New York City. MBA or
MBA-equivalent work experience required. www.tuck.dartmouth.edu/
backinbusiness.

University of Virginia Darden School of Business, Charlottesville,
VA: Re-entering the Workforce is a two-session workshop held around

the country. Contact Connie English in Darden Alumni Career Services at (434) 924-4876 or AlumniCareerServices@darden.virginia.edu for more information.

Independent, Institutional, and Nonprofit Relaunch Programs

American Bar Association: Back to Business Law provides "continuing legal education programs and informal networking opportunities for attorneys who temporarily leave active practice in law firms or corporate settings." www.backtobusinesslaw.org.

Minerva Foundation—Minerva Helping Women Work: Career Exploration Program is a sixteen-week (two days a week during school hours) comprehensive career reentry program with intensive mentoring support. Also six-session Career Exploration Workshop, six-session Job Ready Workshop. In British Columbia. www.theminervafoundation.com/programs/mhww_programdetails.html.

Women@Work Network: Opportunity Knocks career reentry seminars are offered online. Also Inspiration Forums conference calls and Networking Coffees speaker series (in metropolitan New York). www.womenatworknetwork.com.

Women's Enterprise Development Center, Inc.: See above under "Relaunch Scholarships and Grants." www.wedc-westchester.org.

Sample Résumés

See "Sample Résumés of Real Relaunchers."

Career Counselors

According to AARP, "Career counseling and coaching services are booming in the U.S. One result is that you have more choices than ever before. Another result is that people with no special training can represent themselves as career professionals. Check references and credentials, especially for independent professionals. This can get complicated. But it's essential. State governments regulate counselors, but not coaches or other career professionals." (www.aarp.org/money/careers/choosecareer/occupational-info/a2004-05-19-careercounselor.html)

Mary Burton: President, Burton Strategies, New York, NY. burton-strategies@earthlink.net.

Pam Lassiter: President, Lassiter Consulting Career Management Services, Boston, MA. www.lassiterconsulting.com.

Career Counselors Consortium: East Coast directory of career counselors. www.careercc.org.

National Board for Certified Counselors: Counselors in all fields with the National Certified Counselor designation. www.nbcc.org/counselorfind2.

National Career Development Association: Click on "Need a Career Counselor?" for a listing by state. www.ncda.org.

Life Coaches

See "Career Counselors," above; the same caveat applies to life coaches. Life coaches range from the purely practical-minded to the spiritual to the holistic. If you decide to hire one, make sure his or her style and background are right for you.

Persephone Zill: Career and life strategy coach since 1997. www.persephonezill.com.

The Coach Connection: Service to identify and hire a life coach. www.findyourcoach.com/find-your-coach-lvl2.htm#tcc.

International Coach Federation: Coach referral service requiring registration. www.coachfederation.org/ICF/For+Coaching+Clients/Find+a+Coach/Coach+Referral+Service.

Chapter 5. Network, Market Yourself, and Clinch the Opportunity

Relauncher Matchmakers

Career Women: Robust, women-oriented recruitment site with lots of job postings, career information, and links to relevant sites. www.career-women.com.

Flexibility Alliance: Career matching service for employers and relaunching moms interested in full-time, part-time, or flexible work arrangements, and contract consulting. Online community, research, annual sequencing event for women (San Francisco Bay area). www.flexibil-ityalliance.org.

Flexible Resources, Inc.: Search firm promoting flexible work arrangements. www.flexibleresources.com.

Mom Corps: Search firm for contract consulting or part-time work for accounting, IT, legal, and marketing professionals. Offices in Atlanta and Washington, expanding to other cities. www.momcorps.com.

Vista Staffing Solutions: Not for relaunchers per se, but specializes in locum tenens physician and other health care professional placements. www.vistastaff.com/physicians/locum_tenens.php.

W2W Ventures: Career matching service promoting flexible work arrangements, including job shares, contract consulting, part-time jobs, and entrepreneurship, and providing support and resources. Champions program allows women to keep current through classes and contract work, either sponsored by their old employer or funded themselves. www.w2wventures.com.

Freelance Matchmakers

Aquent: Temporary and permanent placement of professionals in freelance, contract, or full-time opportunities. Specializes in creative services, marketing, and health care. www.aquent.com.

Business Talent Group: Matches top-tier talent with employers for consulting or interim assignments; based on the West Coast. www.businesstalentgroup.com.

Guru.com: A robust Web site for freelance talent in creative, IT, business consulting, and office/admin categories. www.guru.com.

Msquared: Provides independent consultants at all management levels as interim employees to companies. www.msquared.com.

Books

See McGovern, Pink, and Huff in "Recommended Books."

Chapter 6. Channel Family Support

Dinner Preparation Centers

Individuals or groups book a two-hour time block once a month to cook a month's worth of prepared meals in a fully stocked kitchen. Menu options change monthly. Some centers offer prepared meals they make for you. Some deliver. Franchising opportunities available! Here are a few of them: www.dreamdinners.com, www.maindishkitchen.com, www.super-suppers.com, www.thesuppershop.com.

Chapter 9. The Relaunch Movement

Organizations and Businesses Serving Relaunchers

Boston College Center for Work & Family: "National leader in helping organizations create effective workplaces that support and develop healthy and productive employees." Research, professional development, workplace partnerships. www.bc.edu/centers/cwf.

Catalyst: "Catalyst conducts research on all aspects of women's career advancement and provides strategic and web-based consulting services globally." www.catalystwomen.org.

Center for Work–Life Policy: Research and policy organization serving member employers concerned with issues of parenting and the workplace. Click on "Resources for On-Ramping" to purchase "Off-Ramps and On-Ramps" study or article. www.worklifepolicy.org.

Families and Work Institute: "A nonprofit center for research that provides data to inform decision-making on the changing workforce, changing family and changing community." www.familiesandwork.org.

Hastings College of the Law Center for WorkLife Law: "A research and advocacy center that seeks to eliminate employment discrimination against caregivers such as parents and adult children of aging parents." Its director, Professor Joan C. Williams, is a prominent writer and researcher on women's work issues, especially as they pertain to law. www.worklife-law.org.

MIT Workplace Center: Redesigning Work, Family, Community Connections: Mission is to build "a mutually supportive relationship between the performance of firms and the well-being of employees, their families, and communities." http://web.mit.edu/workplacecenter.

Mothers and More: A nonprofit membership organization for sequencing women. Through chapters and web offerings, Mothers and More serves 7,500 nationwide. www.mothersandmore.org.

New England Mothers Organization: Job posting board for flexible jobs, newsletter, advocacy alerts, scholarships. www.nemothers.org.

When Work Works: "A nationwide initiative to highlight the importance of workforce effectiveness and workplace flexibility as strategies to enhance businesses' competitive advantage in the global economy and yield positive business results." www.whenworkworks.org.

Women Returner's Network: UK research and lobbying organization. Most valuable part of this site (for UK relaunchers) is the "Links" section. www.women-returners.co.uk.

Chapter 10: What Employers, Universities, and Others Are Doing for Relaunchers

Corporate Relauncher Programs

Goldman Sachs New Directions Program: This program was created "to facilitate networking and professional development opportunities for women who have left the workforce and are looking to return" (from their Web site). Résumés should be submitted to the Careers section of the Goldman Sachs Web site: www.gs.com. Go to Recruitment and Application Process. Continue with Apply Online for Experienced Applicants. Indicate that you heard about Goldman Sachs through "NEW DIRECTIONS" and type the program name in the free format field.

Lehman Brothers Encore Program: "Encore is a Lehman Brothers global initiative designed to facilitate networking and professional development opportunities for individuals, both women and men, who have left the workforce and are interested in resuming their careers in financial services" (from their Web site). Send inquiries and/or résumés to www.encore@lehman.com.

University Relauncher Programs—See chapter 4 resources

Scientific Research Relauncher Grants—Also see chapter 4

Daphne Jackson Fellowships (UK): Funds a two-year half-time position with a corporate or university-based sponsor following a career break of at least two years. www.daphnejackson.org.

European Molecular Biology Organization Restart Fellowships: This two-year fellowship targets research scientists who are returning to the laboratory after taking a career break of at least one year to care for children. www.embo.org/fellowships/index.html.

National Institutes of Health Reentry Grants: Targets women who have been away from lab research from two to eight years. A supplement to an existing NIH research grant of a full-time researcher, the reentry supplement usually funds two years of research but can sometimes cover three. Contact rudickj@mail.nih.gov for more information.

Recommended Books

Babcock, Linda, and Sara Laschever, *Women Don't Ask: Negotiation and the Gender Divide* (Princeton, NJ: Princeton University Press, 2003).

Bolles, Richard Nelson, *What Color Is Your Parachute? A Practical Manual for Job-Hunters and Career-Changers* (Berkeley, CA: Ten Speed Press, 2004).

Bridges, William, *JobShift: How to Prosper in a Workplace Without Jobs* (Reading, MA: Perseus Books, 1994).

Burton, Mary Lindley, and Richard A. Wedemeyer, *In Transition: From the Harvard Business School Club of New York's Career Management Seminar* (New York: HarperCollins, 1991).

Cardozo, Arlene Rossen, *Sequencing: A New Solution for Women Who Want Marriage, Career, and Family* (New York: Atheneum, 1986).

Chira, Susan, *A Mother's Place: Choosing Work and Family Without Guilt or Blame* (New York: HarperCollins, 1998).

Covey, Stephen R., *The 7 Habits of Highly Effective People: Powerful Lessons in Personal Change* (New York: Simon & Schuster, 1989).

Crittenden, Ann, *The Price of Motherhood: Why the Most Important Job in the World Is Still the Least Valued* (New York: Henry Holt and Company, 2001).

————, *If You've Raised Kids, You Can Manage Anything: Leadership Begins at Home* (New York: Penguin Group, 2004).

De Marneffe, Daphne, *Maternal Desire: On Children, Love, and the Inner Life* (New York: Little, Brown and Company, 2004).

Ellison, Katherine, *The Mommy Brain: How Motherhood Makes Us Smarter* (New York: Basic Books, 2005).

Fels, Anna, *Necessary Dreams: Ambition in Women's Changing Lives* (New York: Pantheon Books, 2004).

Friedan, Betty, *The Feminine Mystique* (New York: W. W. Norton & Company, 1963).

Hanson, Janet, *More Than 85 Broads: Women Making Career Choices, Taking Risks and Defining Success on Their Own Terms* (New York: McGraw-Hill, 2006).

Hewlett, Sylvia Ann, *Creating a Life: What Every Woman Needs to Know About Having a Baby and a Career* (New York: Hyperion, 2002).

Huff, Priscilla Y., *101 Best Home-Based Businesses for Women,* revised 2nd edition (New York: Random House, 1998).

Hochschild, Arlie Russell, *The Second Shift: Working Parents and the Revolution at Home* (New York: Viking, 1989).

Ibarra, Herminia, *Working Identity: Unconventional Strategies for Reinventing Your Career* (Boston: Harvard Business School Press, 2003).

Jansen, Julie, *I Don't Know What I Want, But I Know It's Not This: A Step-by-Step Guide to Finding Gratifying Work* (New York: Penguin Books, 2003).

Lassiter, Pam, *The New Job Security: Five Strategies to Take Control of Your Career* (Berkeley, CA: Ten Speed Press, 2002).

Lewis, Susan, *Reinventing Ourselves After Motherhood: How Former Career Women Refocus Their Personal and Professional Lives After the Birth of a Child* (Chicago: Contemporary Books, 1999).

Macko, Lia, and Kerry Rubin, *Midlife Crisis at 30: How the Stakes Have Changed for a New Generation—and What to Do About It* (Emmaus, PA: Rodale, 2004).

McGovern, Marion, and Dennis Russell, *A New Brand of Expertise: How Independent Consultants, Free Agents, and Interim Managers Are Transforming the World of Work* (Boston: Butterworth-Heinemann, 2001).

Pink, Daniel H., *Free Agent Nation: The Future of Working for Yourself* (New York: Warner Books, 2001).

Ryan, Robin, *What to Do with the Rest of Your Life: America's Top Career Coach Shows You How to Find or Create the Job You'll Love* (New York: Simon & Schuster, 2002).

Schwartz, Felice, *Breaking with Tradition: Women and Work, the New Facts of Life* (New York: Warner Books, 1992).

Swiss, Deborah J., and Judith P. Walker, *Women and the Work/Family Dilemma: How Today's Professional Women Are Confronting the Maternal Wall* (New York: Wiley, 1993).

Warner, Judith, *Perfect Madness: Motherhood in the Age of Anxiety* (New York: Penguin Group, 2005).

Williams, Joan, *Unbending Gender: Why Family and Work Conflict and What to Do About It* (New York: Oxford University Press, 2000).

Zappert, Laraine T., *Getting It Right: How Working Mothers Successfully Take Up the Challenge of Life, Family, and Career* (New York: Simon & Schuster, 2001).

SAMPLE RÉSUMÉS OF REAL RELAUNCHERS

Note that some identifying characteristics have been changed.

RACHEL JONES

SUMMARY

Twelve years' experience initiating change, working collaboratively, and planning and implementing programs in nonprofit organizations. Currently pursuing MBA degree with an emphasis in public and non-profit management, expected graduation in 2004.

WORK EXPERIENCE

1993–1995   **Seattle University**   Seattle, WA

Associate Dean of Students

Created and managed campuswide programs that significantly increased new student retention and satisfaction.

Developed and supervised required freshman experience course team taught by faculty and staff.

Mediated disputes between members of the campus community. Provided campus leadership for crisis intervention and response.

Successfully advocated and resolved student concerns and complaints.

1992–1993   Lake Brigg, WA

Private Consulting

Conducted assessments and analysis and provided recommendations for improving campuswide programs and departments that led to institutional change at public and private colleges and universities.

1990–1992   Western College   Bainbridge, WA
Director of Student Activities

Enhanced out-of-classroom experience for students through involvement in student organizations, leadership programs, and volunteer services.

Managed staff, facilities, and budget for campus student center.

1989–1990   Frasier Health Care System   Bainbridge, WA
Training Specialist

Trained 2,000 employees in organization-wide quality improvement program.

Taught management development course for new managers.

Consulted with departmental managers on organizational development issues.

1983–1988   Seattle University   Seattle, WA
Assistant Dean of Students

Planned, implemented, and evaluated orientation program for 8,000 new students.

Designed curriculum and taught leadership course in School of Education.

Directed efforts of 10,000-member parents association including membership drives, publications, and program planning.

Worked collaboratively to change campus perceptions and provide coordinated services for women students on issues of sexual assault and harassment.

GRADUATE WORK & EXPERIENCES

Spring 2002   Business Case Writing   Atlanta, GA

Authored business case about senior leadership transition in a nonprofit organization for class discussion in MBA course at Atlanta University.

Spring 2002   Market Research Project   Atlanta, GA

Created Web-based survey to assess corporate interest in a community service initiative by a nonprofit organization. Collected and analyzed data using the SPSS statistical package. Presented findings and marketing implications for positioning, promotion, and pricing.

Fall 2000   Head Start National   Atlanta, GA
Consulted on a project to assess staff recruitment and retention efforts. Conducted diagnostic interviews and analyzed data. Presented findings and recommendations in written report and presentation to senior management.

Spring 1999   The Puppet Theatre   Atlanta, GA
Assisted faculty member with strategic planning process. Conducted diagnostic interviews and led focus group discussions.

Relevant MBA Coursework:

Fundraising & Development	Policy Analysis in the Public Sector
Consulting	Management of Nonprofit
Marketing Social Change	Organizations

EDUCATION

MBA, Nonprofit and Public Management, Atlanta University, expected 2004.

MS, Higher Education Administration, Seattle University, 1983.

BA, Public Relations/Sociology, summa cum laude, Colgate University, 1981.

VOLUNTEER ACTIVITIES

Country Day School   **Atlanta, GA**
Member, Web Site Development Committee, 2002.
Chair, New Family Orientation Program, 2001–2003.
Treasurer, Parent Association Board. Oversaw annual fund-raising, budget, and investments, 1999–2001.

St. Mark's Parish   **Atlanta, GA**
Family Liturgy Committee and religious education teacher, 1997–present.

REFERENCES

Available upon request.

DONNA SMITH

WORK EXPERIENCE

9/03–present   Mobile County Public Schools   Mobile, AL
ESL (English as a second language) teacher at Ford Elementary School (half-time). Pull-out ESL program teaching students in grades K–6.

11/01–5/02   Montgomery Public Schools   Montgomery, AL
Library assistant and media specialist at Evans Elementary School (half-time). Read to students and led library research and learning games; previewed and processed new books; performed circulation duties.

4/01–6/01   Richardson Unified School District   Richardson, TX
Library media specialist (library tech) at Sable Elementary School (half-time).

1997–2000   Freelance writer and photo stylist   Tulsa, OK
Wrote feature stories for *The Oklahoma Daily,* a daily newspaper, and *At Home in Oklahoma,* an interior decorating magazine. Proofread copy, scouted photo shoot locations, and art-directed interior photo shoots for *At Home in Oklahoma.*

1987–88   Big Clothing Stores, Inc.   Dallas, TX
Merchandise planner. Monitored the distribution and sale of merchandise for 500+ stores.

1981–87   Bank of Texas   Dallas, TX
Commercial loan officer. Serviced secured loan portfolio of small and middle-market companies.

VOLUNTEER EXPERIENCE

2003–04   St. Marks Church   Mobile, AL
Sunday school teacher for physically and mentally challenged children. Bus driver.

1990–2000   St. Johns Church   Tulsa, OK
Sunday school teacher. Elementary education director. Finance committee. President of women's mission group.

1990–2000   **Oklahoma Symphony Orchestra**   Tulsa, OK
                     Society Guild
Publisher of *Guild Notes,* a quarterly newsletter, 1998–99. Gift shop committee, 1999. Assistant treasurer, 1997–98. Gift shop ticket-sales chairman, 1997. Symphony Ball decorations chairman, 1991. Symphony Ball publicity chairman, 1995.

1994–2000   **Blue Ribbon Academy**   Tulsa, OK
Wrote a grant proposal for the school. Member of the Diversity Committee and the Playground Committee. Paid substitute teaching assistant for pre-K class. Lunchroom monitor. Volunteered for numerous school and classroom activities and fund-raisers.

EDUCATION

2003–04   **Mobile District Education Service Center**   Mobile, AL
Teacher preparation and certification program in ESL. Completed all course work and passed ESL ExCET and PPR (EC–12). Will receive teacher certification after completing internship in 5/05.

1983–86   **Texas University**   Dallas, TX
                   Graduate School of Business Administration
Master's in Business Administration.

1977–81   **Rice University**   Houston, TX
Bachelor of arts degree in political science. Crew and track teams. Two summer internships in Washington, DC.

PERSONAL

Mother of two children (aged 14 and 11). Married. Born and raised in Alaska.

CAROL FISHMAN COHEN

EDUCATION

1983–1985 Harvard Business School, MBA, Boston, MA

1977–1981 Pomona College, BA, Economics, Claremont, CA
Recipient of Ada May Fitts Prize, awarded to one woman member of graduating class for outstanding intellectual leadership and influence on other students. Student body president. JV volleyball team.

FULL-TIME EMPLOYMENT

7/87–2/90 Associate, Drexel Burnham Lambert Inc., Corporate Finance, Boston, MA
Participated in numerous private placements of subordinated debt and private equity offerings. Extensive client contact as senior Drexel representative in negotiations.

7/85–7/87 Flextronics, Inc. (now Flextronics International)

3/86–7/87 (Lowell, MA) Part of a management team in charge of start-up manufacturing facility and office. Developed manufacturing prototypes for products of three new customers, including Flextronics's largest corporate customer, and readied them for mass production. This $10 million project (note: 1986 dollars!) involved in simultaneous introduction of 24 new printed circuit board assemblies in two manufacturing locations: Hong Kong and Lowell.

7/85–2/86 (Newark, CA) Managed six accounts ranging from $500,000 to $10 million of Flextronics's revenues. Credited with repeat orders from two of these customers, one over $1 million.

Summer 1984 Summer Associate, Mergers and Acquisitions, Farley Industries, Chicago, IL
Identified, researched, and made recommendations on leveraged buyout candidates for investor William F. Farley.

8/81–8/83 Investment Associate, Capital Research and Management Co., Los Angeles, CA
(American Funds Group, Capital Guardian, Capital Group Cos.) Researched and published in-house equity recommendations. Selected

as special assistant to chairman of the board of Capital Guardian Trust Company. Assisted head equity trader.

PART-TIME EMPLOYMENT AND COMMUNITY SERVICE

11/96–6/01 John Ward Elementary School Parent Teacher Organization (PTO), Newton, MA

6/99–6/01 Co-President. Created strategy for, managed, and emerged as most visible school community leader of successful citywide elementary school redistricting campaign. Established Ward School grant writing program, and authored grant proposal for technologist in residence. Proposal was awarded $10,000 by Newton Schools Foundation (NSF), one of the largest single-school grants ever made by the NSF to an elementary school. Increased school volunteer force by 25%, and broadened scope of involved parents, especially working parents. Shifted PTO focus to math, science, and technology.

11/96–6/99 Treasurer. Established PTO as tax-exempt organization.

6/00–6/01 Co-Founding Member, Newton Public Schools Technology Campaign, Newton, MA

Proposed campaign concept to Newton Public Schools superintendent.

7/92–7/95 Interim CFO, Boston Corporate Finance Group, Boston, MA

Managed office payroll and finances, insurance benefit research and selection, and personnel management. Trained successor full-time CFO.

4/90–4/91 Associate, Bloom and Company, Boston, MA

Met with potential investors and researched companies for possible investment for this small merchant bank.

Spring 1990 Editor, 1990 Annual Report, Anti-Defamation League, Boston, MA

Edited, wrote copy for, and developed presentation concepts for annual report of this nonprofit organization.

ADDITIONAL PERSONAL

11/89–present Mother, four children, born 11/89–7/95. Current ages 5–11. At home full-time since 7/95.

Married. Member, Newton Women's Volleyball League. Enjoy reading, swimming, writing, and motivating people.

e my year

of my pul

Notes

Chapter 1. RElaunch or Not? You Decide

1. Ann Crittenden, *The Price of Motherhood: Why the Most Important Job in the World Is Still the Least Valued* (New York: Henry Holt and Company, 2001; paperback edition, 2002), p. 12.
2. Susan Chira, *A Mother's Place: Choosing Work and Family Without Guilt or Blame* (New York: HarperCollins, 1998; paperback edition, 1999), p. 110.
3. Ibid., p. 112.
4. Judith Warner, "Mommy Madness," *Newsweek* (February 21, 2005), p. 44. See also *Perfect Madness: Motherhood in the Age of Anxiety* (New York: Penguin Group, 2005).
5. Sylvia Ann Hewlett, Carolyn Buck Luce, Peggy Shiller, and Sandra Southwell, "The Hidden Brain Drain: Off-Ramps and On-Ramps in Women's Careers" (New York: Center for Work–Life Policy, March 2005), p. 44.
6. "Parenting Mom Squad," *Parenting* (March 2005), p. 106.
7. Hewlett, Luce, et al., op. cit., p. 52, exhibit 5.5.

Chapter 2. Learn Confidence

1. Interview with Mary Lindley Burton, March 2004.
2. Catherine Guthrie, "Big Story: How Motherhood Makes You Smarter," www.babycenter.com/refcap/baby/emotrecovery/1428975.html.

3. Interview with Patricia Chang, November 2005.

4. Linda Babcock and Sara Laschever, *Women Don't Ask: Negotiation and the Gender Divide* (Princeton, NJ: Princeton University Press, 2003).

5. Jack Canfield Peak Performance Training, www.jackcanfield.com.

6. Interview with Michele Phillips, November 2005.

7. Ann Crittenden, *If You've Raised Kids, You Can Manage Anything: Leadership Begins at Home* (New York: Penguin Group, 2004), pp. 8–9.

8. Guthrie, op cit., and Katherine Ellison, *The Mommy Brain: How Motherhood Makes Us Smarter* (New York: Basic Books, 2005).

9. Dawn Steel, *They Can Kill You ... But They Can't Eat You: Lessons from the Front* (New York: Pocket Books, 1993), pp. 39–40.

10. Ibid., p. 40.

11. Interview with Persephone Zill, October 2005.

Chapter 3. Assess Your Career Options

1. Interview with Marcie Schorr Hirsch and Lisa Berman Hills, November 2004.

2. Interview with Burton.

3. Richard Nelson Bolles, *What Color Is Your Parachute? A Practical Manual for Job-Hunters and Career-Changers* (Berkeley, CA: Ten Speed Press, 2004), chapters 7–9.

4. Mary Lindley Burton and Richard A. Wedemeyer, *In Transition: From the Harvard Business School Club of New York's Career Management Seminar* (New York: HarperCollins, 1991; paperback edition, 1992), chapters 4–8.

5. Herminia Ibarra, *Working Identity: Unconventional Strategies for Reinventing Your Career* (Boston: Harvard Business School Press, 2003; paperback edition, 2004), p. 120.

6. Hilary Stout and Anne Marie Chaker, "Mom for Hire: Industry Springs Up Around Mothers Returning to Work," *Wall Street Journal* (May 6, 2004).

7. James T. Bond, Ellen Galinsky, Stacy S. Kim, and Erin Brownfield,

"2005 National Study of Employers—Highlights of Findings," www. familiesandwork.org/summary/2005nsesummary.pdf, p. 1.

8. Interview with Janet Rowley, MD, May 2005, and www.laskerfoundation.org.

9. Daniel H. Pink, *Free Agent Nation: The Future of Working for Yourself* (New York: Warner Books, 2001; paperback edition, 2002), p. 35.

10. Ginia Bellafante, "Trafficking in Memories (for Fun and Profit)," *New York Times* (January 27, 2005), p. D1.

11. Account based on an interview with Elise Wetzel in December 2005, and Rebecca Lindell, "From the PTA to eBay: This Alum's Entrepreneurial Venture Is a Winning Bid," www.kellogg.northwestern.edu/kwo/sum05/indepth/wetzel.htm.

12. Michelle Conlin, "The Rise of the Mompreneurs," www.businessweek.com/magazine/content/04_23/b3886076.htm?chan=sb.

Chapter 4. Update Your Professional and Job Search Skills, and Prepare for the Interview

1. Interview with Burton.

2. Pam Lassiter, *The New Job Security: Five Strategies to Take Control of Your Career* (Berkeley, CA: Ten Speed Press, 2002), p. 38.

3. The above discussion of elevator stories is adapted from ibid., pp. 38–40, and Lassiter's presentation at the Harvard Business School Charting Your Course Seminar in May 2001.

4. Text of Conan O'Brien class day speech to the Harvard class of 2000, June 2000.

Chapter 5. Network, Market Yourself, and Clinch the Opportunity

1. Bolles, op. cit., pp. 42–44.

2. Ibarra, op. cit., p. 120.

3. Stephen R. Covey, *The 7 Habits of Highly Effective People: Powerful Lessons in Personal Change* (New York: Simon & Schuster, 1989; paperback edition, 1990), p. 188.

4. Lassiter, op. cit., p. 149.

5. This section draws on concepts presented in chapters 2–4 of Lassiter's *The New Job Security* reframed for relaunchers.

6. Ibarra, op. cit., p. 120.

7. Burton and Wedemeyer, op. cit., pp. 22–26.

8. Based on www.85broads.com, an e-mail from Hanson in June 2006, and Janet Hanson, *More Than 85 Broads: Women Making Career Choices, Taking Risks and Defining Success on Their Own Terms* (New York: McGraw-Hill, 2006).

9. Priscilla Y. Huff, *101 Best Home-Based Businesses for Women,* revised 2nd edition (New York: Random House, 1998).

Chapter 6. Channel Family Support

1. Arlie Russell Hochschild, *The Second Shift: Working Parents and the Revolution at Home* (New York: Viking, 1989), p. 8.

Chapter 7. Handle the Job (or Find Another One)

1. Deborah J. Swiss and Judith P. Walker, *Women and the Work/Family Dilemma: How Today's Professional Women Are Confronting the Maternal Wall* (New York: Wiley, 1993), p. 79.

2. Ibid., p. 43.

3. Pink, op. cit., p. 335.

4. Interview with Hirsch and Hills.

5. Ibid.

6. Interview with Nancy Connolly, September 2005.

Chapter 8. Inspirational Relaunchers

1. Interview with Sandra Day O'Connor, March 2005.

2. Interview with Margaret Rayman, May 2005, and her Web site www.surrey.ac.uk/SBMS/ACADEMICS_homepage/rayman_margaret.

3. Heather Peddie account on the Web site for Stanford Law School's Women's Legal History Biography Project, www.law.stanford.edu/library/wlhbp/.

4. Interview with Ruth Reardon O'Brien, November 2005; also ibid.

5. Interview with Katharine Wolf, MD, July 2005.

6. Interview with Dinny Stearns Taylor, November 2005.

7. Interview with Connolly.

Chapter 9. The Relaunch Movement

1. Malcolm Gladwell, *The Tipping Point: How Little Things Can Make a Big Difference* (Boston: Little, Brown & Company, 2000).

2. Katharine Bradbury and Jane Katz, "Women's Rise: A Work in Progress," *Regional Review* (Q1 2005), Federal Reserve Bank of Boston, p. 58.

3. Claudia Goldin, "The Quiet Revolution That Transformed Women's Employment, Education, and Family," *The American Economic Review* 96, no. 2, May 2006.

4. Laraine T. Zappert, *Getting It Right: How Working Mothers Successfully Take Up the Challenge of Life, Family, and Career* (New York: Simon & Schuster, 2002 paperback edition), pp. 12–14.

5. Betsy Morris and Ann Harrington, "Tales of the Trailblazers: *Fortune* Revisits Harvard's Women MBAs of 1973," *Fortune* (October 12, 1998).

6. Arlene Rossen Cardozo, *Sequencing: A New Solution for Women Who Want Marriage, Career, and Family* (New York: Atheneum, 1986), p. 17.

7. Ibid., p. 20.

8. Bradbury and Katz, op. cit., p. 64.

9. Lisa Belkin, "The Opt-Out Revolution," *New York Times Magazine* (October 26, 2003).

10. Sylvia Ann Hewlett and Carolyn Buck Luce, "Off-Ramps and On-Ramps: Keeping Talented Women on the Road to Success," *Harvard Business Review* (March 2005), p. 2.

11. Basic Microdata provided via e-mail by Katharine Bradbury, senior economist and policy adviser, Federal Reserve Bank of Boston, April 2006.

12. Ibid.

13. In a December 2004 interview with Harvard Business School Professor David Moss, he made the "negative signal" observation and was concerned about its ramifications.

14. Susan Lewis, *Reinventing Ourselves After Motherhood: How Former Career Women Refocus Their Personal and Professional Lives After the Birth of a Child* (Chicago: Contemporary Books, 1999), p. xiv.

15. Hochschild, op. cit.

16. Interview with Ellen Galinsky, April 2006.

17. Hewlett and Luce, op. cit., p. 6.

18. Sue Shellenbarger, "Fairer Flextime: Employers Try New Policies for Alternative Schedules," *Wall Street Journal* (November 17, 2005).

19. Arlene Johnson, Karen Noble, and Amy Richman, "Business Impacts of Flexibility: An Imperative for Expansion," Corporate Voices for Working Families report (November 2005), p. 4.

20. Ibid., p. 10.

21. Ibid., p. 12.

22. Ibid., p. 14.

23. Statement made by Anne Erni at the Harvard Business School Annual Women in Business Conference panel The On-Ramp: What You Need to Know Before You Take Time Off and Return to the Workforce, January 2006.

24. Claudia Wallis, "The Case for Staying Home," *Time* (March 22, 2004).

25. Hewlett and Luce, op. cit., p. 1.

26. Interview with Hirsch and Hills.

Chapter 10. What Employers, Universities, and Others Are Doing for Relaunchers

1. Ellen Rosen, "Intermission Over? Now to Raise the Curtain on the Career, Act 2," *New York Times* (June 5, 2005).

2. Interviews with Anne Erni, January 2006, and Fleur Bothwick, Lehman Brothers' European director of diversity and inclusion, March

2006; Encore invitation Web site, www.lehman.com/events/2005Corp/EncoreProgram.

3. Interview with W. Stanton Smith, May 2005, March 2006, and e-mail exchange with Anne Weisberg, senior advisor to the Deloitte Women's Initiative; and June 2006 follow-up conversation with W. Stanton Smith.

4. Interview with Candice Lange and Joan Todd, corporate communications, Eli Lilly and Company, March 2005.

5. Johnson, Noble, and Richman, op. cit., p. 5.

6. Ibid., pp. 21–22.

7. Shellenbarger, op. cit.

8. Alison Stein Wellner, "Welcoming Back Mom: Luring New Mothers and Stay-at-Home Parents Back to Work Needs to Begin Before They Leave," *HR Magazine* 49, no. 6 (June 2004).

9. Interview with Lori Massad, May 2006.

10. Interview with Paige Arnof-Fenn, December 2005.

11. Interview with DeAnne Aguirre, March 2006.

12. Patricia Kitchen, "Nothing Desperate About Housewives' Career Plans," www.newsday.com (October 23, 2005).

13. www.selectminds.com.

14. E-mail to Harvard Business School alumnae from Professor Myra Hart, February 2, 2006.

15. Based on conversations with Corrie Martin, program manager, Tuck Back in Business: Invest in Your Return and Tuck Bridge programs, February 2006, and *Tuck Back in Business* brochure, April 2006. Note: In June 2006, Carol was hired to lead a "Career Chat" for the Fall 2006 Back in Business program.

16. E-mail from Constance Dato English, co-director of Darden Alumni Career Services, April 2006; Back to the Future: Re-entry Program for Women Returning to Work, detailed outline of proposed Zicklin School program distributed at MBA or MIA Women@Work Forum, April 2006; e-mailed invitation to Babson College's Act II program, May 2006.

17. Daphne Jackson Fellowship Web site, www.daphnejackson.org.
18. European Molecular Biology Organization Web site, www.embo.org/fellowships/index.html.
19. Interview with Joyce Rudick, April 2005.

Epilogue: The Future

1. Loretta Chao, "What GenXers Need to Be Happy at Work," *Wall Street Journal* (November 29, 2005), p. B6.
2. Danielle Sacks, "Scenes from the Culture Clash," *Fast Company* (January–February 2006), p. 74.
3. Jyoti Thottam, "Reworking Work," *Time* (July 25, 2005), p. 50, and July 2006 phone conversation with Dawn Bryant, corporate public relations manager, Best Buy.
4. Felice Schwartz, *Breaking with Tradition: Women and Work, the New Facts of Life,* (New York: Warner Books, 1992), p. 50.
5. Felice Schwartz, "Management Women and the New Facts of Life," *Harvard Business Review* (January–February, 1989), p. 1.
6. Louise Story, "Many Women at Elite Colleges Set Career Path to Motherhood," *New York Times* (September 20, 2005).
7. Lia Macko and Kerry Rubin, *Midlife Crisis at 30: How the Stakes Have Changed for a New Generation—and What to Do About It* (Emmaus, PA: Rodale, 2004).
8. Sylvia Ann Hewlett, *Creating a Life: What Every Woman Needs to Know about Having a Baby and a Career* (New York: Hyperion, 2002).
9. Interview with Robyn Davis and Mary McNamara, December 2005.

Acknowledgments

Our first thanks go to the dozens of women we interviewed who shared their very personal relaunch stories with us. We promised them anonymity so we cannot list them here, but we are deeply grateful to them for their openness and insights. We are especially grateful to the six inspirational relaunchers who allowed us to tell their stories in full with their names attached: Sandra Day O'Connor, Margaret Rayman, Ruth Reardon O'Brien, Katharine Wolf, Dinny Stearns Taylor, and Nancy Connolly, as well as to Robyn Davis and Mary McNamara, whose job share we describe in the epilogue.

We also want to acknowledge the many experts, some of whom are also good friends, who helped us with this project by contributing either their professional insights, personal support, or, in many cases, both: DeAnne Aguirre, Heather Balmat, Betsy Blagdon, Katharine Bradbury, Miriam Brilleman, Mary Lindley Burton, Patricia Chang, Ann Crittenden, Alice Freedman, Ellen Galinsky, Connie Glaser, Claudia Goldin, Janet Hanson, Brad Harrington, Myra Hart, Lisa Berman Hills, Marcie Schorr Hirsch, Pam Lassiter, Jennifer Liquori, Corrie Martin, David Moss, Barbara Pagano, Julie Peskoe, Michele Phillips, Jean Rhodes, Janet Rowley, Juliet Schor, the family of the late Felice Schwartz, Jerry Weinreich, Page Wilkins, and Persephone Zill.

Our agent, Geri Thoma, guided us with a knowing hand through the publishing process and through way more than we can ever describe here. Our editor Natalie Kaire's sharp eye and keen sense of our audience helped us make this a much better book, and she never tired of reading it yet another time. Natalie's assistant, Rebecca Isenberg, calmly and efficiently handled numerous details that could have easily thrown the schedule off if left to less competent hands. Production editor Penina Sacks expertly shepherded us through the production process and Claire Brown created our stellar cover. Erica Gelbard worked her PR magic to spread the word. And Rick Wolff had the vision to realize we were on to something, all the more remarkable since he didn't have first-hand knowledge of the problem.

We owe a special thank-you to Alison Poorvu Jaffe for introducing the two of us to each other. One of the great by-products of this book has been our deepening friendship. We can laugh how about how we agreed to be co-authors before we ever met in person (not a strategy we would necessarily recommend to others). What could have been troublesome, or even disastrous, was and is instead the perfect partnership. And, speaking of friends, we are both blessed with many talented and loyal ones whose continued support and enthusiasm have helped us through the many ups and downs of the last few years: Mary Wright Benner, Barbara Berenson, Farran Brown, Jarrett Collins, Lee Rubin Collins, Daphne DeMarneffe, Nicole Diamond, Rivky Eichenstein, Randi Eisner, Lisa Endlich, Al Farrell, Andrea Goldman, Betsy Harper, Gail Hoffman, Sima Jacoby, Lori Kaufmann, Yadin Kaufmann, Lizzie Leiman Kraieman, Debbie Krasnow, Todd Krasnow, Jonathan Lavine, Judy Lepor, Marla Libraty, Susan Lynch, Eileen McLaughlin, Cynthia Morton, Ellen Offner, Abby Rischin, Luciana Silva, Laura Hodges Taylor, Barbara Wallner, and the wonderful women— parts of whose stories are told here—of Harvard Business School's Charting Your Course 2002 NYC seminar.

—Carol Fishman Cohen and Vivian Steir Rabin

I am also indebted to my dear friends and neighbors—the Kreitenberg, Liberman, and Weiss families who have served, uncomplainingly, as backup child care ever since I relaunched. In my case, "it takes a block" to raise five children, earn a living, and write a book all at the same time. My family—the Heald, Neff, Rabin, and Steir clans—has given me unending love and support. Mom, your creativity and perseverance as the author of the musical *Only a Kingdom* have set a shining example for me. My children, Beatie, Yosef, Yisrael, Zev, and Penny, you are my ultimate inspiration and source of joy. Beatie, I am especially grateful for your technical assistance and your willingness to listen to my latest wacko ideas. Doug, my best friend and partner in life, you've been there for me in more ways than I could ever acknowledge. I really appreciate everything you've done for me. And, finally, I offer my deepest thanks to God, for giving me such wonderful friends and family as well as the strength and ability to pursue my dreams.

—VSR

Mom, thank you for your thoughts on the earliest manuscript, and for your constant encouragement during the book writing process. Assorted Cohens, Fishmans, Freedmans, and Mosses, thank you all for surrounding me with the unconditional love that can only come from family. Stephen, my husband and soul mate of twenty years, you make me laugh, cheer me on, tolerate me no matter what, and are always willing to listen to my ideas and give me a thoughtful response. Your perspective is a gift. My incredible children, Michael, Andrew, Sarah, and David, you made my years at home amazing in every way, and you have given me endless feedback about relaunching from a child's perspective. Michael, my "technology department," your expertise was invaluable, but more importantly, your patient, cheerful attitude turned my panic into relief on numerous occasions as I lived at the computer. Andrew, ever watchful of my public image, thank you for all your advice, and for tactfully encouraging me to update my ten-year-old wardrobe. Sarah, your "relauncher song" will always make me laugh, and I thought your book cover design was the best. David, thanks for teaching me how to play Uno and for forcing me to take breaks from working to play so you could beat me. I love you all.

—CFC

Index

CAROL FISHMAN COHEN and VIVIAN STEIR RABIN are cofounders of www.iRelaunch.com, a career break connections company for mid-career professionals in all stages of career break and the employers, universities, and organizations interested in updating and recruiting them. Carol and Vivian are internationally recognized experts on career reentry and speak frequently on the topic. Carol, a former investment banker, lives in Newton, MA, with her husband and four children. Vivian, a former finance and human resources professional, ran her own executive search business prior to founding *i*Relaunch. She lives in Clifton, NJ, with her husband and five children.